GET MORE
MONEY ON
YOUR NEXT JOB
...IN ANY
ECONOMY

GET MORE MONEY ON YOUR NEXT JOB ...IN ANY ECONOMY

REVISED AND UPDATED

Lee E. Miller

New York Chicago San Francisco Lisbon London
Madrid Mexico City Milan New Delhi
San Juan Seoul Singapore Sydney Toronto

1 2 3 4 5 6 7 8 9 0   FGR/FGR   0 1 5 4 3 2 1 0 9

ISBN 978-0-07-162138-0
MHID 0-07-162138-5

McGraw-Hill books are available at special quantity discounts to use as premiums and sales promotions, or for use in corporate training programs. To contact a representative, please visit the Contact Us pages at www.mhprofessional.com.

This book is printed on acid-free paper.

Library of Congress Cataloging-in-Publication Data
Miller, Lee E.
   Get more money on your next job . . . in any economy / by Lee Miller.—rev. ed.
     p. cm.
   Includes bibliographical references and index.
   ISBN 0-07-162138-5 (alk. paper)
1. Career changes. 2. Negotiation in business. 3. Labor contract. I. Title.
   HF5384.M55 2009
   650.14—dc22

                         2008050546

Contents

Foreword

Since Lee Miller launched the first edition of this book back in 1998, things have changed in the job market. Boy, have they ever! Our country is now in the biggest economic mess since the Great Depression. Jobs are disappearing by the thousands. According to a recent survey, nearly half of all working adults say they are worried about layoffs at the place where they work. Many feel lucky to have a job, and if you now say to them, "When you are looking for a job, or staying in a job, you should negotiate for more money," they might look at you as if you were a little nuts.

Well, let us start with two fundamental truths, one concerning you, one concerning employers:

Truth 1: In any economy, it is reasonable for you to seek to be paid what you are worth.

Truth 2: In any economy, it is reasonable for an employer to seek to hire you and keep you for the lowest salary you are willing to accept.

Between these two truths lies negotiation. Salary negotiation.

Salary negotiation would never happen if *every* employer in *every* hiring interview or performance review were to mention, right from the start, the top figure it was willing to pay you at the current moment. *Some* employers do, of course, but most employers don't. Hoping they'll be able to get you for less, they start *lower* than they're ultimately willing to go. This creates *a range*. And that range is what salary negotiation is all about.

For example, if the employer wants to hire somebody for no more than $20 an hour, it may start *the bidding* at $15 an hour—in which case, the employer's *range* runs between $15 and $20 an hour. Or if the company wants to pay no more than $30 an hour, it may start the bidding at $22 an hour—in which case, the employer's *range* runs between $22 and $30 an hour.

So why do you want to negotiate? Because if a range *is* thus involved, you have every right to try to discover *and get* the highest salary that the employer is willing to pay *within that range*.

The employer's goal is to save money if possible. Your goal is to bring home to your family, your partner, or your own household the best salary that you can for the work that you will be or are doing there. Nothing's wrong with either goal. But it does mean that when an employer starts the bidding lower, salary negotiation on your part is proper and expected. Ditto when it comes to asking for a well-deserved raise. Moreover, salary is not the only thing that you can negotiate about. There are many other forms of compensation that you can ask for if you know how to negotiate, including bonuses, stock, benefits, perks, training, time off, and flexible scheduling, just to name a few.

Negotiation is Lee Miller's strong suit. A Harvard-trained lawyer, Lee spent over 20 years as a senior human resources executive in a career that included being the head of human resources for TV Guide, USA Networks, and Barneys New York. During the course of his career in human resources, he hired and negotiated compensation with hundreds of employees.

Miller now writes a career column for the *New Jersey Star Ledger*, and he has decided to share his in-depth knowledge of negotiating compensation and benefits with you in this rewritten, updated, truly insightful book. It belongs in everyone's career library.

Richard Nelson Bolles
Author of *What Color Is Your Parachute**

---

*Richard Nelson Bolles's highly acclaimed bestselling book *What Color Is Your Parachute? A Practical Manual for Job-Hunters and Career-Changers* (Ten Speed Press, Berkeley, Calif.) was first published in 1970. The book has been revised and reissued every year since, and in 2009, it was published as the *Job-Hunting in Hard Times Edition*. As of 2009 there were 10,000,000 copies in print.

Acknowledgments

I would like to thank Richard Nelson Bolles, author of the bestselling book *What Color Is Your Parachute?*, for writing the foreword to this book; Louis Amendola, executive vice president of merchandising for Brooks Brothers, for helping me write the chapter "Dressing the Part to Enhance Your Ability to Negotiate (and Your Career)"; and Joyce Strawser, dean of the Seton Hall Stillman School of Business, for her help with the introduction and for demonstrating to me once again the huge financial impact that even a small failure to negotiate can have. I would also like to thank Melissa Anchan of the Milano School and Bernard Gumbs of Seton Hall for their research assistance.

In addition I would like to extend thanks to the following individuals for their thoughts and contributions: Cathy Black, president of Hearst Magazines; Janice Reals Ellig, a partner in the executive search firm of Chaddick and Ellig and author of *What Every Successful Woman Knows*; Carol Raphael, chief executive officer of the Visiting Nurse Service of New York; Dr. Patricia Farrell, professor of clinical psychology at Walden University; Peter Handal, chief executive officer of Dale Carnegie Training; Davia Temin, chief executive officer of Temin and Company; Lisa Gersh, former president of the Oxygen Network; Ted Pilonero, president of the Joseph Group; Vivian Eyre, president of Partners for Women's Growth, Inc.; Lena West, chief strategist at xynoMedia Technology and author of the e-book *The Blogosphere Cluebook* (2007); Carolyn Wall, former publisher of *Newsweek*; Ron McMillan, coauthor of *Crucial Conversations: Tools for Talking When Stakes Are High*; Jan Hopkins, former anchor of CNN's *Street Sweeps*; Jerri DeVard, a marketing consultant and former senior vice president, brand management and marketing, at Verizon Communications;

Randy Kahn, a managing director at Citigroup's Salomon Smith Barney; Jill Krumholz, a recruiter with Charleston Partners; Alaina G. Levine, director of special projects at the University of Arizona; David Gammel, president of High Context Consulting; motivational speaker Camille Leon; Ali Croft, public relations director for Just Drive Media; Linda Seale, former senior vice president of human resources at MTV; Bob Corno, a financial advisor at the Mason Companies; and Maxine Hartley, an executive coach with Right Associates.

Introduction

If someone offered you an investment opportunity that would enable you to earn $480,000 in exchange for very little time or money and virtually no risk, would you be interested? Well, that is what negotiating one additional $2,000 raise early in your career would be worth to you over the course of your working life because the $2,000 would be compounded through your future raises and promotions.[1] And that figure reflects only the lost income; it does not include the effect the raise would have on your pension, social security, bonuses, and stock options, all of which are normally tied to base salary. Learning how to negotiate for better salary and benefits is one of the best investments anyone can ever make.

This book is for anybody who is contemplating changing jobs, seeking a raise, or aspiring to be promoted. That includes just about everyone. The techniques I describe can be applied equally effectively regardless of the job you are in. CEOs, executives, managers, salespeople, systems engineers, programmers, Web designers, first-line supervisors, and administrative assistants—all can benefit from a better understanding of how to negotiate their compensation.

In a constantly changing world, with mergers, takeovers, downsizing, rightsizing, and plain old-fashioned layoffs, very few of us can expect that we will continue to work until our retirement for the first employer that hires us. My father had one employer for almost all of his working life. I've had seven different employers since I graduated from law school, not including teaching, writing, and consulting.

---

[1] Getting $2,000 less in salary starting at age 25 will amount to $199,653 in lost income alone by the time you reach 65, assuming that your average raise each year is 4 percent during the remainder of your career, including any promotions. That lost-salary figure results from the compounding effect, over the remainder of your working life, of basing each subsequent raise on an initial salary $2,000 higher. And if those foregone earnings were invested and earned even a modest return of 5 percent a year—half the average return of the S&P 500 Index stocks over the past 20 years—that $2,000 raise would be worth $479,784 by the time you were 65.

A case in point: I left the practice of law to become the corporate vice president of labor relations at Macy's following an unanticipated transfer. I had been a partner in the Washington, D.C., office of a large national law firm and was about to be transferred to their Chicago office. For several months I had been working in Chicago each week and returning to Washington on weekends. Under pressure, I reluctantly agreed to the move. A friend of mine who was aware of my situation called to see if I would consider leaving the law firm and going to work for a corporation. He had been contacted about a human resources position with Macy's for which he thought I was a perfect fit.

At the time, Macy's was the premier department store chain in the nation. Everybody knew Macy's: the world's largest department store, the Thanksgiving Day parade, and the best training program in retail. The work sounded challenging. I liked the people I knew there. It was in New York, where I had grown up and where my parents still lived. So I decided to talk to them.

I flew to New York and met with Dave Brown, the senior vice president for human resources, to whom this position would report. We hit it off instantly. After spending about an hour with him, I met with other executives in the corporate offices. Then I flew back to Washington.

The following week I received a call from Dave's secretary asking me to meet with some people in the operating divisions. That Friday I flew back to New York. In the morning I was put through a series of interviews. Then I had lunch with Dave. After lunch I met with both the chairman and the president of the company.

By this time it was obvious that I was being seriously considered for the position. To this point there had been very little talk about the terms of employment. I knew the base salary that Macy's wanted to pay because I had been told that during the first interview. I had done my own research to determine the benefit and the stock option plans that the company offered. Since I was aware that certain plans were available only to senior vice presidents, I had expressed concern about the position being at the vice president level. Other than that, there had been no discussion about salary or benefits.

After my meeting with the chairman, I thought I would be flying home. Instead, Dave called me into his office and offered me the job. He told me how impressed everyone was with me. He went over the compensation package and addressed my concern about the title, explaining that corporate vice presidents were considered to be on the same level as divisional senior vice presidents. Therefore, I would receive the same benefits as a divisional senior vice president.

We talked for a while. Dave made a few changes to the package in response to various issues that I raised. Then he excused himself for a few minutes and left. When he returned, he told me he had gone to see the chairman. He said that everyone really wanted me to join the company. He was hoping that he could go back to the chairman right then and tell him I would be starting in a few weeks. To make sure that I felt good about the deal, he offered me something that he knew I was not expecting—a sizable signing bonus.

I didn't know what to do. Dave needed to hear that I really wanted to work for Macy's. He expected an immediate answer. Although I didn't have to give him one, not doing so would not be a good way to start off my relationship with a new boss. I was excited about the job. The compensation package was very fair, but I thought that, with a little more time, there might be some room for improvement.

I had been an employment lawyer for eight years. I had negotiated labor contracts with unions and settlements in employment lawsuits; I had advised employers on compensation packages and employment contracts; I had read numerous books on how to negotiate; I had even taken a course on negotiations when I was at Harvard Law School. Yet negotiating about my own future was very different and much more difficult.

Since that time, I have negotiated hundreds of employment agreements—as a lawyer; as a human resources executive at Macy's, Barneys New York, USA Networks, and TV Guide; and more recently as a consultant. As a career coach, I have also advised executives ranging from midlevel managers to CEOs when they were negotiating compensation. Many of the deals I have negotiated resulted in multipage, formal, written contracts dealing with every aspect of the employment relationship. Others have consisted of oral agreements confirmed by simple letters outlining key terms that were agreed upon earlier. How a deal is structured and documented depends on a number of factors: the specific circumstances of the negotiations, the particular employer, common practices in the industry, the level of the position, and the relative bargaining power of the parties. The basic process, however, is the same.

The purpose of this book is to share with you some of the secrets that I have learned over the years. By the time you finish reading, you will have learned how to get the best possible deal when changing jobs, seeking a promotion, or asking for a raise. You will also have learned how to make sure that you actually get what has been promised and how to keep it in the event that your boss leaves or the employer is taken over. This book will prepare you to handle every step of the negotiations for a new job, beginning even before the first interview and continuing right through your acceptance of the final offer. In addition, you will learn how to get a raise or a promotion even when times are tough. Without having to go to law school or spending years becoming a compensation expert, you will understand how to develop a strategy that enables you to achieve your personal objectives. You will also learn what to do when your prospective boss is pressing you for an immediate answer to an unexpected offer.

How did I respond to Dave's surprise offer? I told him that I was excited about the possibility of coming to work for Macy's. I said if it were up to me alone, he could go back to the chairman right then and there and let him know that I was accepting the offer. However, since this decision would affect not only me but my family as well, I said that I needed to talk it over with them. It was a true statement because I wanted to discuss the move with my family before accepting the offer. However, it also served my purposes in the negotiations. Not only did it satisfy Dave's need to know that I really wanted the job, but it also allowed me the time I needed to consider the offer objectively. Moreover, it kept the negotiations open and let me later come back to him to seek any modifications that I needed in order to "convince my family" that this was the right thing to do.

In a recent Society for Human Resources Management survey, 8 out of 10 recruiters said they were willing to negotiate salary and benefits with the job candidates they were seeking to hire, yet only about a third of the candidates surveyed said they felt comfortable negotiating salary and benefits. As the calculations set forth at the beginning of this introduction clearly demonstrate, not negotiating can be a costly mistake. Moreover, research shows that people who attempt to negotiate their salary and benefits in an appropriate way are actually perceived more favorably than those who don't negotiate at all. My experience as the head of human resources at USA Networks, TV Guide, and Barneys New York bears those findings out. If candidates didn't negotiate with me when I was recruiting them, it raised doubts in my mind as to how effectively they would negotiate for the company when they had to.

So why doesn't everyone negotiate when they are offered a job? Most people don't negotiate because they don't know how and they don't understand that they are expected to do so. Others are afraid that they may damage their relationship with their future boss or even lose the offer.

Understanding the process will keep that from happening and will enable you to increase your income by tens of thousands or even hundreds of thousands of dollars over the life of your career.

There are some basic principles that will help you successfully negotiate your salary and benefits without alienating your new employer. These principles govern every type of employment negotiation (see the chapter "Principles for Negotiating: The 11 Commandments of Employment Negotiations"). Mastering them is essential to your career and financial success. However, every negotiation is unique. You need to tailor your approach to accommodate not only your goals but also the needs of your prospective employer. Therefore, the book also sets out 25 specific negotiating strategies to get more money, better benefits, and greater job security. These strategies can be highly effective when used in the right situations.

What if the economy is bad? Most people are happy just to have a job when times are tough, and they assume that they can't get a significant salary increase in their current job or in a new job (particularly if they are unemployed). But those are not accurate assumptions. The fact is that whether the economy is good or bad makes no difference if you know what to do. This book will teach you how to negotiate and get what you want, no matter what the state of the economy.

You will be taught how to analyze the various situations you may face during the negotiating process and determine the best way to handle each. You will also learn when and how to make adjustments. This book cannot take the place of advice from an attorney when a legal question arises, but it will help you develop a strategy to execute that legal advice. Most important, it will teach you how to prevent a prospective employer or recruiter from taking advantage of you and not paying you the salary and benefits you deserve.

The Secret to Negotiating in Any Economy Is Not to Have the Employer Negotiate with You

Let them come to you.

—Jeremy Irons

When I was hired as a senior associate at a Washington, D.C., law firm, the country was in the midst of one of the worst recessions since the 1930s. Yet I was able to negotiate a 50 percent salary increase. Was this due to my unique skill as a negotiator? I wish that were the case. I was in my twenties, and this was the first time I really had to negotiate about my own compensation. In hindsight, I made lots of mistakes. The things I did do right, though, were to negotiate with the right employer at the right time and ensure that they believed I was the right candidate, before we ever talked seriously about money. Those are the three keys to successfully negotiating your compensation even when times are tough.

Salespeople understand this. What is the first thing a car salesperson does when he senses that you are interested in buying a particular car? He takes you out for a test drive. He wants you to feel the wind in your hair while your favorite music is playing on the car's state-of-the-art sound system. He has you envision yourself pulling out of the dealership and driving that car home. He wants you to fall in love with that car. Once you do, the price will not stop you from making that purchase. You will find a way to pay for the car, and the salesperson will help you. What you won't do is negotiate effectively because you have already decided you absolutely must have that car. The same thing happens with employers. Once they decide that you are the "best candidate," they will ordinarily find a way to meet your compensation requirements. People buy what they want, not what they need, and they do what they want, not what they should. Those psychological imperatives are impervious to the state of the economy. Good economy or bad economy—we find a way to pay for the things we *really* want.

In general, when the economy is weak, employers tend to be tight with their money. They try to keep costs down. They look at the positions being filled in terms of what the people filling them can do for the organization. Employers are aware that they have the upper hand when negotiating with employees. Most important, when times are tough, employees believe the myth that they are not in a position to negotiate—a myth employers are only too happy to perpetuate. What you need to remember, however, is that you are not dealing with employers in general negotiating with employees in general. You are dealing with a *specific* employer who is considering hiring *you*. That makes all the difference in the world.

I would be lying if I told you that it isn't easier to negotiate for more money when the economy is booming. Yet no matter what the state of the economy, if you are talking to an employer that really wants to hire you, *for you* the economy is good. Convince the employer that you are the right candidate for the job. Then make sure that you keep the employer focused on "recruiting" you. If you do that, whatever is happening elsewhere in the economy will not matter.

When an employer or a recruiter seeks you out, it greatly increases your bargaining power. If you want to be able to negotiate more effectively, take steps to make that more likely to happen. The best way to do that is to expand your professional network and enhance your Internet presence.

Instead of waiting for candidates to come to them, recruiters are searching the Internet to identify the best candidates for open positions, including individuals who may not be looking for a job at the moment. This practice will continue, and likely even intensify, during periods when the economy is weak because that is when employers become even more serious about finding employees that can make a difference. Search engines like Zoominfo.com, which pulls together information about individuals from Web sites across the Internet, are now commonly used by recruiters to identify potential candidates. Having your name appear where people doing the hiring are likely to look is important if you want to be found.

Recently, for example, Jill Krumholz, a recruiter with Charleston Partners, was conducting a search to hire a senior benefits professional for a large global technology company. As Krumholz described it, "The first thing I did was to Google the term 'global benefits conference.'" By looking at the conference presenters, she was able to identify several individuals that might be right for the position. After doing further research, she contacted a few of those individuals and was able to find from among them a well-qualified candidate to present to her client. Having been sought out by the prospective employer, the candidate, who at the time was not looking for a job, was in an excellent position to negotiate her compensation package.

To maximize their ability to negotiate in any economy, savvy careerists are taking advantage of these "passive candidate recruiting" trends and are creating a powerful Internet presence so that the next great job opportunity *will find them.* In that way their name pops up when recruiters and prospective employers are looking to fill a position for which they might be appropriate, even when they are not actively in the job market.

That Internet presence starts with an online profile, one that describes who you are professionally. Web sites like MySpace.com and Facebook.com allow you to post profiles that are both social and professional, while others like LinkedIn.com focus only on professional profiles. In addition to helping those seeking to fill positions "discover" you, having an online professional profile facilitates networking with other professionals. The larger your professional network, both online and offline, the more likely someone will recruit you, greatly increasing your bargaining position.

Being involved in professional associations significantly increases the likelihood that you will be recruited. It not only enhances your network but it also provides you with greater professional legitimacy. Make sure that your profile appears in directories of professional associations and Web sites like 3StepNetworks.com that specialize in creating an Internet presence for professionals and business executives. Consider joining associations featured on those Web sites to enhance your Internet presence.

Even when you are actively looking for a position, your legitimacy, and therefore your negotiating leverage, will be enhanced by the Internet presence you have created. According to Lena West, chief strategist at xynoMedia Technology and author of the e-book *The Blogosphere Cluebook* (2007), "Employers routinely run Web searches of candidates' names and all known e-mail addresses before they consider someone for a promotion or a new job." So not only do you want to create an Internet presence, you also want to ensure that it presents you in a positive light.

There are many ways to increase your professional stature on the Internet beyond posting a profile to the high-traffic networking Web sites:

▶ In addition to joining professional organizations, participate in online discussions of topics on their Web sites. Offer insights on the important issues facing your profession. Ask and answer questions. Offer help to others whenever you can.

▶ Have something to say that is insightful about the industry online. Write a blog that comments on current issues facing your industry. If you don't have the time to write a blog, write comments on the blogs of others in your field. (For those of you not familiar with blogs, they are online commentaries that you write and that are easy to set up and manage through sites such as blogger.com or yahooshine.com.) You can also answer industry-related questions on Web sites that post questions such as answers.yahoo.com or LinkedIn.com.

▶ Write reviews on Amazon.com about current books being read by people in your field.

The Internet is not the only way to increase the likelihood that you will be recruited. Don't merely join professional organizations; become active in them. Join committees, attend meetings and conferences, write articles for their publications, and volunteer to be a speaker. Stay in touch with people with whom you have worked even after you change jobs. Get involved in civic and religious organizations. Offer help and advice to people in your professional network whenever possible. Send them articles that might be of interest to them. Periodically drop them a note just to keep in touch. The people in your network are the ones who are most likely to recommend you to recruiters and let you know of job opportunities that might be of interest to you.

Even if you are the one to approach the employer or you are seeking a raise from your present employer, you change the negotiating dynamics by changing how the employer views the situation. Once the employer has decided that you are the one it wants, you can create a situation in which the employer feels like it is recruiting you rather than negotiating with you.

Eileen Habelow, Northeast regional vice president of Randstad, a worldwide staffing agency, recently gave a bigger raise than she had planned because of the way her employee approached the topic. She asked this individual to take over a troubled account and offered him an increase in salary, but the way he responded caused her to rethink the amount she had offered.

He told her that "he was flattered that she had thought of him for this tough job and was excited by the challenge even though it required him to leave a secure position where he is doing extremely well." That simple statement reminded her that not only was he the best choice to solve her problem with this account but also that accepting this position entailed both financial and professional risk for him. So even though she believed he would accept the job at the salary she had initially offered, when he asked for a larger increase she gave him one.

When the person hiring or promoting you recognizes that he needs you, he is willing to pay more. His focus is on recruiting you and making you feel good about the opportunity rather than on negotiating with you to save a few dollars on your salary. When they view the situation in that light, employers will not only give you more, they will do so gladly. It is your job to make sure that they never forget that they are trying to recruit you. How do you do that? All the techniques described in this book are based on that premise. Use them.

When times are tough you need to adjust your priorities. It is even more important that you ensure you have the tools necessary for success. Get agreement on staffing, budget, expense account, and the other tools you need to be successful before you accept the offer rather than letting them become issues after you start work.

When the economy is weak, raises are also harder to come by and sometimes are constrained by organizational guidelines. So you may want to negotiate your first raise as well. This is particularly effective if the salary being offered is less than you were hoping for and you cannot get the employer to increase it significantly. For example, you could say: "I understand that you don't have any more money in the budget now, but let's agree on some first-year goals, and if I achieve them, we can agree that my salary will be adjusted at that time to the level we have been discussing." Alternatively, you may want to negotiate the criteria necessary to receive your year-end bonus. You can also seek a guaranteed minimum first-year bonus if it will take some time for the changes you intend to implement to have their full impact. Guarantees are particularly important if bonuses are based on a standard formula (for example, an increase in sales or the improved profitability of your group).

Timing is also critical. Let the employer put the first offer on the table. (See the chapter "Principles for Negotiating: The 11 Commandments of Employment Negotiations," Commandment 5, "Use Uncertainty to Your Advantage.") Avoid, as much as possible, discussing compensation until your prospective employer has already decided that you are the one she wants to hire. Do that tactfully and in a way that will not upset your prospective employer. At the same time, if you handle it correctly, an employer trying to recruit you will not want to press the issue for fear of angering you.

If you can delay discussions about salary, or keep them vague, until an employer wants to hire you, you can often get an offer without providing detailed salary information. If hiring managers do not have that information, they will be forced to base their offer on your market value rather than your current salary.

Depending on when your salary history is requested, here are some possible ways you can respond:

▶ *Questions about salary on the application.*   The issue of what you are currently earning is likely to arise before you even start the interview process, when you are asked to fill out an application. Most applications have a section that asks for salary history. Many online job postings and ads in newspapers also ask for this information. Some even warn that you won't be considered if you don't provide salary information. Sometimes you can simply ignore the request. Other times you can deal with this question by stating that you "will discuss it in person." Occasionally, you will not be considered for a job if you do not provide this information; more often than not, though, if you have marketed yourself well, you will be able to get an interview without disclosing your current salary.

▶ *Questions about salary from the interviewer.*   When the interviewer asks you about your salary, your goal remains the same— delay talking about it, or keep the discussions vague. You might try saying something like, "It is not about the salary; it is about the job. If it's the right job for me and I am the right person for it, salary won't be an issue." Then you can turn it around and ask what the employer has budgeted for the position. If you have to talk about compensation, be general and talk about your total compensation. For example, if your salary, potential bonus, and stock options are worth $75,000, maximize it by saying something like, "My total annual compensation is in the high five figures."

▶ *Questions about salary from the recruiter.*   Recruiters generally seek salary information for a different purpose. Since they usually are paid based on a percentage of your first year's compensation, it is in their interest for the offer to be higher. They want to know your salary to avoid recommending a particular candidate only to find out later that the employer and the candidate cannot agree on salary. Therefore, the tactics that work with companies to avoid discussing salary will not work with most recruiters. They will insist on having salary information. Providing the information to recruiters, though, will hurt your ability to negotiate. Remember that recruiters work for the employers and whatever you tell the recruiters will usually be passed on to those employers.

Even though an employer generally has a salary range for a position, that range is never set in stone. The goal is to get all the key players to really want to hire you before talking about salary. Once an employer falls in love with a candidate, negotiating is the last thing on his mind; instead, his focus is on getting that individual to accept the offer. The employer will find ways to pay you more if he has to in order to get you to accept the offer.

Getting a prospective employer to fall in love with you requires an understanding of what the people making the hiring decisions care about. While in most organizations there is a common set of shared values referred to as the "organization's culture," we don't interview with an organization. We interview with individuals. For most jobs you will have to interview with more than one person. The individuals that interview you will each see the job being filled somewhat differently. They will each define the perfect candidate as the perfect candidate *for them*. To convince any particular interviewer that you are the one for the job, you need to figure out what she cares most about.

What someone is looking for in a candidate usually can be found in his answer to the question, "What can the candidate do for me?" Individuals tend to see the answer to that question differently depending on their role in the organization. Someone working in human resources will have a different view of what is important than will someone in finance, and both will differ from that of your future boss when it comes to what qualities they are seeking in a job candidate.

The human resources executives are usually looking for the easy, obvious choice—someone who will be readily accepted by everyone involved. That way they can fill the position quickly and move on to other work. They also don't want to take risks. Human resources executives need to be able to justify why they believe someone is the "best" candidate for the job. If the candidate has all the right skills and experience but fails on the job, no one will blame them for recruiting someone who was "clearly wrong for the job." On the other hand, if the human resources executives favor someone who doesn't fit the job specifications exactly and then that candidate doesn't work out, even if the individual is otherwise outstanding, the human resources executives are likely to face criticism. So typically human resources executives opt for the safe choice. Bear that in mind when you interview with them, and show them how you meet all the important qualifications for the job. Make sure that the interviewer is comfortable that you are not a risky choice. Focus on how you have successfully handled similar challenges in the past.

What do finance executives care about? They want someone with whom they will be able to work—someone who knows how to develop, and stay within, a budget and who can help reduce expenses or generate additional revenues. Those are the skills you typically want to emphasize when you are interviewing with a financial executive.

The hiring manager, your future boss, wants someone who can help solve her most pressing problems, whatever they are. Hiring managers are likely to have very immediate needs, and they want someone who can help them take care of those needs. In today's competitive business environment, your prospective boss is looking for someone that can have an immediate impact. Hiring managers tend to focus on whatever they deem to be their most important needs at that moment. The most important question you can ask the hiring manager is, "What is it at work that keeps you up at night?" The answer to that question will help you determine what your future boss really cares about. That is what you need to concentrate on. If you can show how you can help the hiring manager resolve those issues, you have gone a long way toward winning her over. Once you do that, the salary negotiations will be easy. Be prepared with specific examples of the things that you have done that are likely to relate to the immediate problems your future boss is facing.

While you are the same person with the same skills, experience, and personal qualities no matter whom you are interviewing with, what you choose to emphasize will make all the difference in the world. Remember each person who interviews you sees the job being filled slightly differently based on how he interacts with that position. When you are talking about your ability to do the job, what you choose to talk about is primarily a matter of emphasis. The more each of those people feels that you share his values, the more he will want to hire you. That will in turn result in his being more amenable to giving you what you want in order to ensure that you accept the position and feel good about doing so. Deferring discussions about compensation until after you have convinced the key decision makers that you are the right candidate for the job will enable you to maximize your ability to negotiate in any economy.

SUMMARY OF KEY POINTS

▶ Being recruited increases your bargainng power; be proactive in creating the conditions that will result in the right employers and recruiters finding you.
▶ Build a professional network.
▶ Create an Internet presence.
▶ Become active in professional and civic organizations.
▶ Get a potential employer to "fall in love with you" by understanding how the hiring process works.
▶ Determine what each individual who interviews you really cares about.
▶ Focus your interview answers on what is important to the interviewer.
▶ Defer compensation discussions until after a decision has been made to hire you.
▶ Keep the employer focused on recruiting (rather than negotiating with) you.

Everything You Need to Know about Using the Internet (and Other Sources of Information) to Help You Negotiate

Always be more prepared than the other guy.

—Senator Phil Gramm

Preparation for salary negotiations always begins with the Internet. It is an invaluable source of easily accessible compensation information. Just search under the term "salary" and you can locate dozens of useful Web sites. Using a variety of career-based Web sites, you can gather information about salaries and benefits at employers where you might be interested in working, as well as at their competitors and at similar companies in other industries.

Many of the Web sites that provide information on salary and benefits are free to site visitors although they may offer additional information to paid subscribers or to those who are willing to purchase individual reports. Others can be accessed only for a fee. The amount of available salary information on the Internet is virtually limitless; knowing the best places to find the specific information you need will save you time and effort. Several of the best compensation Web sites are described below.

Salary.com (www.salary.com)

Several of the major job search engines, including Monster.com and Vault.com, offer Salary.com's Wizard as a tool for their users to research salary for specific positions. The Salary.com Wizard allows you to retrieve information by job title and location. Say, for example, you are an executive assistant in Kansas City and are looking for a similar position with another employer. The Salary.com Wizard shows you what other executive assistants in Kansas City earn. The site includes a brief job description of a typical executive assistant so that you can compare it with a position you are considering to ensure that it is a good match. If the job description isn't a match, the Wizard suggests comparable job titles that might be a better fit—for example, administrative assistant or executive secretary.

Once you settle on the applicable job description, the Salary.com Wizard will display the distribution of salaries for executive assistants in the Kansas City area as a bell curve with markers at the 10th, 25th, 75th, and 90th percentiles. The Wizard will display the data with and without bonuses factored in, as well as showing you the median amount that employers spend on base salary, bonuses, social security, 401(k) and 403(b) plans, disability insurance, health care, and pensions, as well as the amount of time off they offer. Another available feature is a salary breakdown by pay period, assuming a biweekly paycheck, so that you can view your actual take-home pay after deductions. In determining this figure, the Wizard considers federal and local withholding rates, but it lets you enter the other types of deductions you want calculated in the paycheck.

The Salary.com Wizard also allows you to compare salaries for similar positions in various cities throughout the country. For example, you could compare what executive assistants in the Midwest earn with those on the West Coast or with the national average. Combining this feature with the Salary.com Cost-of-Living Wizard will assist you in analyzing the financial impact of relocating.

Another valuable feature that Salary.com offers is its partnership with Monster.com. When you search for salary information about a particular position on Salary.com, a part of the results page includes Monster.com job listings for specific openings with that title, providing you with up-to-date salary information as well as other possible positions for which you might want to be considered.

Salary.com provides free salary information for specific positions, by years of experience and location. It gives you a range, showing the high, low, and average salaries as well as information on the cost of living in the regions you are interested in. The site also offers premium content for which you must pay a fee. Premium information includes salary information by company, location, experience, education, and industry as well as the rationale behind compensation offers made by specific employers.

PayScale.com (www.payscale.com)

Like Salary.com, PayScale.com allows you to determine the going market rate for the specific jobs you are interested in. One of the unique features of PayScale.com is that it has you complete an online questionnaire that enables you to match what you do with comparable positions to ensure that you are looking at the right positions. It also features a "what-if" section, so that you can change variables based on factors such as relocation and education, to see how changing those variables would likely alter your compensation. PayScale.com also has a function that enables you to calculate a cost-of-living adjustment for different cities as well as comparable salaries for the same job title in different cities. If you register on the site, you can save information about various job offers you are considering and compare them against one another.

PayScale.com also offers a premium membership, which provides anonymous, anecdotal salary information from individuals at various companies. Once you have entered your job and career information, the site generates a report on each employer that you specify. It also generates industry data for comparison. Another unique premium feature offered by the site is that it generates anonymous profiles of people in similar jobs. These profiles consist of information that other customers entered when creating their accounts. As such they are fairly detailed and may be more up to date than the reports since they are inputted on a regular basis by users. A premium membership also allows you to run reports using specific criteria, such as nursing salaries in hospitals with varying bed counts.

SimplyHired.com (www.simplyhired.com)

SimplyHired.com is primarily a search engine that looks for job postings throughout the Internet on other career and employer Web sites. As a result, SimplyHired.com offers real-time information reflective of current job postings. SimplyHired.com also offers a feature that allows you to find the average salary for a job in the city in which you live and compare it to the average salary of the same position in other cities, based on the job postings its search engine finds.

Taking advantage of a partnership with the social networking Web site LinkedIn.com: every job posting on SimplyHired.com includes a button that connects to LinkedIn.com and shows people that you know who work for that particular employer (a LinkedIn.com account is required to use this feature). This facilitates networking with individuals who work at employers that you are interested in and provides another avenue to gather salary and benefits information, as firsthand employee knowledge will be an invaluable source of information about the inside workings of an employer. Its partnership with LinkedIn.com provides a useful tool for obtaining valuable information that can be helpful during their job search, including during salary negotiations.

Vault.com (www.vault.com)

Vault.com is a career-based Web site that offers a wide range of salary information. Certain sections of the site may be accessed for free, but some of the most useful information the site offers is available only to premium ("Gold") members. The site is updated frequently, with much of its information being as recent as only a few days old. Some of Vault.com's highlights include the following:

▶ *Salary surveys by industry.* These cover almost 50 fields such as retail, fashion, advertising and PR, technology, financial services, government, and health care. These surveys include testimonials from current and former employees and can include salary information, opinions on management and organizational culture, and perks unique to the companies surveyed. For instance, one survey noted that all employees of a particular financial services firm are eligible for a 20 percent discount on personal cell phones.

▶ *Employer snapshots.* These provide a summary of information about an employer including recent news articles, history and culture, excerpted pros and cons from employees, and a special section with tips from insiders on getting hired by that organization.

▶ *Vault.com Salary Central.* Here you can find current salary information in three specific sectors: consulting, law, and financial services. The legal section, for instance, contains salary and bonus information for employees at hundreds of top law firms throughout the United States and United Kingdom, broken down by years of service within the firm. The consulting section is broken out between management consultants and tech consultants, but both include information about actual salaries and expected bonuses, based on number of years of service and so on. The financial services section includes information on accounting, investment banking, and investment management salaries. Criteria reflected include, for example, whether employees have certain certifications (and if so how many) and whether employees have graduate degrees.

Vault.com provides job postings, industry data, and employer data, as well as job-specific information. There are also industry surveys, employee interviews, and reports on specific employers. Vault.com is subscription based, unlike many other premium sites where you have to pay per report.

Other Sites

Depending on your specific needs, budget, and/or industry, a variety of other online sources can be helpful when you are preparing to negotiate salary, including the following:

- ▶ *GuideStar.org (www.guidestar.org)*. This Web site focuses on nonprofit organizations. Among other features, the site provides access to current job postings for nonprofits as well as the IRS 990 reporting forms for listed organizations, which show the compensation of the top five highest-paid staff members.
- ▶ *Glassdoor.com (www.glassdoor.com)*. Glassdoor.com contains information from employees about the salaries, benefits, and company culture of thousands of employers. In order to register so you can use the site, you have to provide information about your own employer, which is made available anonymously to other users. This feature provides valuable, detailed, up-to-date information about specific employers.
- ▶ *Riley Guide (www.rileyguide.com)*. This Web site provides a compilation of links to other sites that offer free salary surveys. Many of these sites are industry specific.
- ▶ *CareerOneStop (www.acinet.org)*. This Web site (also known as America's Career InfoNet) offers a wealth of career information covering everything from salaries and benefits to negotiation to career descriptions. This site also has links to other helpful career sites.
- ▶ *U.S. Department of Labor, Bureau of Labor Statistics (data.bls.gov/oes/search.jsp)*. This database tool located on the

agency's Web site creates customized salary reports for generic job titles in a variety of industries and sectors.

▶ *IEEE Salary Survey (www.ieeeusa.org/careers/salary/)*. Free to members of the Institute of Electrical and Electronics Engineers, this database contains a wide variety of salary information specifically dealing with the technology sector.

▶ *Pam Pohly's Net Guide (www.pohly.com)*. This site contains a list of sites that provide salary-related information for the health care industry.

Other general career Web sites that have salary calculators are Yahoo's Hot Jobs (hotjobs.salary.com/) and Monster.com (www.monster.com). Careers (www.careerjournal.com), which is owned by the *Wall Street Journal*, and JobStar.org (www.jobstar.org) also provide salary information.

Hoover's (www.hoovers.com) provides valuable information about salaries and stock ownership of key executives as well as organizational structure. In addition, it identifies key competitors for each listed company. Knowing an employer's key competitors will enable you to find out about the salary and benefits that those companies offer, which can be tremendously useful in employment negotiations. For example, if you were negotiating to be the director of marketing at Pepsi, how helpful would it be to know the compensation of the director of marketing at Coca-Cola?

In addition to the online survey type of information described above, as part of your preparation you should check the job boards for recent postings of jobs at your level. This will provide up-to-the-minute salary information on positions similar to the one you are negotiating about. In addition to providing valuable market information, you may want to apply for some of the positions you come across (see Strategy 13).

Information about publicly traded companies—including the salary of the five highest-paid employees along with their bonuses, stock, stock options, deferred compensation, and other benefits—can be found in their proxy statements, which are readily accessible online. The proxy statement will also describe various benefit plans as well as the eligibility requirements for participating in those plans. Proxy statements (Schedule 14A) and other documents that public companies are required to file can also be readily accessed through the EDGAR database, which can be found on the Internet on the Securities and Exchange Commission Web site at www.sec.gov/edgar/searchedgar/webusers.htm.

You can go directly to the filings of the company you are looking for by opening the location in your Web browser and adding the company's name at the end of the following string:

http://www.sec.gov/cgi-bin/srch-edgar? insert company name

Because the browser identifies the company by adding words to the search, you must use a Boolean format at the end of the string, connecting each keyword in the company name with a

+and+

to identify the organization. For example, Sun Microsystems becomes

sun+and+microsystems

Thus, the full string to locate Sun Microsystems documents is

http://www.sec.gov/cgi-bin/srch-edgar? sun+and+microsystems

You can also generally obtain a proxy statement and other useful information by contacting a company's investor relations or public affairs department or by contacting the Securities and Exchange Commission, a U.S. government agency in Washington, D.C.

Unless you are being considered for one of the top five jobs in a public company, you are unlikely to find out exactly what the person who previously held the position earned. However, no matter what the level of the position you are seeking, you should be able to develop an estimated salary range by determining the compensation of other executives at the company and at competitive firms.

Finally, don't forget to check the employer's own Web site. It may provide information about salary and benefits. It also may include job listings from which you can glean useful salary information. Be sure to do a Google search for the employer's negotiator by name to find out everything you can about him or her as well. Also, visit the Web sites and directories of professional associations. Often they'll not only provide salaries for positions in a particular industry but also ranges based on geographic location and experience level.

Other Sources of Information

While the Internet is the easiest way to gather relevant salary information, it is not the only available source of infomation. In fact, the best sources of information about an employer, including salary and benefits information, are employees and former employees. For any particular employer that you might be interested in, you will want to talk with employees and ex-employees. Current employees can provide you with up-to-date information on salaries and benefits, as well as the types of salary increases that have been given over the last few years. They can also help you understand the organizational structure of the employer.

Former employees can also provide you with valuable information. While that information may be dated, it can be adjusted to reflect estimated salary increases that have been granted since they left. At the very least, this information will enable you to determine the relative importance of different positions within the organization. Their lack of current information is more than offset by their greater willingness to talk about sensitive issues such as compensation. You will be surprised how many of your friends or acquaintances know employees and ex-employees of various companies. All you have to do is ask.

With the advent of social networking sites such as LinkedIn.com, Facebook.com, MySpace.com, and Classmates.com, employees and ex-employees are easier to find and to network with. Alumni associations, professional organizations, charities, and religious organizations are also avenues through which you can identify individuals to network with and obtain information about employers you are interested in. Once you have made a connection, try to arrange a face-to-face meeting rather than relying only on e-mail or telephone communications. You will get a lot more information from someone if you can get him or her to sit down with you over a cup of coffee than you will get via e-mail exchanges or telephone calls.

Accountants and lawyers can also be valuable sources of information. Although ethics prevent them from disclosing confidential information about their clients, they may have knowledge about other employers that they have had dealings with. If the information is not confidential, they are generally willing to share it with you.

Regardless of the level position you are seeking and the industry in which you work, using the Internet can help you prepare for salary negotiations. Doing your homework ahead of time, and having an understanding of the market rate for the position as well as a firm's general compensation structure, will help you achieve your goals when it comes time to negotiate your salary.

Summary of Key Points

▶ Before you begin to negotiate, do your homework.
▶ Determine the market value for the position by using the tools available on various career Web sites.
▶ Get as much information as you can about the salary and benefits offered by the specific employers you are interested in.
▶ Use the Internet (as well as other avenues) to connect with both current and former employees.
▶ Find out as much as you can about the organizational structure.
▶ If a move is involved, look at the cost of living in the area you are considering.
▶ Find out everything you can about the employer's negotiator.
▶ Review information on the employer's Web site.

Beyond Research

PREPARING TO NEGOTIATE

To act effectively, we still must have a plan. To the proverb which says "A journey of a thousand miles begins with a single step," I would add "and a road map."

—FLETCHER BYRON

Although preparation is a good idea in most endeavors, it is critical in negotiations. It is the one facet of the employment process in which the applicant can have an advantage over the employer. Typically, employers do little or nothing to get ready for negotiating with a job candidate once they have decided to make an offer. Their focus throughout the hiring process is on finding someone who can fill a perceived need.

After an employer identifies the candidate it wants to hire, the primary focus turns to getting that individual to accept the job and begin work as soon as possible. While the employer will likely have given some thought to the general financial parameters for filling the position, it almost certainly will have spent no time developing a negotiating strategy.

Normally the only actual limits on what an organization can offer are budgetary constraints and organizational structure. Since most compensation systems, particularly in small companies, are not rigidly structured, employers generally have a great deal of flexibility in what they can offer. As a practical matter, often the only real constraint on what can be offered comes from the employer's negotiator not wanting to look foolish.

Thus, provided that what you are seeking can be accommodated within the budgetary limitations and organizational constraints the negotiator has to live with, almost any arrangement that is considered reasonable is likely to be acceptable. In fact, if you can convince your future boss that the budgeted compensation is not competitive, the employer will often be able to find additional money elsewhere.

Organizational constraints are more difficult to overcome. For example, no matter how reasonable your salary demands are, it will be exceedingly hard to convince an employer to pay you more than it pays your boss. It will be even more difficult to convince your future boss of the need to do so. (Salespeople who work on commission are sometimes an exception to this rule.) However, preparation will enable you to negotiate better terms within those organizational constraints. Sometimes you may even be able to get the employer to adjust the organizational structure to accommodate your legitimate compensation requests. Properly presented, your prospective boss may even be supportive of your efforts to increase the amount budgeted for the position because it might provide an opportunity to advocate for a salary increase for himself as well.

As stated above, ordinarily employers do not prepare to negotiate with the individuals they are recruiting. Initially they decide what qualifications are needed for the position. Then they determine approximately what they are willing to pay for those skills, based on their budget and where the position falls in the organizational hierarchy. If the employer has done any preparation at all, it will be to determine the market rate for the position in question. What information the employer has will ordinarily have come from market surveys or from informal contacts with other employers to determine what employees in comparable positions earn. These comparisons will generally be made, if at all, at the time the organization develops a budget for the position. Even if market research has been done, often the information has become dated by the time the position is eventually filled.

Preparing to Discuss Your Current Salary

Most potential employers will want to know what you are currently earning. Employers and recruiters will usually inquire about your current compensation at a relatively early stage in the hiring process. When and how you answer that question can have a significant impact on the ultimate success of the negotiations. To the extent that a prospective employer has detailed information about your current compensation package, the employer will use it in determining how it structures its offer of employment.

For a position at the same level as your current job, a new employer will typically offer a 10 to 15 percent increase in salary. The increase will be greater if the new position involves a promotion or entails substantial risks, such as the imminent possibility of a merger or takeover. Similarly, if the job involves relocating to a more expensive part of the country, the offer will normally include a differential to cover the increase in the cost of living. In virtually every instance, however, your current salary will weigh heavily in determining the amount of the offer you receive.

How to answer the question "What are you currently making?" is dealt with in detail later (see Strategy 1). Obtaining the information necessary to support your salary demands before you begin negotiating is critical to prevent an outcome predetermined by your current salary.

If you were buying a car, wouldn't it be helpful to know the lowest price at which the dealer would be willing to sell the car? With proper preparation you can determine, within a range, what salary a prospective employer should be willing to pay in order to hire you. Once you know what that range is, you should be able to maximize your salary within it. Unless your future employer can be convinced to adjust the salary range upward, the top of the range will serve to limit your salary. To get a prospective employer to rethink the salary range, you must first understand how employers set salaries.

Let's assume you are the controller for a midsized company. You aspire one day to be chief financial officer. Since the chief financial officer where you work is 45 years old, has been with the organization for most of his career, and is not likely to be promoted, you've decided to look elsewhere for a job that offers greater opportunities for advancement. Another reason you are considering other job possibilities is that your salary has lagged behind that of your peers elsewhere because of your employer's weak financial position.

Just as you start to put your résumé together, a headhunter calls to ask if you would be interested in the controller's position for a large computer manufacturer. The employer is looking to groom someone to be chief financial officer when the incumbent retires in two years. The recruiter thinks you have the perfect background for the job. You ask what the position pays. She responds: "It depends on the experience of the individual." Then she asks you how much you are currently making. You deftly avoid giving a direct answer to that question (see Strategy 1). Then you immediately begin the task of trying to determine the salary range that would be appropriate for the position.

How Employers Set Salaries

There are four primary determinants of salary: (1) the job's relative position in the organization's hierarchy, (2) the market rate for the position, (3) the candidate's present salary, and (4) the department's budget.

Where the position fits into the organization's hierarchy defines the outer limits of potential salary. Normally employees will not be paid more than their boss, less than their subordinates, or much differently from their peers. Within those parameters, what job candidates are offered will be influenced most by their current salary. An individual's current salary generally ends up playing a critical role for a number of reasons. In the first place, it can be easily ascertained by a potential employer. Its reliability is not subject to challenge since the candidate has provided the information. Moreover, in the absence of a competing offer, a prospective employer will assume that a job candidate will be happy if he is able to improve his compensation by an incremental amount. Consequently a candidate's present salary serves as a benchmark against which the reasonableness of the employer's offer will be judged.

An offer can also be influenced by the market rates for similar positions. If you can demonstrate that an offer is below market, it is likely to be improved. The best evidence of what your skills can command in the job market though is what another employer is willing to pay. Most organizations will at least match a competing offer if they want to hire someone, provided that the offer is within their organizational and budgetary limitations. In the absence of a competing offer, salaries at key competitors and information from general salary surveys can be used to determine the market value for a particular position [see the preceding chapter, "Everything You Need to Know about Using the Internet (and Other Sources of Information) to Help You Negotiate"].

Budget plays a role only to the extent that the employer can't afford to, or doesn't want to, pay the market rate. In that case, the candidate will often be compensated in other ways, such as with stock or stock options in lieu of a competitive salary. Alternatively, to accommodate budgetary constraints, an employer may accept someone who is willing to work for less than the market rate. Candidates may be willing to do so because they are unemployed or because the job constitutes a promotion and they do not have all the qualifications that would ordinarily be required for the position.

You know your current salary. You will find out very early in the hiring process whether the employer cannot afford, or is unwilling, to pay the market rate. Therefore, in order to prepare for negotiations properly, you need to gather information about the organization's hierarchy and determine the market rate for the position. The prior chapter dealt with how to determine the market rate for a given position using the Internet and other available resources.

To understand the organization's hierarchy, the employer's Web site is a good place to start. If you are negotiating with a public company, its annual report and proxy statement also contain a great deal of useful information. The "proxy statement" is a document that is prepared by the company and sent to its shareholders annually, prior to the election of directors. It is required by law to include certain information, including the salary of the five highest-paid employees along with their bonuses, stock, stock options, deferred compensation, and other benefits. For not-for-profits, the Form 990 they are required to file with the federal government provides similar information. The proxy statement will also describe various benefit plans as well as the eligibility requirements for participating in those plans. This information can also be readily obtained via the Internet or from the company directly [see the preceding chapter, "Everything You Need to Know about Using the Internet (and Other Sources of Information) to Help You Negotiate"]. As discussed in the previous chapter, employees and former employees are invaluable sources of information about an organization's structure.

Developing a Negotiating Strategy

Once you have determined the likely compensation range for the position, how can you use what you have learned to your advantage? Let's look at how you might be able to use the information in the situation described previously where you have been approached by a headhunter. You know what the current chief financial officer, your future boss, is making from looking at the employer's proxy statement. From current and former employees, you can get an idea of the approximate salaries of other director-level employees. With that information, you can figure out approximately how much the employer is willing to pay for the position.

Once you can get the chief financial officer to offer you a salary at that level, there are only two ways to improve upon it. One way is to convince your prospective boss that the employer's salaries, at least in his department, have fallen below market levels and in order to attract top quality talent, the employer needs to adjust the entire salary structure upward. Of course, that would generally include the boss's salary as well. If salary surveys and key competitor data show that the chief financial officer and the controller's positions are being undervalued, you as the candidate can provide this information to your future boss. He can then use the difficulty in recruiting you not only to have the controller's salary adjusted upward but also to argue for improvement in his own compensation as well. Armed with that ammunition, he could become the strongest proponent within the organization for increasing the controller's salary.

Another way an employer can respond when confronted with information that a salary offer is not competitive, without disrupting its whole salary structure, is by increasing the offer in ways that do not affect the overall salary structure. For example, the employer could agree to pay you a signing bonus, to provide you with additional stock options, or to agree to an early performance review.

Let's look at how one of my clients, Jack, used his knowledge of the organization's structure in a similar situation. Jack was vice president of human resources for a division of a Fortune 1000 company. He was being recruited by a competitor, a smaller but more profitable company, to fill a similar position. Historically, the head of human resources at his prospective employer had always been a vice president, although the position reported directly to the company's president. After researching the organization, Jack determined that only senior vice presidents were eligible for certain benefits. Among the benefits senior vice presidents received were a company car and participation in a stock option plan.

After a job offer was extended to him, instead of trying to negotiate for additional salary or benefits, Jack indicated that he would love to come to work for them but that a lateral move, even for more money, did not make any sense in his situation. Since he had experience negotiating leases, he suggested that he take on the additional responsibilities of handling real estate and running the corporate office, with the title of senior vice president of administration. In view of the fact that the human resources position already reported to the president, the title change did not pose any major organizational problems. Because Jack had done his homework and understood the organizational structure, he knew that his compensation package would automatically increase significantly if he was hired at the senior vice president level. So instead of negotiating the salary, he negotiated for a senior vice president's title (see Strategy 4).

It is also useful to learn whatever you can about the person negotiating on behalf of the employer. The negotiator will usually be your future boss or someone in the human resources department. Talk to people who know that individual. Learn where he or she lives. Ask about his or her interests.

Find out about the person's negotiating style. As recommended in the previous chapter, do a Web search (e.g., a Google search) using the negotiator's name. Then think about how this information might be of use. If, for example, the negotiator has a working spouse, that individual is likely to be sympathetic to problems that your spouse will face as a result of having to relocate. The more you know about this person, the easier it will be to negotiate with him or her.

Another aspect of your preparation is to anticipate issues and rehearse your responses to them. You can always take a break before you respond to any issue being raised for the first time. However, if you have anticipated the issue, you will be better able to offer a well-thought-out response. Your position will be persuasive because you are prepared; but at the same time it will appear to be spontaneous. This not only will give you credibility but will also highlight the importance of the issue to you. As a result, you may get the issue resolved to your satisfaction right then and there. At the very least, you will have positioned yourself well to deal with the issue later on.

As part of your preparation, you should develop ready responses to all the major issues that you anticipate will arise. Otherwise, you may weaken your bargaining position by appearing not to be able to respond to a key point being made by the employer's negotiator. Politicians use this type of preparation very effectively. For example, during the 2008 presidential campaign Barack Obama had a standard "stump speech" that hit on all the major themes of his campaign. During the presidential debates, when a difficult question arose, he was able to draw on his speech, even though it may not have answered the question exactly. The answer was still effective, even to people who had heard it before. To people who had never heard it, the effect of giving a "spontaneous," articulate, and well-thought-out response to the question was compelling. You want to be able to use your prepared responses in the same way.

You need to understand not only the constraints placed upon the employer but also your own priorities. What is it that you want? What are you unhappy about in your current job? Examining your priorities is an important part of your preparation. Once you have determined what they are, it is a good idea to write them down. Ask yourself what is important to you, and then ask someone who knows you well the same question—that is, what does he or she think is important to you. Is it salary, bonus potential, title, job security, stock, severance, freedom to be creative, autonomy, a supportive boss, access to necessary resources, state-of-the-art equipment, status, or perks? Make a list of what your negotiating priorities are, and rank them in order of importance. Referring to this list periodically during the negotiations will help keep you focused on your objectives.

Understanding your needs will also help you determine what type of employer you want to work for. Start-up companies may not be able to offer you the market rate salary but can typically offer stock or stock options. In one deal that I worked on with a start-up, we were able to overcome the company's cash flow problems by proposing that, since the company could not afford to match my client's current cash compensation, instead it would provide my client with a large equity stake. A satisfactory agreement was reached after each side took the time to understand both the objectives of the candidate and the limitations on the employer.

In any negotiation there will be trade-offs. If you consider your own priorities in light of the employer's needs, you will know when it is possible, for example, to trade salary for stock ownership. You will also be able to walk away from a prospective job once you determine that the employer cannot offer the type of compensation package you want. That can sometimes be the most important decision you make during the negotiations (see Strategy 25).

SUMMARY OF KEY POINTS

▶ Most employers don't do much to prepare for negotiations with the individuals they are seeking to hire.
▶ Proper preparation can provide you with an advantage in the negotiations.
▶ Understand how employers set salaries.
▶ Learn everything you can about the person handling the negotiations for the employer.
▶ Determine your priorities.
▶ Understand the constraints the employer must contend with.
▶ Be prepared to discuss your current salary.
▶ Develop a negotiating strategy.
▶ Anticipate issues and prepare responses to those that you expect will arise.
▶ Identify the trade-offs you are willing to make.

Dressing the Part to Enhance Your Ability to Negotiate (and Your Career)

Being the one guy at the clambake with a pocket square in your linen sport coat doesn't make you a gentleman among cretins; it makes you overdressed. But it is better than being the guy wearing a tank top at the wedding.

—MAXIM MAGAZINE

While attending a meeting of the Professional Speakers Network, the president of the organization came up to Camille Leon, a motivational speaker from Los Angeles, and asked, "Does having 'secretary hair' get in the way of your success?" At the time she had long straight hair almost to her waist. She promptly went out and had it cut and styled. After receiving the comments about her hairstyle, Leon also began to pay attention to the differences between secretaries and women managers in the corporate settings where she consulted. Then she "threw away her sweaters," noting that "secretaries tended to wear sweaters but the female managers almost always wore jackets." Not only did she start booking more business thereafter but she was also able to negotiate higher consulting fees.

Your appearance will have a significant impact on how successful you are not only in your negotiations but also in your career. So I asked Louis Amendola, executive vice president of merchandising for Brooks Brothers, to help me write about how both men and women should dress in order to enhance their legitimacy and give them the aura of authority that facilitates getting promoted and effectively negotiating compensation.

The key to maximizing the impact you have in your negotiations, as well as in all the other facets of your career, is to always dress appropriately for the position you aspire to as well as for the occasion. While expectations about dress differ from industry to industry, everyone has certain expectations about how a person "in authority" should look. The way people dress and how they carry themselves form the foundation of how others view them. Police officers, judges, and doctors for example, all dress so that you know instantly that they are functioning in a role that sets them apart from the rest of us. In virtually every field, individuals with higher status dress differently. Dress appropriately for the industry and the position you are seeking. That will require dressing differently in Los Angeles, Chicago, or New York City. Similarly what works in Los Angeles won't work in Paris or Singapore. It will also make a difference if you are working in financial services, entertainment, or retail industries.

Lou offered some general tips on how to dress to enhance your legitimacy when you are interviewing for a job and negotiating your compensation:

▶ Wear the best clothes you can afford, and make sure they are well tailored.

▶ Be current, but not trendy, in terms of fashion.

▶ Take time with your appearance so you look "well put together" but natural. Periodically check to be sure your makeup is right, your tie is straight, and your shirt is tucked in.

▶ Make sure your clothes are cleaned and pressed. Your trousers should have a crisp crease.

▶ Your nails should be clean and well manicured.

▶ Your hair should be neat and styled.

▶ Pay particular attention to your choice of accessories: shoes, tie, watch, outerwear, and briefcase.

▶ Polish your shoes. It completes the look. A beautiful suit and unpolished shoes suggest that you are dressing differently in an attempt to impress.

For men, suits are still equated with authority in most industries. A classic wool suit that is well tailored and stylish, contemporary but not too trendy (unless you are in an industry such as entertainment or fashion where trendy is expected) will serve to project the right image. Even if business casual is the dress code for your industry, a sports jacket without a tie will help you project the right image.

Choose your ties carefully. They complete the picture. You can use your ties to express your personality—bold or conservative—but they should be high quality and contemporary. Take your cues from the men's magazines, newscasters, and top executives in your organization. Ties should also coordinate with your shirt and suit. If you have any doubts, a good salesperson or personal shopper can help you. Mickey Mouse ties are a definite "no-no," and team logo ties should be hauled out only on the day after your favorite team has won a championship game. Unless you are an academic, bow ties probably aren't a good choice either.

Lou recommends "learning to tie your tie properly." Ties should be tied with either a Windsor or half Windsor knot. He adds, "Keep your collar buttoned, and don't loosen your tie when you are in a meeting." While men's suits can be worn for several years, men's shirts and ties need to be replaced every year. "Styles change, and shirts show signs of wear after about a year."

Women have the advantage of being able to show a little more personality in the way they dress. Dresses are almost always appropriate as long as they are not too revealing. Tasteful skirts or pants and a blouse also convey the right image. A well-tailored jacket can enhance the look.

Good tailoring is just as important for women as it is for men. Be sure the sleeves and skirt are the right length. An inch can make all the difference between chic and dowdy. Also pay attention to details such as the accessories and shoes you wear. Shoes should be high quality, stylish, and well polished. Women should update their shoes at least annually. When it comes to makeup and accessories, less is more. Makeup shouldn't overpower the outfit, and neither should perfume. Lou warns "not to overaccessorize outfits, especially with too much jewelry." Earrings should not be too large, and clothing should not be too tight. Pay attention to your choice of handbags because other women will.

Sometimes as part of the recruiting process you may be invited to a social function. Dress appropriately for the type of function. Whether a picnic, barbecue, or pool party at the boss's home, no matter how informal, these are still very much business functions. Clothes that are too tight, too short, low cut, or see-through are never appropriate. Young people have to be particularly cognizant of how they dress and look. Alaina G. Levine, director of special projects at the University of Arizona, recalls how when she was younger, she began to dress in business suits so that she would be taken more seriously. It worked. Now that she is more established, she continues to wear business suits even in the more casual environment she finds herself in at the university. "People treat you differently when you dress that way. At networking events, for example, if you are wearing a suit, people look at you as a person of authority." According to Levine, "It never hurts to be a little bit more formal than the people around you, as long as you are appropriately dressed for the occasion. That will enable you to stand out in a positive way."

Look at how successful people in your field dress, and let that guide you. Always dress for the position you aspire to rather than the position that you currently hold. Whether it is the right suit or having the proper accessories, dress in a way that visibly demonstrates that you are the right person for the job.

Decision makers, consciously or subconsciously, often consider whether someone looks the part in deciding whether to hire or promote the person. How someone dresses can play a major role in those decisions. How you look also can impact how you are paid and how effective you are when you negotiate compensation.

The image you present is something that you should never leave to chance. Determining how to dress in order to create the right image for yourself is as much a part of your preparation as determining what the market value for your position is. One element of being able to influence others is the ability to establish your legitimacy—branding yourself with that aura of authority that establishes instant credibility. To do that, you should dress the way the people that you are seeking to influence expect someone in authority to dress.

SUMMARY OF KEY POINTS

▶ How you dress can have an impact on how successful you are when negotiating compensation as well as in advancing your career generally.

▶ Dress appropriately for the position you aspire to as well as for the occasion.

▶ Look at how successful people in your field dress and let that guide you.

▶ Wear the best clothes you can afford, and make sure they are well tailored, cleaned, and pressed.

▶ Pay attention to your choice of accessories (that is, shoes, tie, watch, outerwear, and briefcase).

▶ Take care with your grooming (that is, hair, nails, and so on).

▶ Polish your shoes.

▶ Determining how to dress is an important part of your preparation for negotiating compensation.

Principles for Negotiating

THE 11 COMMANDMENTS OF EMPLOYMENT NEGOTIATIONS

Important principles may and must be inflexible.

—ABRAHAM LINCOLN

Taking into consideration those things that make employment negotiations unique, together with general negotiating and influencing concepts, I have developed a set of core principles that I refer to as "The 11 Commandments of Employment Negotiations." These principles serve as general guidelines applicable in every employment negotiation. They should always be kept in mind when you are using the specific negotiating strategies described elsewhere in this book.

Commandment 1: Be Prepared

Senator Phil Gramm attributes his success in both politics and business "to always being more prepared than the other guy." That is good advice when it comes to managing your career as well. It is the first rule in employment negotiations. More than in any other type of negotiation, preparation is critical when negotiating the terms of your employment. The more information you have, the more successful you will be. This is so important that I have devoted a full chapter to preparing for employment negotiations (see the chapter "Beyond Research: Preparing to Negotiate"). Suffice it to say that preparation is the single most important aspect of ensuring that you get the best deal possible at whatever stage you are at in your career.

Commandment 2: Recognize That Employment Negotiations Are Unlike Other Types of Negotiations

Employment negotiations differ from other types of negotiations. Certain techniques should be avoided even though they may be effective in other situations. Employment negotiations are not a one-shot deal like buying a house or a car. They differ even from ongoing negotiations involving a series of deals being worked out between the same parties. When the employment negotiations are over, you will have to work with your former "adversary" on a daily basis; more important, your career success may well depend on the person with whom you have just finished negotiating. Therefore, even though you want to get the best possible deal, you need to proceed in a way that will not tarnish your image. After all, the negotiations are the employer's first real view of you as an employee.

By the same token, your future boss will want you to feel good about joining the organization and to feel that what you have agreed to is fair. Moreover, your boss will want you to be motivated to put forth your best effort once you begin work. Once an employer has decided that you are the person for the job, its primary concern is not to negotiate the least expensive compensation package that it can get away with. Rather, its main focus will be on getting you to accept the job. As a result, employment negotiations are unusual in that both sides share that same basic goal.

Commandment 3: Understand Your Needs and Those of Your Prospective Employer

Any employment negotiation is going to involve trade-offs. To be successful, you need to examine your own priorities. What is it that you want? Are you comfortable with a lower salary and a larger equity stake? Do you feel confident that you can satisfy the requisite criteria to earn a bonus? Are you able to handle dramatic swings in income from year to year? How important is job security? How much do you value a Cadillac benefit plan? What is the minimum salary you are willing to accept?

Understanding your needs will also help you determine the type of employer that you want to work for. For example, a family-owned business may be able to provide a competitive salary but may not be willing to offer significant equity to a nonfamily member. On the other hand, a start-up company may not be able to pay market salary, but it will typically make stock, or stock options, available to its employees.

Regardless of the type of organization, a prospective employer may not be able to give you exactly what you want. There are numerous institutional constraints on how much an employer can pay for a given position or what kinds of benefits it can offer. By understanding what can and cannot be done, you will be able to determine what you need to ask for. Moreover, you won't expend significant negotiating capital seeking to obtain benefits or other terms that would be provided to you as a matter of course.

By understanding your own needs, you can focus on those things that are most important to you. From there it is a matter of making trade-offs and being creative in structuring the package to suit your needs (see Strategy 10). If, for example, you have children about to enter college, deferred compensation or equity may be less important than a signing bonus or a larger salary. On the other hand, if you are free to take risks, you may be willing to accept a lower salary in return for equity.

Understanding your own priorities, and what an employer can offer within its own organizational and budgetary constraints, will enable you to determine what trade-offs are possible in order to maximize your compensation package. This knowledge will also allow you to obtain those things that are most important to you and will prevent you from wasting time with an employer that cannot offer the type of compensation package that you need. Walking away can sometimes be the most important decision you make during a negotiation (see Strategy 25).

Commandment 4: Understand the Dynamics of the Particular Negotiations

Sometimes you will have skills or experience that are in great demand. Or you may be uniquely qualified to fill a particular need an employer has. Hiring someone quickly may be important, and you may be the only qualified candidate to have made it through the interview process. Similarly, if you have been able to defer any significant discussions about compensation until the employer has determined that you are the best candidate for the job, your bargaining position will be greatly strengthened even though there are other qualified candidates available. These are enviable positions to be in.

On the other hand, you may in fact be one of several candidates the employer is considering, any one of whom the company would be happy to hire. Under those circumstances, compensation may be the key factor in determining who gets the job. Sizing up the situation and understanding the relative position of each of the parties will help you determine when to press your advantage and when to hold back.

Commandment 5: Never Lie, but Use the Truth to Your Advantage

Honesty is important. If you don't share my view that it is wrong to lie, then I hope you can be persuaded that it is ineffective to do so, especially when you are dealing with your future employer. If you lie, sooner or later you are likely to be caught. Once you are, you lose all credibility. Even if you don't lose the job opportunity, you will be placed at a tremendous disadvantage. More important, your future credibility once you are in the job will be irreparably damaged.

By the same token, complete candor will not be rewarded. You should never lie but neither should you feel compelled to simply blurt out everything you know. You are not required to answer any specific question directly unless the answer helps you achieve your objectives. You are free to determine what you want to say and how you want to say it.

One aspect of preparation is to understand those areas that may be problematic so that you can rehearse how to handle them when they come up. How you respond to certain questions, including any hesitation on your part, will communicate valuable information. Therefore, it is important to determine ahead of time how you are going to reply to difficult questions when they arise. That will enable you to provide answers that are not only in line with your strategic purposes but are also truthful.

Commandment 6: Understand the Role That Fairness Plays in the Process

When you buy a car, you are trying to negotiate the lowest possible price, and the dealer is trying to get the highest. Even when you are contemplating a series of business transactions, you are still going to try to negotiate the best possible deal, taking into account the ongoing nature of the relationship. As in those situations, in employment negotiations the candidate's goal is to get as much as possible. However, the employer's objective ordinarily is not to negotiate the least expensive deal but rather to hire the best candidate for the job. This is almost always true if you are dealing with your future boss rather than a recruiter or someone from the human resources department.

The guiding principle for most employers in determining what they will agree to is fairness. In order to hire someone they want, within the constraints of their budget and organizational structure, employers will usually agree to anything they deem fair and reasonable. Appeals to fairness are the most powerful weapon available in employment negotiations. Sometimes such appeals may even convince employers of the need to adjust their salary structure or increase the amount of money they have budgeted for a position.

Be able to justify every request you make in terms of fairness. If the cost of living is higher where you're going, it is only fair that your salary be increased sufficiently to compensate for the higher cost of living. If interest rates have risen dramatically since you purchased your current house, it is reasonable to ask your future employer to subsidize your home loan. If comparable employees in similar organizations are given 1 percent of the employer's stock, you should be treated the same. Your prospective employer will want you to accept its offer and to feel that you have been treated fairly. Understanding how to invoke fairness as a negotiating principle can mean the difference between success and failure.

Commandment 7: Use Uncertainty to Your Advantage

The more information you convey to your potential employer about your bottom line, the more you are limiting yourself. If an employer is not certain what it will take to recruit you, its initial offer is likely to be close to its best offer. What the company offers may even be more than you would have asked for in the first place.

In most types of negotiations you want to let the other side make the first offer. Since potential employers almost always present the initial offer, they will try to determine beforehand what it will take to get you to accept the job. Often employers use headhunters to obtain information about your current compensation, benefits, stock plans, and so on. They want to know what you are seeking and if there are any particular issues that might create problems in recruiting you. With that information, prospective employers will be able to determine the minimum package they need to offer.

Although potential employers may not offer you as little as they can get away with, if you have divulged too much information, they will likely not offer you as much as they otherwise would. By not disclosing exactly what your current compensation package is or exactly what it will take to get you to leave your current position, you force a potential employer to give you its best offer.

Commandment 8: Be Creative

You may not always be able to get everything you want, but you want to be sure to get everything that you can. Focus on the value of the total package. Be willing to make trade-offs to increase the total value of the deal. Look for different ways to achieve your objectives. Limit your "requirements." When you lock yourself into a position, you constrain your ability to be creative. The fewer things you must have, the more you will be able to get.

If you are creative, you can package what you want in ways that are more agreeable to the employer. You'll be able to find creative "trades" that will enable you to withdraw problematic requests in return for improvements in those areas where there is more flexibility. By doing so, you can maximize the value of the package that you negotiate.

There are limits as to what you can achieve no matter how creative you are. In the end, you still must get the employer to agree to those elements of the deal that are critical for you to have. If you are not able to do so, or if you have to give up too much in order to get what you need, perhaps this is not the right job. Before, however, you insist on any particular term in your employment package, be sure that it is really essential. Most aspects of any offer are really only money in one form or another. As such, their value can be readily ascertained and easily traded for something of equal or greater value (see Strategy 10). By insisting on a particular item, you may be giving up something of greater value; you may even be giving up your chance to get the job altogether.

Commandment 9: Focus on Your Goals, Not on Winning

Too often when people negotiate, winning becomes more important than the actual objectives they are seeking to achieve. This tendency is particularly problematic when you're dealing with employment. Not only is it necessary to achieve your goals, it is also important not to make your boss feel like a loser. Remember, this individual's support is vital to your long-term success. He or she will determine the direction your career takes. You will have gained little by negotiating a great deal if in the process you alienate your future boss.

Commandment 10: Know When to Quit Bargaining

One sure way to lose everything you have achieved through your negotiating efforts is to be greedy. There comes a point in every negotiation when you have obtained everything that you could reasonably have hoped to achieve. At that point you should thank the person you are dealing with and accept the position.

If you don't recognize when to stop negotiating, you run the risk of having the company decide that it made a mistake by offering you the job in the first place. Most organizations will want to treat you fairly and make you happy, but few want to hire a prima donna. Being perceived as greedy or unreasonable may cause the offer to be withdrawn. Even if it does not, you will have done immeasurable harm to your career. Irving Younger, a law school professor who taught trial tactics when I was at Harvard Law School, admonished us that once you make your point cross-examining a witness, "Stop. Shut up. Sit down." Those words of wisdom apply equally when negotiating with a prospective employer.

This brings us to the eleventh and most important commandment, the importance of which cannot be overemphasized.

Commandment 11: Never Forget That Employment Is an Ongoing Relationship

Employment negotiations are the starting point for your career with a new employer. They set the tone for the employment relationship. Get too little and you will be disadvantaged throughout the remainder of your working life; push too hard and you can sour the relationship before it even begins. How you handle the initial negotiations can have an impact, for better or for worse, on how successful your tenure with the organization will be.

Following the 11 Commandments of Employment Negotiations and employing the strategies described throughout the remainder of this book will enable you to effectively negotiate the terms of your new employment. Once you've done so, you will be able to start your new job confident that you have obtained the best deal possible, and if you do your job well, there will be additional opportunities to negotiate further improvements as time goes on.

25 Proven Strategies for Getting More Money, Better Benefits, and Greater Job Security

Success depends on three things: who says it, what he says, how he says it; of these three things, what he says is the least important.

—JOHN, VISCOUNT
MORLEY OF BLACKBURN

In chess, every move evokes a countermove designed to deny the other side an advantage. In negotiating, particularly in the employment context, if you select the appropriate strategy, there are no countermoves. The proper negotiating strategy makes use of the existing dynamics of a situation. As in judo, the right strategy turns your adversary's needs to your advantage.

The principles of negotiating, which I refer to as "The 11 Commandments of Employment Negotiations," are general guidelines that apply in every employment negotiation. They need to be kept in mind at every stage of the process. In addition, there are specific techniques and tactics that can be used in certain situations. To make them work, you don't need a lawyer or an agent. All you need is to be able to evaluate the circumstances and determine which strategies are appropriate for the situation.

Will every one of the techniques discussed in this chapter work in every negotiation? The answer clearly is no. However, if you understand your prospective employer's agenda, you will be surprised at how easily you can identify the right strategies to use.

Depending on the level of the position you are being considered for, the negotiations may consist of a single discussion or extend over a period of weeks or even months. For many positions you will have only a limited opportunity to negotiate. In that case you will need to get everything you want on the table quickly. On the other hand, if the job is at a significantly high level or the organization wants to recruit you badly enough, the negotiations may take place over a period of time. Under those circumstances timing becomes a factor. In any particular situation, you may be able to use only one of these strategies. In most negotiations, you will be able to use several. You will have to determine which strategies are best under the circumstances.

Selecting which strategies to use, and determining when to use them, takes planning. If you understand the organization's priorities, you can anticipate the issues that are likely to arise during the discussions. It is important, however, to remain flexible. Whether a particular tactic will be effective often depends on how things develop. The right strategy will succeed because it takes advantage of the negotiating dynamics that exist at a particular moment. Delay too long and you may miss your opportunity. Begin before you have laid the proper foundation and you may not achieve the desired result. Of course, a negotiating strategy will almost always fail if you haven't properly analyzed the situation confronting you.

For example, most employers want the people they hire to feel that they are being treated fairly. At the same time, employers don't want to be taken advantage of. Therefore, strategies that rely on a sense of fairness can be used in most employment negotiations. However, you can't appeal to a sense of fairness when a negotiator is so competitive that winning, or at least not appearing to lose, is more important than the actual outcome achieved. Similarly, strategies such as bypassing the negotiator or blaming the lawyers will work only in certain well-defined situations.

The discussion of the strategies that follows will enable you to recognize those situations in which either the individuals involved or the negotiating dynamics lend themselves to certain approaches. You will learn not only how to use the strategies but also when each can be applied to maximum effect. The examples are based on real-life situations. After you have finished reading this book, you will understand how to effectuate a particular strategy (and you will also be able to recognize when one is likely to blow up in your face). Then, when the right moment arises during negotiations, you will be able to execute the appropriate strategy and achieve your goals. Properly applying these strategies will allow you to start your new job secure in the knowledge that you have obtained the best deal possible.

1

Making the Most of Your Compensation

DISCUSSING YOUR CURRENT SALARY

When you tell the truth, you never have to worry about your lousy memory.

—H. JACKSON BROWN, JR.

Often I have been brought in by a client near the end of a negotiation to help resolve a particularly difficult issue or to work out the final details of a contract, the basic terms of which have already been agreed upon. At that point I can usually get the client a little more money or slightly better terms; I can also help resolve any outstanding issues or identify problems that haven't been considered. What I am no longer able to do is help the client negotiate the best possible package because the major opportunities to improve an offer usually occur early on in the discussions.

The importance of doing the right things before negotiations even begin is brought home to me time and time again. I received a call seeking advice from a business acquaintance whom I will call Rick. He related the following story. Rick had received a call from a recruiter at a well-known search firm. The search firm had been retained to find a chief operating officer for a small manufacturing company that had just been purchased by a private investment group.

The recruiter described the company as having been poorly managed by its prior owner, a large conglomerate, but one with enormous potential.

The investors were looking for an entrepreneur who could bring their cost structure into line, market their product aggressively, and prepare the company to go public in a few years. The recruiter explained to Rick that the salary might be a little low but that he would be given a significant equity position. If the company was successful, his stock would more than compensate him for any loss of salary. After some further discussion about the employer, the recruiter asked Rick what his current salary was. He responded that his "base salary was $100,000."

Rick's response to the recruiter's question was reflexive. It was the response most people make when they are asked about their salary. It was also the wrong response. The best response would be to avoid divulging one's current salary at such an early stage in the process. This may be difficult to do; however, it is not impossible. To be able to respond properly to an inquiry about your current compensation, you must prepare ahead of time. When this question comes up, as it inevitably will, you need to have a well-thought-out response. Be comfortable enough with what you are going to say so that there is no hesitation. You can then move quickly to another subject without focusing undue attention on the issue.

Consider the impact of what Rick told the recruiter. A candidate's current salary is the single most important factor employer's use in putting together an initial offer. As a general rule, if a new job doesn't involve a promotion or a relocation to a higher-cost area, an employer will offer a 10 to 15 percent increase over the employee's current salary. Even when a promotion or relocation is involved, an employee's current salary will be the employer's starting point in deciding what to offer.

Based on the way the situation was described to him, Rick could expect to be offered a base salary at or slightly below his current salary level, plus a substantial grant of stock or stock options to compensate for the employer's inability to increase his salary. Unfortunately for Rick, his salary disclosure enabled the employer to match his current salary and offer him enough equity, in light of that salary, to make it worthwhile for him to change jobs. That is exactly what happened.

Rick is an honest guy and a terrific marketer. But he had spent his entire career with one company, and so he was not experienced in employment negotiations. Because Rick did not have a strategy for dealing with the predictable question about his current salary, the answer he gave served to limit the amount of the salary he was offered. Fortunately, I was able to help him increase the number of stock options he was given. Even so, if Rick had answered that salary inquiry differently, he might have been offered a larger salary initially and would still have been able to negotiate a significant equity stake.

At some point during the hiring process you will certainly be asked and will be expected to answer questions about your salary. You should answer those questions honestly but not without first having given careful thought to your answer. When responding to questions about your compensation, bear in mind the fifth commandment of employment negotiations: "Never Lie, but Use the Truth to Your Advantage." Not only is it wrong to lie about your current salary, it is a tactical error as well. Your current salary can readily be confirmed by your current employer. In fact, you may even occasionally be asked to provide a copy of your last W-2 form after you are hired. On the other hand, as Rick learned the hard way, complete candor works to your disadvantage.

How can you make the most of your current salary when discussing it without lying? The simplest way is to consider the value of your total compensation. When providing salary information, include not only base salary and bonuses but also benefits such as car allowances, reimbursements for professional and club dues, expense accounts, deferred compensation, stock and stock options, pension benefits, 401(k) plans, company-paid insurance, and so on. If possible, avoid being too precise, at least during preliminary discussions. How should Rick have responded? Instead of stating that his base salary was $100,000, he could have countered with something like this:

EMPLOYER: What is your current salary, Rick?

RICK: Last year my total compensation was approximately $150,000.

This response takes into account not only Rick's $100,000 base salary but also his bonus of $25,000 and his approximately $25,000 stock option grant, perks, and other benefits. Even better, he could have responded that his current compensation was between $150,000 and $175,000, depending on his bonus. Alternatively he could have simply stated that his salary was in the low six figures. Finally, Rick could have tried to deflect the employer's question by asking his own question such as what had the company budgeted for the position.

By including the value of all the elements of his compensation package and not providing a detailed breakdown, Rick would be taking advantage of the seventh commandment: "Use Uncertainty to Your Advantage." This would force a prospective employer to carefully consider the value of the job, rather than Rick's current salary, in determining what to offer. In this way the employer would be encouraged to put forth its best offer. It would not be able to determine an appropriate offer simply by adding an amount to Rick's current salary that would seem sufficient to entice him to change jobs. These same techniques work whether your salary is $50,000 or $500,000.

If you are asked specifically about salary and can't avoid the subject, be sure to describe your salary in its most favorable light by including bonuses and other cash payments as a part of your salary. By describing your compensation in this manner, you are communicating that you take for granted the fact that you will earn a bonus and consider it to be part of your basic compensation package.

Because your bonus may vary from year to year, it offers a certain amount of flexibility (without being dishonest) in the way you describe your compensation. Moreover, the inherent variability of bonuses allows you additional opportunities to create uncertainty with a prospective employer. For example, if the bonus you earned last year was much larger than what you anticipate receiving this year, describe your compensation in terms of what you earned last year. If, on the other hand, you expect that this year's bonus will be larger than last year's, discuss what you expect to earn this year. Thus you could say that you are earning $75,000 in base salary and expect to receive a $15,000 bonus this year. If the last time you received a large bonus was several years ago, when you were given $25,000 because of your extraordinary work on a particular deal, you can talk about earning bonuses of between $10,000 and $25,000. Even better, you could describe your bonus as "up to $25,000." You could also talk about the bonus program in general, describing your bonus *potential*, which is the maximum possible bonus you could earn. Be aware, however, that eventually someone will probably ask about the bonuses you have actually received.

If you expect to receive a bonus or a raise this year, be sure to include it in the valuation of your current compensation. For example, if you are expecting a $10,000 raise in the next month, you should state that "my base salary will be $85,000 when I receive my performance review next month." The same purpose would be served, and some additional uncertainty created, by changing that slightly and stating that "my base salary will be at *least* $85,000 when I receive my performance review next month." This positions your compensation in its most favorable light.

Equally important, the failure to take into consideration an impending raise or bonus in describing your total compensation can seriously disadvantage you when you accept a new position. For example, if a new employer offers you a 15 percent increase in your present salary but you are anticipating a 10 percent raise from your current employer, your actual compensation will not have increased significantly over what you would have earned had you not changed jobs. In fact, it may not actually result in a significant increase at all if you have to wait more than a year before you are eligible to receive a performance review and possible raise from your new employer. The problem can be exacerbated if your annual bonus is due at the same time as your performance review.

If Your Salary Is Low Because You Have Been with the Same Employer for Many Years

A problem you may encounter if you have been with the same employer for a lengthy period of time is that your salary has not kept up with the market. If your current salary is used as the basis for setting the salary at a new job, you will continue to be paid less than you are worth. Since women on average earn less than similarly situated men, using their current compensation will likely be particularly disadvantageous for most women. If you are underpaid and you allow that to happen, you will remain underpaid.

Under these circumstances it is critical to concentrate the discussion on the market rate for the position and avoid or delay discussing your specific salary for as long as possible. Having information as to what other organizations are paying for similar positions will help you focus the employer on the value of the job, as opposed to your current salary.

To avoid having an employer use your current salary to determine what it will offer you, know what you are worth, disclose as little about your own current salary as possible, use other offers, and be willing to walk away. If you have to disclose your current salary, not only should you make it clear that you know that you are being underpaid but you should also explain the reason why without being apologetic about it. For example, you might state, "Employers are paying between $70,000 and $90,000 for graphic designers. Although I have been earning only $55,000 at the Cheapo Graphics Company while I have been mastering CAD technology, now that I am fully proficient, I expect to be paid the going rate." Whatever the reason for your below market salary, be prepared to explain why you have been willing to accept it and, without being defensive, to demonstrate what other employers are paying people with similar skills.

If You Are Already Earning More Than the New Position Pays

The opposite problem arises if you are currently earning more than the employer is contemplating paying for the position. In that situation, you need to be very careful about how you communicate your current salary. If you describe your current compensation in a way that is clearly outside the range for the job, you probably won't be considered further. On the other hand, if you lock yourself into a position early on by stating that the proposed salary is acceptable, you probably will not get an opportunity to significantly increase the compensation at a later stage in the process.

The best way to handle the situation is to defer the discussion of salary until the employer has had a chance to understand the value you can bring to the position. If you cannot put it off, as described above, describe your current salary without being too specific. For example, Rick could describe his compensation as in the "$100,000-plus range" or in the "low six figures." If that doesn't work, simply reverse the techniques we have been discussing. Thus you could mention only your base salary without discussing bonuses or anticipated raises until later. Focus on your interest in the content of the job and the long-term opportunities the employer offers, and indicate that you are flexible with regard to salary. Once you have convinced the employer that you are the best person for the job, even though you have stated your flexibility in terms of compensation, you can still try to negotiate a better offer.

Whatever your particular situation, it is critical that you develop a strategy for answering questions about your current salary. These questions will invariably be asked at an early stage in the process before it is in your best interest to provide that information. If you are not prepared, you will answer reflexively, as Rick did. By doing so, you will miss a critical opportunity to improve the offer you receive.

SUMMARY OF NEGOTIATING POINTS

▶ Avoid discussing your current compensation for as long as possible.
▶ If you have to talk money, describe your total compensation, not just base salary.

► Take into account anticipated raises and bonuses.
► Describe your compensation in its most favorable light.
► Never lie.
► Avoid being too specific.
► Create uncertainty.
► Be prepared with market data if your current salary is below the market.
► Carefully prepare and rehearse your responses to questions about your current salary.

2

Asking for More

YOU CAN'T GET WHAT YOU DON'T ASK FOR

*You may be disappointed if you fail, but you are
doomed if you don't try.*

—BEVERLY SILLS

Early in her career, Ali Croft, public relations director for Just Drive Media, was offered a job at eBay for $55,000. When she responded that the offer was "a bit lower than she was expecting," the human resources manager asked her "what it would take" to get her there. Ali asked for $60,000. She was ultimately offered $62,000, and her boss later told her that she was impressed that Ali had asked for more money.

Most people ask for too little when they accept a new job. Generally job candidates are flattered to have received an offer and are excited about the job opportunity. They may not want to do anything that could jeopardize the offer. Often candidates don't even consider the possibility of asking for anything more. When they are really interested in the position, many individuals accept the employer's initial offer with little, if any, negotiating.

Most employers, on the other hand, try to find out exactly what job candidates are earning and offer them just enough more to make it worth their while to change jobs. Imagine that you are not particularly excited about a new opportunity. Since you don't really care if you take the job or not, you find it easy to ask for more money. Surprisingly, you will often actually get what you ask for. Even if you don't get everything you are looking for, in response to your requests, the company is likely to improve its initial offer.

Why do most people ask for too little? Often they are just afraid that they will look foolish. Many of my clients, at least initially, come to me for advice because they are uncomfortable with the negotiating process. Most have never negotiated the terms of their own employment before. Typically when they come to me, they tell me that they just want to make sure that they are not missing anything important. When I suggest that they might want to try to negotiate a better deal, I get mixed reactions. Some of my clients, obviously, have come to me for that express purpose. Others say that they don't want to negotiate. However, if I tell them that executives in similar positions usually get this or that additional benefit, they all ask for specifics so they can go back and ask for the benefit. Is this just envy? ("If other CFOs get this, I want it too.") It could be, but I don't think so. Once they know they can ask for the benefit without looking ridiculous, they almost always do. In fact, they may feel that not doing so will make them look foolish, particularly to their peers.

Why You Should Always Ask for More Than You Expect to Get

The obvious reason to seek more than you expect to get is that you just might get what you ask for. Certainly you will get more than if you don't ask at all. More important, asking provides you with room to negotiate. By definition, negotiating requires give-and-take. If the person you are dealing with simply agrees to everything that you ask for, you are almost certainly asking for too little. Otherwise, by agreeing to all your requests, the other party would risk looking inept to his or her superiors. Ordinarily for an agreement to be reached, there has to be some sense that each side has made concessions or modified its proposals in order to reach a mutually satisfactory outcome. If your initial position sets forth exactly what you want, then either you won't reach agreement or you'll have to take less in the end in order to close the deal.

I began my career as an employment lawyer negotiating collective bargaining agreements with labor unions. It is something I enjoyed doing, and I learned a great deal from the experience. In certain industries labor negotiations are conducted in the following manner: one company negotiates a contract with the union, and each of the other companies in the industry go through the exercise of bargaining—only to agree, in the end, on the same basic terms as those agreed to by the first company. This negotiating approach is referred to as "pattern bargaining," and it was very common at one time. The automobile industry has historically negotiated this way. For example, the United Autoworkers might first choose to negotiate an agreement with Ford before it begins to negotiate with Chrysler and General Motors.

As a young labor negotiator, I was told a story that I use whenever I teach negotiating to MBA students. Although I do not know the specific individuals involved, I have no doubt it is true. The story involves a company in an industry that engaged in pattern bargaining. Shortly before this particular company entered into negotiations with its union for a new collective bargaining agreement, a new chief executive officer was appointed. The new CEO had spent years in the industry and knew it very well. Although he had never been required to take part in labor negotiations, he understood that everyone always agreed to the same basic contract. So rather than waste time mechanically going through the motions of bargaining, he decided to personally go to the table at the start of the negotiations and explain to the union that the company would simply agree to the same annual increase of 50 cents an hour that the other companies in the industry had already agreed to. That way they could all get back to work without wasting a lot of time and effort getting to where everyone knew they would eventually end up. The union refused the CEO's seemingly reasonable offer and its bargain stance actually became tougher. After months of unsuccessful attempts to reach an agreement, the company finally had to give its employees an increase of 55 cents an hour in order to conclude the negotiations.

The point of this story is that negotiating is a process. The new CEO tried to short-circuit the process and ended up having to pay more as a result. If negotiations are handled properly, there is something therapeutic about them. Everyone feels that the end result is fair. Even though both sides don't get everything they want, or perhaps *because* both sides don't get everything they want, the parties walk away feeling that they did the best they could. It is a curious process, but it seems to work reasonably well. By asking for more than what you expect the other side to agree to, you leave yourself room to bargain. This approach will allow you, through the give-and-take of negotiations, to find out what the other side is willing to provide and to get everything possible, yet have everyone leave feeling good about the final agreement.

Asking for more than you expect to get is a basic negotiating technique referred to as "anchoring." However, there is a difference when it is done in the context of employment negotiations. When you buy a car, you can initially make an absurdly low offer if you want. In fact, it might not turn out to be quite as ridiculous as you thought. In any event, this type of bargaining is perfectly acceptable. Any car dealer who thinks you are seriously interested in purchasing a car will find a way to get you to discuss a more realistic price. At worst, you can go to another dealer and make a more reasonable offer the next time.

In employment negotiations you lose credibility if you take unreasonable positions. If your judgment or negotiating skills are brought into question, you run the risk of losing out not only on the specific bargaining point at issue but on the job opportunity itself. Therefore, in the context of employment negotiations, this strategy is more appropriately labeled "ask for more but be sure your requests are reasonable." Ask for everything that you can arguably justify. This will almost always be more than the employer is willing to agree to, leaving you room to bargain further.

Your preparation should include being able to provide a rationale for any request you might want to make. For example, you might base a request for a higher salary on market data. Similarly, you can ask for a particular benefit, or payment in lieu of that benefit, because you are receiving it from your current employer or because others in similar positions at other organizations receive it. Sometimes individual circumstances, such as a very low mortgage rate or the nonrefundability of your child's tuition in private school, may give rise to a specific request. At other times you may be looking to restructure a proposal in a way that is more favorable to you rather than simply seeking additional benefits. In the case of bonus criteria, for instance, you may want to propose alternatives that are more advantageous to you. Be prepared to show why your proposal makes more sense than what the employer initially suggested.

How you frame your requests is also important. Ask for what you want; do not make "demands." It is best to appear reasonable not only in what you ask for but also in how you ask for it. Even if you are one of the rare individuals who is in a position to make demands, that approach is almost never as effective in the long run as thoughtfully bringing the employer around to your point of view. If you truly have sufficient bargaining leverage, you will be able to get what you want without either angering or humiliating the person negotiating on behalf of the organization. Tact is important since you may have to work with that person in the future. If you are negotiating with your future boss, it goes without saying that how you negotiate will affect your future career.

Remember, always leave yourself room to modify your requests. Most employers won't grant all of them. In rare instances, a prospective employer won't agree to any. However, as long as you can give a plausible reason for what you are seeking, it is unlikely that the employer will hold the mere fact that you asked against you. If the truth be told, most employers expect you to negotiate, and at certain levels, failing to do so may lead them to wonder if they made the right choice in selecting you.

Asking for more does not mean that you should attempt to renegotiate every aspect of an offer. That would be a waste of your time and would quickly result in a loss of credibility. Instead, focus on those areas where you believe the employer has more to give. At the same time, emphasize those items that are most important to you. Similarly, by raising a number of different issues, you will be able to come to a resolution by conceding on some issues in return for the employer agreeing to give in on others. That is the essence of negotiating.

SUMMARY OF NEGOTIATING POINTS

▶ Don't be afraid to ask for more than you think you can get.
▶ Leave yourself room to negotiate.
▶ Be reasonable in what you request.
▶ Be prepared to justify what you are asking for.
▶ Remember that how you ask is important.
▶ Avoid making "demands."

Compensation, Benefits, and Perks Checklist

Here is a list of some of the items you might want to ask for when you negotiate compensation. The list is not intended to be all inclusive but rather is only intended to set forth some of the possibilities.

- ☐ Base salary
- ☐ Signing bonus
- ☐ Timing of your first salary review
- ☐ Annual performance bonus (amount and eligibility criteria)
- ☐ Guaranteed minimum annual performance bonus (at least in the first year)
- ☐ Reimbursement for home office expenses (for example, Internet services)
- ☐ Laptop computer
- ☐ Cell phone or BlackBerry or iPhone
- ☐ Training
- ☐ Payment of professional membership dues
- ☐ Paid subscriptions to the *Wall Street Journal*, business magazines, and/or professional journals
- ☐ Expense account
- ☐ Tuition reimbursement
- ☐ Stock options
- ☐ Restricted stock grants
- ☐ Discounted stock purchases
- ☐ Pension and/or 401(k) (generally available to all full-time employees and not negotiable)
- ☐ Health benefits (Some aspects are covered by benefit plans, but others may be negotiable or available as payments in lieu of the actual benefits.)
- ☐ Deferred compensation
- ☐ Profit sharing
- ☐ Financial, tax, and/or estate planning services
- ☐ Legal planning services
- ☐ Company car and/or mileage reimbursements
- ☐ School tuition for children
- ☐ Financial assistance for day care
- ☐ Relocation cost reimbursement
- ☐ Loan to purchase home
- ☐ Potential forgiveness of loans based on agreed-to criteria (tenure and/or performance)
- ☐ Gym membership
- ☐ Club memberships (rare these days)
- ☐ First- or business-class air travel (on flights of a certain duration)
- ☐ Flexible work schedules
- ☐ Tax gross-ups for taxable benefits
- ☐ Severance and termination provisions

Some of the listed items may be covered in organization-wide benefits plans, the specifics of which may not be subject to negotiation. However, even if a benefit is not provided by a particular benefit plan and the organization has no interest in changing that plan to include the benefit, if you can make a case as to why you should have it, or if you currently receive it and would be giving it up by joining the new organization, you can always seek an increase in your salary or a cash payment in lieu of the benefit you are losing.

3

Seek and You Shall Find

THE TACTICAL USE OF QUESTIONS

It is often how the question is framed that determines the answer that is received.

—JUDGE SLOVITER

You have been offered a position with a new employer. Happily, everyone has agreed on most of the terms of employment. You are in the process of negotiating with the vice president of human resources about severance in the event things don't work out. The conversation goes something like this:

YOU: Do you have a severance policy?
VP: No. Not a formal one.
YOU: An informal one?
VP: Yes. One week per year of service.
YOU: In the event that the company is taken over or if for some other reason I lose my job, I think a year would be more appropriate. After all, I am giving up a very secure job and moving my family across the country.
VP: No one ever gets more than six months.
YOU: I really don't feel, with all the corporate restructurings taking place, that I could relocate my family without more security than just a six-month severance package.

That is a reasonable response. It is possible that the employer will agree to give you a larger severance package, at least in the event of a takeover. If the employer doesn't change its position on this issue, however, you have a problem. You either have to back down and risk losing credibility or call the employer's bluff and risk losing the job.

A better approach might be to respond with a question. For instance, the last exchange could have been handled this way:

VP: No one ever gets more than six months.
YOU: No one?

Unless the vice president of human resources answers "No one!" you will probably be able to get a severance package of greater than six months. By forcing the vice president of human resources to admit that some people have received larger severance packages, you change the nature of the debate. Instead of arguing about whether it is possible to give you a better severance package, you will now be able to focus on whether your situation merits the same consideration as that of others who received additional severance. Since the vice president of human resources will be reluctant to discuss the specific circumstances of individuals who were given more than six months of severance, it is likely that the employer will find a way to accommodate your request.

Ask if there are any special compensation programs (bonus plans, stock option plans, supplemental executive retirement or medical plans, deferred-compensation plans, and so on) that key executives receive. Determine who is eligible to participate in those plans. If you are not at that level, inquire about lesser programs available to people in positions similar to yours. Find out how many employees are eligible to participate in those plans. If what your prospective employer has been telling you about the importance of your position does not match up with the number and type of employees who participate in the plans that you are eligible for and those you are not, simply asking those questions may result in your being included in a better plan. If your position is not included in benefits plans that you think you should be eligible for, and you cannot negotiate a more appropriate level for your position, this may not be the right job for you (see Strategy 25).

Questions are a very useful negotiating tool. To begin with, they are generally not threatening. In addition, people like to appear knowledgeable and will usually share a great deal of information if you just ask. Moreover, most people find it difficult to lie in response to a direct question. And a negotiator's evasive response to a direct question, in and of itself, provides you with valuable information.

Questions may be designed to elicit information, or they may be intended to make a point. How you ask questions is important. Several techniques used by courtroom lawyers can prove very effective in salary negotiations.

Silence is one way that lawyers get information when they are questioning witnesses. After a witness answers, rather than ask the next question, they simply remain silent and see if the witness continues talking. This technique works equally well when negotiating (see Strategy 23).

Acting as if you don't understand something is another way of gaining additional information. When you ask lots of questions and look like you need assistance, people will instinctively want to help. This technique is sometimes referred to as the "Columbo approach," after the TV detective played by Peter Falk, who by acting hopelessly confused was always able to get the criminal to give him the necessary information to solve the case. Because you are seeking help, the defenses of the person with whom you are dealing will be lowered. As a result, that individual may unintentionally provide you with valuable information that you can use to help make your case.

When you are negotiating with a prospective employer, you have to be careful how you use this technique. You should not use it too often. Limit this approach to situations about which you would not be expected to be knowledgeable. After all, the company is hiring you because it considers you to be experienced. You don't want to do anything to undermine that belief.

One of the goals of asking questions during negotiations is to try to keep the other party talking. The more someone talks, the more information you will gather. An added benefit is that questions help you develop a relationship with the person with whom you are negotiating. Having a personal relationship with the employer's representative is always valuable during the negotiating process, particularly when issues are difficult (see Strategy 9). As discussed above, one way to encourage someone to talk is simply to remain quiet and listen after you ask a question. To be even more effective, acknowledge your interest in what is being said by looking directly at the speaker after you ask your question and occasionally nodding in agreement (see Strategy 23).

As illustrated by our first example, another technique lawyers use is to paraphrase what has just been said in question form beginning with "you never" or "you always" or words to that effect. This technique is particularly effective when an organization is relying on a policy or practice to deny an otherwise reasonable request. For example:

VP: Relocation is governed by our relocation policy.
YOU: The relocation policy controls regardless of the circumstances?
VP: Except in very unusual circumstances.

Once you have gotten that concession, you are well on your way to making the case that yours is also an "unusual circumstance." You can then follow up by asking, "Under what circumstances have exceptions been granted in the past?"

By encouraging the negotiator to talk, you increase the likelihood of obtaining information to support your position. What you learn in this way can provide insight into what the employer is thinking. Moreover, knowledge gained directly from the negotiator is not subject to challenge.

The use of questions not only provides you with valuable information but it also makes those responding feel that they are working with you, not negotiating against you. After all, when people answer your questions, they are helping you. If you treat the negotiations as an effort to work together to resolve the obstacles that might prevent you from joining the organization, you will end up getting a better deal (see Strategy 5). In addition, by involving the other side through the question-and-answer process, you will provide an additional impetus for the employer's representative to want to conclude the negotiations successfully (see Strategy 8).

Another helpful form of questioning is simply to ask why, particularly when you are responding to a statement like "We can't do that" or "That is our policy." Asking why calls for a reasoned response. Once you obtain a justification, you will be able to argue persuasively that the reason given is inapplicable in this instance. Asking a question like "How can we work this out?" can also sometimes prove helpful.

Finally, if all else fails, you can ask the negotiator what he or she would do in your situation. This approach is often very effective in changing the negotiating dynamics. It frequently causes the other side to try to come up with a solution to the problem, rather than convince you that no problem exists. Since the negotiator understands what is possible, he or she can usually find an acceptable solution within the framework of what the employer can live with.

Recruiting is a lot like courtship. Little things can kill a deal. If discussions aren't handled properly in the early stages, ardor can quickly wane. When it comes to employment decisions, emotions often play a critical role. Unless seemingly small issues are quickly and satisfactorily resolved, one side or the other may conclude that it has made a mistake. Often deals fall through without the other person ever really knowing why.

I recall one negotiation that seemingly was going to break down over a relatively minor issue. However, a well-timed question put the negotiations back on track. I was representing an executive in California who was being recruited by a Connecticut firm. We had worked out all the major issues—salary, bonus, and stock options—to my client's satisfaction. The employer had a generous relocation policy that dealt with most of my client's concerns. But it provided for only a 30-day temporary living allowance. My client's daughter was a senior in high school, and he felt he could not move his family until after she graduated. He described his situation to the employer and asked for temporary living expenses for a period of one year until his daughter finished high school. The employer insisted that it could not deviate from its relocation policy. Although the company had been very accommodating in every other area, it would not budge on this issue.

In light of the total package, even a full year's temporary living allowance would not have amounted to a large sum of money. I tried to convince my client to give in on the issue and to use it as leverage to improve some other aspect of the deal (see Strategy 24). He wouldn't hear of it: "If they are going to be so unreasonable about temporary living expenses, this is not where I want to work." Just when I thought the deal was about to collapse, a timely question allowed us to conclude the negotiations successfully.

What was the insightful query that helped us salvage the negotiations? It was simply "Why?" More specifically, I told the employer's negotiator that I really couldn't understand why we were arguing about the temporary living allowance. It was not that much money in terms of the total package, and in light of my client's particular circumstances, paying for temporary living expenses for a year while he lived away from his family seemed only fair. The negotiator explained that the reason the relocation policy was written in stone was that the organization previously had a bad experience with a senior executive. After receiving temporary living expenses for well over a year, the executive couldn't get his wife to move and he returned to his previous employer. Knowing why the negotiator would not agree to a seemingly reasonable request allowed us to resolve the problem relatively easily. We entered into a written agreement that stated if my client did not move his family to Connecticut at the end of the year, he would repay the temporary living expenses. The negotiator could then agree to modify the relocation policy for my client without the fear of being made to look foolish.

Not every problem can be fixed simply by asking a question. Not every deal can be saved. However, rather than arguing about an issue, sometimes asking the right question can break an impasse. Questions are not adversarial. They can be used to frame the terms of the debate. Questions can be directed in a way that brings the other side around to your point of view. Moreover, the question-and-answer process encourages the parties to work together. It focuses them on finding a mutually acceptable solution. If enough questions are asked, they often provide the insight the parties need in order to come to terms.

SUMMARY OF NEGOTIATING POINTS

- ▶ Use questions to gain an understanding of the employer's positions.
- ▶ Encourage the employer's negotiator to talk.
- ▶ Listen.
- ▶ Be quiet after you ask a question.
- ▶ Paraphrase what has been said in question form, adding "you always" or "you never" or words to that effect.
- ▶ Ask why.
- ▶ Frame issues by using questions.
- ▶ Use questions when you reach an impasse.
- ▶ Ask questions as a way of encouraging the parties to work together to solve problems.

4

Negotiating the Position, Not the Salary

Choose a job you love, and you will never have to work a day in your life.

—CONFUCIUS

You just finished a series of job interviews with Wetscape Company, the maker of small, portable computers that are rented at resorts, hotels, airports, and bars. The president of the company is very excited about the product and has spent the last hour telling you about its many potential uses. She then offers you the position of director of sales, the job that you were interviewing for, at an annual salary of $120,000. A significant number of stock options are included as part of the compensation package. You respond by stating that you would be happy to take the job but only if you are given a $10,000 annual expense account. How do you think the company's president will react? Even if that request is reasonable, the timing and the manner in which it is being made virtually guarantee that it will not be well received.

Although employment negotiations differ from other types of negotiations, when it comes to salary and benefits, employers and employees still have distinctly different interests. Employers may not offer you as little as they can get away with, but they do not want to pay you any more than they believe is reasonably necessary.

There is usually room to maneuver. Yet many people don't negotiate at all when they are offered a new job. They decide whether they want the

job and either accept or reject the offer. If they negotiate at all, it is usually to attempt to resolve some particular problems that they anticipate will
arise. Typically the issues they raise have something to do with their move
or their families' needs. Those people who do try to improve the financial
terms of the initial offer tend to approach the process as they would any
other negotiations. This quickly turns the negotiations into a zero-sum
game. Prospective employers will view the negotiations that way as well,
with every dollar they give you being treated as one less dollar they have
to spend elsewhere.

Employment negotiations need not proceed in that fashion. Treat the
process more like a courtship than an adversarial proceeding. Bear in mind
that once an employer decides to hire someone, the primary goal becomes
convincing that individual to join the organization. It is to your benefit to
avoid turning the recruitment process into a traditional zero-sum negotiation.

By recognizing the different dynamics governing employment negotiations, you can take advantage of the one interest that all applicants and
employers share—the job. Whenever the negotiations become difficult, talk
about the position. If your prospective employer balks at your salary request,
discuss your ideas about how you would handle the job. Ask about opportunities to increase market share, improve customer service, or reduce costs.
Talking about the job will immediately change any interaction from an
antagonistic one to a collaborative one.

Employers are not looking to hire someone whose primary interest in a
position is money or benefits. There will always be some other job with a
higher salary or better benefits. Employers want someone who is excited about
the organization and the job opportunity. If you keep that in mind, you may
be able to achieve your objectives of more money and better benefits in ways
that your prospective employer will not consider to be at its expense.

Remember my client Jack? He was able to get a better benefit package
by convincing his future employer to give him additional job responsibilities and upgrade the position to that of senior vice president. He negotiated
the position, not the compensation. Even if he had not been able to get the
position title upgraded and gain the benefit package that went along with
the title, the added job responsibilities increased the value of the position.
With those additional responsibilities, the employer could readily afford to
pay Jack a higher salary without feeling that it had lost anything.

This technique is particularly effective when the position you are seeking is budgeted for less than you currently earn. Let's say that you see an

advertisement in the *Wall Street Journal* for a job that sounds exactly like what you have been looking for. The employer is offering up to $60,000, depending on experience. You have the right background for the position, but you are currently making $65,000. What should you do? You could forget about pursuing the position. Or you could avoid discussing salary until you've convinced the employer that not only are you perfect for the job but you also can do even more with the position than your prospective boss expects. When you negotiate the position, salary will almost always follow.

Whatever the issue, you will be a lot more persuasive with your future employer if you discuss the job rather than your compensation. For example, if you treat your expense account as a perk, what you are able to negotiate will likely depend on the level of your position. On the other hand, if you focus on what you need in order to do your job effectively, the reaction will be entirely different. Instead of asking for a bigger expense account, try channeling the conversation this way:

YOU: I'm very excited about the possibility of being in charge of sales for your Midwest region. The salary you are offering is very fair. I think we would work very well together. However, I have one concern.

FUTURE BOSS: What's that?

YOU: I have been very effective in my current job because I spend most of my evenings and weekends entertaining clients. I'm concerned that my expense account won't be sufficient for me to continue to be able to do so.

FUTURE BOSS: You don't have to worry about that. We'll make sure you get whatever you need. What did you have in mind?

YOU: I was thinking $10,000 should be sufficient for me to really impact sales.

FUTURE BOSS: If that's what you need, I think we can handle that.

Whenever you hit a rough patch in the negotiations, talk about the job. Stress how excited you are about the possibility of working there. Try discussing all the great things you will be able to accomplish if the position is properly structured. Always bear in mind that it is a lot easier to negotiate the position than it is to directly negotiate for an increase in compensation.

SUMMARY OF NEGOTIATING POINTS

▶ Treat the negotiations as a continuation of the recruitment process.

▶ Seek opportunities to enhance the job responsibilities and the job level.

▶ Discuss skills and experience that would qualify you for more responsibility.

▶ Whenever possible, focus on how your requests will help you do your job better.

▶ If the negotiations become difficult, talk about the job.

▶ When you negotiate the position, salary will follow.

5

Creating a Win-Win Situation

Learn to listen. Opportunity could be knocking at the door softly.

—FRANK TYGER

Traditional bargaining theory is based on an analytical approach that I like to refer to as "circle analysis." There are two sets of circles: One set of circles overlaps and one set does not. The circles represent the bargaining parameters of each of the parties to the negotiations.

Identifying Common Interests

Overlapping circles indicate that the parties have mutual interests. An agreement is possible within the area where the circles overlap. Take, for example, an employer that is willing to pay an annual salary of between $60,000 and $80,000 for the position of director of transportation. Assume that the person the employer wants to hire is willing to accept the job if the salary is at least $70,000 a year. Using traditional negotiating analysis, we conclude that the candidate will be hired at a starting salary of somewhere between $70,000 and $80,000.

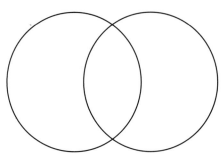

In the example just described, most people would consider the negotiations to be a complete success if the employer agreed to a salary of $80,000. A truly effective negotiator needs to be able to convince an employer to adjust its thinking and improve upon what it initially believed was the maximum amount it could offer. To do that, you have to show that what you are proposing is not only better for you but better for the employer as well.

To get the best possible package, be creative in approaching employment negotiations. Instead of simply seeking a salary of $80,000, which is the most a candidate could hope for under traditional bargaining theory, a win-win strategy seeks to determine the circumstances under which the employer might be willing to pay more than $80,000. Perhaps the employer would agree to pay a base salary of $70,000 plus a bonus of up to $25,000 if certain performance criteria are satisfied.

Win-win negotiating calls for a different mindset. It demands creativity. It also requires spending time exploring the other party's needs and desires. Once you understand what the employer's objectives are, you can craft proposals that not only satisfy its needs but also work to your advantage.

Remember the employer that would not agree to pay for extended temporary living expenses because a senior executive had abused that policy in the past (see Strategy 3)? Let's assume you were negotiating with that company and were asking for a signing bonus. It is unlikely that an organization that has had a history of problems with executives leaving after a relatively short time would agree to pay a signing bonus. But it might consider doing so if you agreed to pay back the bonus if you left within a year. That would eliminate its concern about paying a signing bonus and having you leave shortly thereafter, with the financial loss and embarrassment that would cause. It does nothing, however, to satisfy another of the company's concerns: reducing executive turnover.

Once you understand the employer's needs, you can propose a win-win solution. Instead of a signing bonus, you could suggest a forgivable loan to be used for the down payment on a house. This type of loan does not have to be paid back if an employee remains with the employer for a specified period of time, usually three to five years. The arrangement satisfies your financial objectives. It enables you to buy a home in the area, even encourages you to do so. Unlike the signing bonus, which you could spend any way you wanted, a forgivable home loan benefits the employer as well. A home loan allows you to buy a nice house in the neighborhood of your choice. It encourages you to relocate your family. Your spouse and children will quickly become part of the community. Once they have comfortably settled in, it becomes less likely that you will want to disrupt their lives with another move any time soon. The solution also gives you a financial incentive to stay—at least until the loan is forgiven. This is a win-win solution. It helps the company reduce turnover and the resulting disruption and loss of productivity. At the same time, it provides you with the additional compensation you are seeking.

Creativity is the key to developing win-win solutions. Identify what each party's real interests are and try to find ways to satisfy them. Instead of simply trying to divide up the pie, you are looking for ways to enlarge it. If you succeed in finding a win-win solution, everyone is better off.

Let's go back to our circles again. Only this time, you find yourself in a negotiating situation in which the circles don't overlap. For example, you receive an offer from an organization you would really like to work for. You are perfect for the job. The prospective employer considers you to be the ideal candidate. However, you will accept the job only if the salary is at least $70,000 a year. Unfortunately, the employer has budgeted only $60,000 for the position.

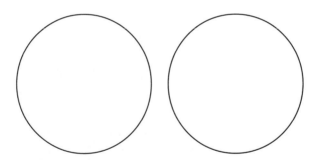

Under traditional bargaining theory, reaching a mutually acceptable agreement is not possible. There is no match between your needs and those of the employer. In circle analysis terminology, there is no overlap. According to this school of thought, you might as well start looking for a different job because there is no way you will be able to reach an agreement that allows you to accept this one.

Let's assume you are an intuitive negotiator. You want the job, and you have not been sufficiently schooled in the art of negotiating to know what is obvious to any good circle analyzer—that you can't get the job on terms acceptable to you. Once you find out that the most the employer is willing to pay is $60,000, what do you do? You explore what the employer's real needs are.

You discover that the company is losing sales because orders cannot be filled fast enough and its distribution costs are too high. You can readily identify more than $100,000 in cost savings, and by reducing the time it takes to fill orders, you should be able to cut the number of canceled orders in half. So you propose accepting the base salary that the employer initially offered plus a bonus based on cost savings and reductions in the number of canceled orders. You calculate that you can earn an additional $20,000 bonus and possibly more under the system you are proposing. If you achieve those results, you would be very pleased with the compensation package.

The employer will also be happy. It gets to hire someone with your experience, something the company did not think it could afford. Moreover, it is able to do so with the base salary that was budgeted for the position. If you achieve the results necessary to qualify for the proposed bonus, your new employer will be glad to pay it. You will have solved two major problems for the company and will have increased its profits by much more than your bonus. This is win-win negotiating. By looking at both parties' real interests and finding ways to satisfy them, you have created an agreement where, at first glance, none seemed possible.

Recently I had the opportunity to work with a client to improve her compensation package using a similar approach. My client was a marketing executive with a large company. She was negotiating with a small publishing company to become the new chief operating officer. She was eligible for a $50,000 bonus with her current employer at the end of the year (see Strategy 6). The new company wanted her to start immediately but was not willing to compensate her for the lost bonus. The owners of the company considered their compensation package to be very generous. Basically they were unwilling to pay her any more until she proved herself. So I had my client propose that she be compensated for the lost bonus at the end of her first year, but only if she achieved certain agreed-upon goals. The employer was willing to accept that proposal because it provided a win-win solution. If she achieved the agreed-upon performance objectives, the company would be glad to pay the additional money because of the increased profit that resulted from her efforts.

Every deal cannot be salvaged by win-win negotiating. If the reason the employer will not pay more than $60,000 for the director of transportation job has to do with organizational structure, there may not be any way to solve the problem through win-win negotiating. Once you understand why the company is unwilling to pay more than $60,000, you can at least explore possible ways to overcome its concerns. For instance, you might be able to persuade the employer to place the position at a higher level so you could be paid more money without disrupting the organization's salary structure. Perhaps you have certain unique skills and experience that would allow the position to be redefined by adding responsibilities to the job, thereby increasing its value to the organization. That solution would satisfy your salary needs by placing the position at a higher level and at the same time satisfy critical business needs of the employer. If, however, paying more than $60,000 for the position would require raising the salary of a large number of other executives, it would make no economic sense for the company to increase its offer. No amount of win-win negotiating can change that, although a signing bonus might allow the company to pay you more money without impacting its basic salary structure.

There are two different ways to develop a win-win solution. To employ the strategy effectively, you need to understand the difference between these two approaches. One type of win-win negotiating is based on identifying common interests and developing proposals that benefit both the employer and you. As illustrated by the last example, agreeing to a lower base salary in return for the opportunity to earn a generous bonus based on results important to the company is, by definition, a form of win-win negotiating.

The same can be said for accepting stock options in lieu of a portion of your salary if, for example, you are joining a start-up company. The employer benefits by being able to hire someone it might not have otherwise been able to afford. You benefit if the employer does well as a result of your efforts because the value of those options will rise dramatically. Since the stock options do not increase in value unless the company's stock goes up, you do well only if the company does well. This is the epitome of a win-win negotiating solution.

The second type of win-win negotiating involves identifying benefits that the employer can provide at less cost than their value to you. If, for example, you are being recruited to work for a retailer, you might seek a clothing allowance for the purchase of apparel sold by the company. Since the cost to the company for this merchandise is less than what it would cost you to purchase the clothing at retail, it is in your interest as well as the company's to provide some of your compensation in the form of a clothing allowance. Moreover, the company has an interest in its executives using the products it sells. Executives who use the company's products can better relate to its customers. They also become walking advertisements for those products. In this way everyone benefits.

Similarly, a better job title may be very important to you, but it may not be that significant to the employer, particularly if it does not involve a more expensive compensation or benefits package. By taking advantage of the different values you each place on various items, you may be able to enhance your total package significantly without dramatically increasing the cost to the employer. When this type of discrepancy exists, an "add-on" negotiating strategy may be appropriate (see Strategy 17).

If you understand how to develop win-win strategies, you will be able to negotiate a better deal. Even if initially it does not appear that the employer can satisfy your objectives, you needn't automatically give up on an otherwise good employment situation without first exploring ways to satisfy each party's needs. In one situation that I worked on, in which my client was being recruited by a start-up company, we were able to overcome the employer's immediate cash flow problem by proposing that the company provide a large equity stake to my client in return for a deferral, for one year, of half his starting salary. A satisfactory agreement was reached only after both sides took the time to understand each other's needs as well as the limitations on what the employer could do.

In every deal you should look for ways to improve your situation by helping the other side improve its own position. That way the negotiations will not be a zero-sum game. The employer will have more to give because it will be getting more. This is truly where negotiating becomes an art.

Summary of Negotiating Points

▶ Identify the employer's needs.
▶ Identify areas of common interest.
▶ Develop proposals that maximize benefits for the employer as well as for you.
▶ Be creative.
▶ Explore different options.
▶ Look for benefits that you value more than they cost your prospective employer.

6

Timing Your Departure

Leave them while you're looking good.

—ANITA LAOS, *GENTLEMEN*
PREFER BLONDES

You normally cannot control when the job you want opens up or when a recruiter calls about an employment opportunity. Moreover, once you have accepted a job, your new boss will almost always want you to start as soon as possible. Like most people, you will also want to begin your new job as soon as you can without leaving your former employer in a bind. Nonetheless, it may not be in your best financial interest to do so. As a result, start dates sometimes become issues in employment negotiations.

If there is some flexibility as to the start date, you may be able to time your departure so that you do not lose benefits for which you are about to become eligible. Even if a prospective employer insists on your starting immediately, you may be able to keep the negotiations going long enough to accommodate your scheduling needs. Similarly, most employers will understand that it may take some time to transfer projects you are working on to others. You may be able to use your need to do so to delay your departure date and avoid not losing benefits unnecessarily.

The timing of a job change may be significant for a number of reasons. Eligibility for certain benefits often depends on an employee continuing to be employed through a designated date. For example, bonuses, restricted stock, stock options, pensions, and 401(k) plans are all typically contingent on an employee remaining employed for a specified period of time. For benefits governed by an employer's benefit plans—pension plans, 401(k) plans, and stock option plans—the time period before the employee is given unre-stricted ownership of the benefit is referred to as the "vesting period." Rights may vest all at once, as in the case of a pension that becomes fully vested after five years. On the other hand, as is typically the case with stock options and restricted stock, a certain portion of each grant (e.g., 25 percent) vests annually.

If you are about to receive your annual bonus, or if grants of restricted stock or stock options will soon vest, you need to take that into considera-tion when negotiating your compensation at a new job. Clearly, leaving an organization shortly before your pension vests may result in a significant financial loss. Even after you are fully vested, it will cost you money to change jobs immediately prior to being credited with an additional year of service for pension purposes, or right before you become eligible for this year's company match in your 401(k) plan.

Most employers will agree to compensate you for the value of any bonuses, stock, or pension benefits lost as a result of changing jobs. Other-wise, it would often not make sense for you to take the job. Reimbursement for the loss of benefits is usually relatively easy to negotiate. However, in order to be compensated for the loss of these benefits, you need to know enough to ask. You also need to be able to calculate (or have your account-ant calculate) the value of these benefits. If you are given cash in lieu of a benefit afforded favorable tax treatment, be sure to take that into account in calculating the amount you need to receive. For example, not being able to defer payment of taxes on pension or 401(k) benefits or, in the case of stock, of not getting the benefit of the more favorable capital gains tax rate requires that the employer include the amount of taxes you will incur upon receipt of payment in lieu of the benefit in determining the amount you need in order to be made whole.

Although employers will generally compensate you for lost benefits, they will include the cost of these payments when determining the value of the total package that they are offering. Even though in fairness it shouldn't be considered, money paid to compensate for lost benefits will ordinarily result in less money being available for salary and other benefits. This is par-ticularly true when the problem is resolved, as it typically is, by means of a cash payment at the time of hire. Even if you are told otherwise, your new employer almost certainly has factored these costs into the value of the total package. Any such payments that are made will result in a corresponding reduction in other elements of the deal. Thus, for example, if an employer is already compensating you for a lost bonus, it is unlikely to agree to give you a signing bonus as well. If it does, you can guarantee that the bonus will be reduced by an amount equal to the amount of the lost benefits the employer has already agreed to pay for.

The best strategy therefore is not to have to ask your prospective employer to compensate you for lost benefits. Rather, you should try to time your departure to minimize the loss of bonuses, stock options, or other benefits. Thus, if you resign shortly after receiving your performance bonus or after this year's portion of your stock option award vests, you will not have to be compensated for not receiving those items. Instead, you can get a signing bonus or some other benefit, in addition to what you have already received from your former employer.

Timing Your Departure to Maximize Your Pension Benefits

To the extent that you can do so without sacrificing other objectives, try to time your departure so that you maximize the credit you receive for service under your pension plan. Because of the way the pension laws are written, years of service for pension purposes may not be the same as the actual number of years you have been with the organization. For purposes of determining the amount of your pension, employers are required by law to credit you with a full year of service in any year that you work 1,000 hours or more. Most pension plans are set up on a calendar-year basis. A full-time salaried employee works 1,000 hours by the end of June in any given year. Therefore, if your employer has a calendar-year plan, you can get an additional year of pension credit simply by terminating your employment after June 30.

If you have complete control over the timing of your departure and can do so without losing a bonus or additional stock rights, you may be able to earn an additional year of pension service with your new employer as well. One executive I was advising was able to enhance his pension benefits by controlling the timing of his departure precisely. He left his former employer on July 6, thus receiving an additional year of credit under his former employer's plan. This was particularly important because it gave him the five years of credited service required to vest under that plan. By carefully timing his departure, he was able to avoid losing all his pension benefits.

The executive started work with his new employer the following week, on July 9, and was thus also able to work 1,000 hours for his new employer in that same calendar year. As a result, he received an additional year of credited pension service under his new employer's plan as well. By carefully timing his departure, he gained thousands of dollars in future pension benefits. Moreover, he avoided having to ask his new employer to compensate him for lost benefits. Instead, he was able to negotiate a higher salary and a signing bonus.

Timing Your Start Date to Increase the Value of Your Stock Options

Timing may also affect the value of any stock options you are granted. Certain types of options, called "incentive stock options" (ISOs), by law must be priced at the market price on the date that they are granted. Other types of options may have similar restrictions spelled out in the plan under which they are awarded. Thus, for example, a new hire may be granted an option to purchase a certain number of shares of company stock at the market price on the employee's starting day. The stock price on that day is referred to as the "exercise price" or the "strike price." The recipient of the grant will, at some future date, be able to exercise those options and buy that number of shares of stock at the exercise price. If the stock goes up in value, when the options are exercised the employee will be able to purchase the stock for less than the market price. The employee will earn an immediate profit equal to the difference between the exercise price and the market price on the day the options are exercised.

Let's assume, for example, that Carla is able to get Small Manufacturing Company to give her options to buy 1,000 shares of stock at $5 a share, the price of the stock on the day she begins work. Three years later she exercises those options when Small Manufacturing Company stock is selling for $10 a share. Carla has to pay only $5,000 to exercise those stock options. She can then turn around and sell the stock for $10,000, making an immediate profit of $5,000.

Since the exercise price is determined by the market price on the day the options are granted, the employee's starting date can have a significant impact on how much those options are ultimately worth. If the price of the employer's stock is increasing, the sooner an employee starts work, the more valuable those options will be. If the price of the stock falls after the employee begins work, the options may turn out to be worthless. Thus, if the stock market is rising or if you anticipate that the company's stock will increase regardless of overall market trends, it may be in your interest to begin work as soon as possible, even if that results in the loss of benefits from your current employer. On the other hand, you may be able to rearrange your plans so that the timing of a grant works to your advantage.

During one negotiation I was involved in, the date on which stock options would be granted became a major point of concern. My client had planned to conclude the agreement with his new employer, take a previously scheduled four-week vacation in Europe, and then resign his current employment (with reasonable notice) in order to start the new job. However, my client also wanted to lock in a low option price in a rapidly rising stock market. To deal with this issue, we were able to get his new employer to agree to allow him to begin his employment immediately and then take his vacation as an employee of the new company. In this way he received the benefit of any increase in the value of the stock that occurred while he was away on vacation.

You cannot ensure receipt, from your former employer, of every benefit for which you might be eligible simply by controlling the date of your departure. Different benefits will come due at different times during the year. Your bonus may be scheduled for July, whereas the employer match on your 401(k) plan may not be made until December 31. If you get a job offer on December 10, you probably would not want to delay starting your new job until July solely to get your bonus, even if you could. However, you might want to start your new employment after January 1 so that you receive the employer match on your 401(k) contributions.

An awareness of the importance of timing may be worth thousands of dollars in additional benefits that you might otherwise have lost. It may also eliminate the need to ask a prospective employer to compensate you for the loss of benefits, thus enabling you to seek other compensation from your new employer instead.

Summary of Negotiating Points

- ▶ Determine when your bonuses, stock, and other benefits are earned.
- ▶ Plan the timing of your departure to maximize receipt of those benefits.
- ▶ Ask to be compensated for any benefits you lose because of timing.
- ▶ When seeking to be compensated for lost benefits, be sure to include in the amount you are seeking the cost of having to pay taxes on any payments in lieu of those benefits.

▶ Remember that employers, in valuing the total compensation being offered, will take into account any payments made to compensate you for lost benefits.

▶ When planning your departure, keep in mind that for most pension plans you have to work only 1,000 hours in a year to get a full year of pension credit.

7

Using the Follow-Up Memo as a Negotiating Tool

"The horror of that moment," the King went on, "I shall never never forget!"

"You will though," the Queen said, "if you don't make a memorandum of it."

—LEWIS CARROLL, THROUGH
THE LOOKING GLASS

In most types of negotiations, you want the other side to make the first offer. The reasons are obvious. The other side's first offer may be more than you would have asked for. In that case you are truly fortunate because you know that a satisfactory agreement can be readily reached. Anything additional that you obtain is "icing on the cake." You don't have to worry about not being able to reach an agreement and can focus 100 percent of your energies on improving the terms of the deal.

Employment negotiations differ from other types of negotiations in that the employer almost always makes the first offer. If you have been successful in not disclosing too much about your current compensation or what it would take to get you to leave your current job, you are in an excellent position to take advantage of this fact (see Strategy 1). Even if the employer's initial offer is not acceptable, it is still advantageous to receive that offer first. It provides you with information. It commits the employer. Most important, it allows you to control how the negotiations proceed. You can identify the issues you want to discuss and determine the order in which you bring them up.

To the extent that you can control the agenda, you can often determine the direction the negotiations take. Doing so will generally improve your bargaining position. You can affect the order in which issues are discussed by the way you respond to the employer's initial offer. For example, you could respond to each element in the initial offer point by point, or you could begin by addressing one or two selected items, leaving the rest for later. In this way you can gain control of the process.

Let's assume an employer offers you a salary that you feel is too low. You have several choices. You could simply ask for a higher salary. Or you could attempt to change the structure of the employer's offer completely and come back with a totally different type of proposal. You might try to restructure the compensation package so that it includes a performance bonus or provides you with equity. You might even propose taking a lower salary if the bonus potential or stock option grant is large enough. We will examine specific responses to particular types of proposals in discussing other strategies. The point here is that you can control how the negotiations proceed by the way you respond to the employer's proposals. Using a follow-up memo or e-mail can be an effective way to exert control over the process.

Lawyers have a saying: "He who controls the drafting of the documents controls the deal." That is the reason every good employment lawyer wants to be the one who drafts the agreement. Normally agreements are reached first through discussions and then those agreements are reduced to writing. Rarely is every detail covered during the initial discussions. When the terms of the agreement are reduced to writing, the party drafting the document can clarify any points that have been left vague and can incorporate its view as to how points that have not been covered should be resolved. The drafter can also suggest solutions to problems that he or she becomes aware of during the drafting process but that were not identified during the discussions. Once an agreement is reduced to writing, as long as it is consistent with the basic terms that have been discussed and agreed upon, it takes on a certain legitimacy just by the fact that it exists. The other side is then left to try to negotiate changes to the language of the document.

In the employment context, it is the employer who typically prepares the documents. If there is a formal contract, it is almost always drafted by the employer's lawyer. Typically, however, the only document that details the terms of the agreement is an offer letter written by the employer. Ordinarily it is difficult for an employee to gain control over the drafting of employment documents. However, by judicious use of follow-up memos or e-mails, you can occasionally wrest control of drafting the final documents away from the employer. If a formal contract is not contemplated, you may be able to preempt the employer's offer letter by promptly sending a confirming letter or e-mail of your own. In it, you set forth your understanding of the terms that have been agreed upon and ask your future employer to confirm the agreement by signing and returning a copy of the letter to you.

A particularly effective technique is to send a follow-up e-mail after each discussion. This would mean that after each negotiating session (or as is more often the case, each telephone call), you would immediately send an e-mail confirming the points that have been agreed upon. In this way, even if your new employer drafts the final documents, those documents will have to be consistent with your e-mails. In that way you gain some control over the drafting process.

Follow-up e-mails can also help you influence how the negotiations proceed. The next conversation after your follow-up e-mail will almost always focus on that e-mail, not on the discussion that preceded it. Let's say, for example, you have just reached agreement on a salary package that includes a potential bonus equal to 100 percent of your base salary. In your confirming e-mail, you could state that you will be calling the next day to discuss bonus criteria. You could even suggest what the criteria should be. Or you might mention other areas that you want to discuss. In either event, you are controlling the negotiating agenda. Since the outcome of negotiations often depend on timing, when you raise an issue can be critical. Follow-up e-mails can be effectively used to implement strategies that depend on timing (see Strategy 11).

A follow-up memo or e-mail can be particularly effective in responding to an initial proposal, before it is reduced to writing. Let's assume that you just had a conversation with the president of Small Company who wants to offer you a job but can't afford to pay you what you are currently earning. After outlining the offer, the Small Company president tells you that he will send you a letter setting forth the offer in more detail. You could wait to receive the letter and then address the issues that concern you, or you could seize the initiative and e-mail him a note that states something along the following lines:

Dear Small Company President:

I am very excited about the company and the job opportunity we discussed. I understand why you feel that a company of your size cannot match my current base salary. Your description of Small Company's transportation management needs, however, leads me to believe that I can immediately contribute to the company's bottom line. My experience in transportation management with Big Company should enable me to bring about immediate savings in your delivery costs.

I am so certain I can save you money that I would be willing to accept a base salary less than I am currently earning if you could provide a bonus payable only if I reduce your delivery costs. I would suggest a bonus of 10 percent of what I save the company in delivery costs during my first year of employment.

I will call you tomorrow to discuss how we could structure my compensation on the basis of the savings I could generate for the company. I look forward to talking to you then.

Yours truly,

Transportation Manager
Big Company

By sending this e-mail before you receive a formal written offer, you transform the dynamics of the negotiations. The president of Small Company has not yet formally committed himself to a proposal. He can accept your suggestion without "losing face." Or he can come up with a proposal of his own that would provide you with the additional compensation you require.

Effective use of a follow-up e-mail or memo will enable you to defuse a potentially difficult situation in which each side has staked out a position from which it is hard to retreat. Instead, the follow-up e-mail or memo provides a way for you to continue your discussion with the president about how to bridge the gap between your current salary and what Small Company can afford. The focus of the discussion is now firmly where you want it to be—on how Small Company can manage to pay you more so that you can join the firm.

The follow-up e-mail or memo is not merely a means of recording the terms that have been agreed upon. Properly used, it is a strategic tool to control the flow of the negotiations and to refocus them when they are not proceeding as planned.

Summary of Negotiating Points

▶ Maintain control over the negotiating agenda.

▶ Respond to proposals in ways that shape what will be discussed, and in what order.

▶ Use follow-up e-mails or memos to set the negotiating agenda.

▶ Bear in mind that the person who drafts the employment documents can affect the substantive terms of the deal.

▶ Use follow-up e-mails or memos to gain control of the drafting process.

▶ Remember that follow-up e-mails or memos can not only be used to record the parties' agreements but can also be used as strategic negotiating tools.

8

Creating a Stake in the Outcome

I consider my ability to arouse enthusiasm among men
the greatest asset I possess.

—CHARLES SCHWAB

Tim had been talking to a well-known New York–based retailer for several months about the possibility of becoming the company's director of advertising. He was one of several candidates being considered. Finally the company decided to offer him the job. By the time it got around to making the offer, Tim's interest in the position had cooled. In the interim he had been talking to another company about a similar position. So when the salary offer from the retailer was lower than he had expected, Tim expressed his disappointment with the offer. The company responded that it was limited as to what it could do because of the organization's salary structure but indicated that the job offered a tremendous opportunity for advancement. Tim repeated that he thought the salary was low and would have to think it over. Tim added that, although he was very interested in the job, he was also talking to another company.

About a week went by when he received a phone call from the company's president, to whom he would be reporting. The president wanted to know what he had decided. Tim again stated how excited he was about the possibility of coming to work for him. Because of the salary, however, he was having a difficult time making a decision, particularly since the other company he was speaking to was offering significantly more money. Despite the lower salary, he was still seriously considering the offer. He asked for a little more time. Two days later the president called him back and offered him more money. Simply by continuing to express his interest in the position, Tim was able to get the employer, which by this time already had a significant stake in the outcome, to substantially increase its offer.

In his book *Bargaining Games*, Keith Murnighan describes a game called the "Dollar Auction" that he uses when he teaches negotiating seminars. In the game, people are given the opportunity to bid for a $20 bill. The bidding must increase by at least $1 with each bid. The highest bidder pays whatever is bid and gets the $20 bill.

What makes the game interesting is that the second-highest bidder also has to pay, forfeiting whatever he or she has bid. The top two bidders each pay, but only the highest bidder receives anything for his or her effort. Invariably the same thing happens every time this game is played.

The bidding starts at $1 and rapidly goes up $2, $3, $4, until the bid is over $10. By $15 there are usually just two bidders and the bidding slows down. Then one of the bidders gets cute and decides to jump his or her bid to $19. That person sits back, feeling quite proud of his or her negotiating brilliance. Without fail, however, after a brief pause the remaining bidder raises his or her bid to $20.

This creates a dilemma for the $19 bidder. The bidder can quit, in which case he or she loses $19, or the bidder can go to $21. Almost every time the $19 bidder will go to the $21 bid. Then the battle begins. The bidding continues to $30, $40, $50. Each party tries to scare the other into quitting. The bidding often exceeds $50 and occasionally can go as high as $100.

No reasonable person would pay $100 for a $20 bill. So what is really going on here? At first the dynamics of the situation are about the money and the game. At some point the objective changes to trying to protect the money you have already committed. Thus, when you bid $21, you will lose only $1 ($21 minus the $20 you win) rather than the $19 you will lose as the second-place finisher. Eventually it's no longer about money or even winning the game; it's about not looking foolish.

When you are negotiating about your future employment, you want the other party to develop a personal stake in getting you to accept the offer. This is sometimes referred to as "gaining commitment." As in the Dollar Auction, the commitment of the employer tends to intensify as the negotiations proceed. One's desire to ensure a successful outcome increases geometrically with the amount of time and effort invested in the process. This phenomenon of "escalating commitment" reflects the basic human tendency of not wanting to admit to having made a mistake. In order to justify previous commitments of time or money, people often go to extraordinary lengths to prevent a project from failing, even when it would make economic sense to abandon the project. Why? To avoid looking foolish.

The concept of escalating commitment often comes into play during employment negotiations. As time passes an employer may become committed to hiring you without any conscious effort on your part. This will work to your advantage, even though you are unaware of what is occurring. If you understand how to gain an employer's commitment or to recognize when this has occurred, you will be able to use that knowledge to your advantage.

Simply by keeping the discussions going in a positive manner for an extended period of time, up to the point at which you begin to look unreasonable, you increase the likelihood of the negotiations concluding favorably. An employer that has spent a significant amount of time and effort negotiating a deal becomes committed to completing it successfully and becomes increasingly willing to compromise in order to ensure that occurs.

As time goes on, the employer will grow impatient to conclude the negotiations and may even become concerned that you won't accept the offer. As a result, the employer will increase its efforts to satisfy your needs. A friend of mine describes how this phenomenon worked for her when she was being recruited as senior vice president of human resources for a major New York advertising agency. When the company offered her the position, she raised a number of issues. She asked about parking, car allowance, club dues, and so on. She also asked if the company could send her a description of the benefit plans. These discussions took place over the course of several days. The employer agreed to some of her requests but could not agree to others. A few days later she received a call from the chairman of the company, who offered her a substantially higher salary than had originally been proposed. Obviously, the company was committed to hiring her and had become concerned that she might not accept the job. So the chairman made her an offer that he knew she could not turn down.

Although employment negotiations usually are completed in a matter of days or at most weeks, time tends to work in the candidate's favor. That is because the person negotiating on behalf of the employer does not want to look foolish for having wasted a substantial amount of time and effort trying unsuccessfully to put the deal together. You can also extend the process by asking for information. You can ask to review the benefits plans, for example. You can also ask for clarification of various points you have discussed. E-mails are a good way to raise noncontroversial issues that may require some form of clarifications.

You can, however, overplay the waiting game. If the negotiations go on for too long, the employer will begin to wonder whether it has made a mistake in extending you the offer in the first place. After all, one reason the employer was interested in you in the first place was that you seemed so excited about the job. So it is important that you do not give the appearance of delaying, even though you are in fact controlling the pace of the negotiations. Of course, throughout the process you should continually reassure your prospective employer that you really are excited about the job.

One way to build commitment and control the pace of the negotiations is to tackle some of the easy issues first. Once those issues have been raised and resolved, the other party starts to gain a stake in ensuring that you accept the position. In resolving the easy issues, you begin to build a relationship that can carry over to negotiating the more difficult ones. Another way to get the negotiator to make an investment in the process is to ask questions that take some time and effort to answer. You can also ask for time to "think things over" before you respond.

Another way to prolong the negotiations is to defer an issue while you seek advice from your lawyer or accountant (see Strategy 16). This tactic works particularly well when you are dealing with technical issues, such as an agreement not to compete. An added advantage is that as a result you will be able to take a more informed position on the issue when you do finally discuss it. In fact, most people do need advice on technical employment issues. While the discussions about these subjects are being postponed, you can attempt to resolve the issues you want to address first.

If the selection and recruitment process has taken a long time, the employer already has developed a level of commitment to hiring you. You can increase that commitment during the course of the negotiations. Your future boss strengthens her commitment, for example, whenever she talks to others in the organization about you. Whether she recognizes it or not, by so doing she has placed her credibility on the line. She will not want to look foolish in the eyes of her boss or her peers. After that emotional bridge is crossed, she will do everything possible to get you to accept the offer. If you are aware of these psychological dynamics, you are much more likely to get what you want.

Once your future boss becomes committed to hiring you, any additional benefits or increases in compensation needed to achieve that result will seem less significant. It becomes easier to gain small concessions—improve the package a little here, add a little more money there—in order to complete the deal. The more public the commitment, the more important it becomes for you to accept the offer.

SUMMARY OF NEGOTIATING POINTS

► Devoting time and energy to the negotiating process leads an employer to develop a psychological commitment to ensuring its success. Do everything you can to encourage that commitment.

► Control the pace and agenda of the negotiations.

► Use e-mails to extend the process.

► Try to have a number of meetings and discussions with the employer's negotiator.

► When appropriate, take time to seek the advice of your lawyer or accountant.

► Use time to your advantage.

► Continually reassure your prospective employer of your interest in the job.

► Recognize when an employer has become committed.

► Take advantage of a clear commitment to promptly conclude the agreement.

9

Disagreeing without Being Disagreeable

BEING LIKABLE AS A NEGOTIATING STRATEGY

If you argue and rankle and contradict, you may achieve a temporary victory—sometimes; but it will be an empty victory because you will never get your opponent's good will.

—BENJAMIN FRANKLIN

After Macy's filed for bankruptcy, it was forced to lay off a large number of employees. The company even hired someone from outside to handle the terminations in the corporate offices. Management understood that it would be difficult for insiders to carry out the terminations because these people were friends and colleagues. The person who was brought in to handle the dismissals had no such reservations. She quickly dispatched the employees who were no longer considered essential and provided them with a standard severance package.

Some people tried to negotiate a better severance package but without much success. One employee bypassed this individual and went directly to the senior vice president of human resources, whom she had known for years, to discuss her dismissal (see Strategy 21). She accepted the firing graciously and asked only that, in light of the number of years she had worked for the company, the amount of the severance be increased. She appealed to the senior vice president as a friend and reminded him that she had one child in college and another about to start. Her request was granted. The head of human resources, because of his relationship with the employee, could not say no.

Personalizing the Issues

It is never easy to fire someone, but it's a lot easier if you don't know the person. Then it's just a matter of "objectively" looking at the needs of the employer and determining who stays and who goes. As they say, "It's not personal." Not so when you know someone. It's much harder if you have met the spouse and children, gone out for drinks, and worked closely together. The same is true when you are hiring. The more you like the candidate, the harder it will be to refuse reasonable requests made during the negotiations. Accordingly, one of your objectives as a job candidate should be to get the people you are dealing with to like you.

How do you do that? Think about all the people you enjoy spending time with. What characteristics do they share? Most people cite qualities like being witty, charming, talented, successful, smart, attractive, and well informed. Of course, these are the qualities possessed by the people we see on television and in the movies, people whom we wish we could have as friends. (Actually it is the characters they play that we really want as our friends.) I don't know about you, but I scarcely count Brad Pitt, Charlize Theron, Scarlett Johansson, and Will Smith among my friends. In real life, the qualities that most of us are attracted to in friends are enthusiasm, a sense of humor, and genuine affection. The third quality is the most important. We all tend to like people who like us and make us feel important.

It is much harder to say no to someone you like than to someone you don't really know. Therefore, part of your negotiating strategy should be to get to know the employer's negotiator on a personal basis and to let that person get to know you. One way to do that is to ask lots of questions, not only about the issues you are discussing but also about the organization and about that person and his or her job. Talk about things other than just the terms of your employment. Show an interest in the negotiator as a person. What does he like? Where does she live? Does he have a family? Try to identify common interests. Talk about your kids. Talk about her kids. Talk about golf. Talk about local sports teams. Anything the negotiator is excited about is probably a good topic to discuss. It is only common sense, however, to avoid topics such as politics and religion, which can evoke strong emotional reactions.

Although being likable probably helps in every type of negotiation, it is particularly beneficial in employment negotiations. Your future employer will want you to feel good about joining the organization. This is particularly true if you are bargaining with your future boss. Your boss has a personal stake in ensuring that you are satisfied with the outcome of the negotiations. Your boss wants you to start work excited about the job and feeling good about the way you have been treated. The more your future boss likes you, the more he or she is going to want you to accept the job and the harder he or she will try to make you happy. Being likable makes it that much more difficult for a prospective employer to refuse reasonable requests that you make.

Try to personalize the issues being discussed. If the job requires you to move, ask the negotiator about his experiences when he moved to the area. Seek advice. Not only will the negotiator be flattered but he is also likely to provide you with valuable information. Your inquiry will also make it easier to get additional relocation benefits when you subsequently discuss the terms of the move. When you use this approach, the negotiator is more likely to relate to the problems you face and will be more willing to help you resolve them to your satisfaction.

Remember the traits people look for when choosing friends? The same qualities that make you desirable as a friend make you an attractive candidate for employment. When choosing among otherwise qualified applicants, managers want to hire people they like and who are excited about the job. A sense of humor never hurts either.

Not everyone can be funny, but you certainly can laugh at someone else's jokes and go out of your way to show that you like the people you are dealing with. All it takes is a little effort to demonstrate excitement about the organization and the job. Whenever possible, show that you are really interested in the position. That is good advice when you are trying to get a job offer. It is no less important when you are negotiating the terms of that offer. Emerson once said: "Nothing great was ever achieved without enthusiasm." Successful executives instinctively know this. The one quality most hiring executives look for in a candidate is enthusiasm. Make it work for you.

Suppose, for example, that you are interviewing in New York City, an area with a high cost of living, and you don't feel the salary being offered is sufficient. You could tell the employer that the offer just isn't good enough. Or you could say that you are really excited about the job but have some concerns about the cost of living in New York since you are coming from Bentonville, Arkansas. By using the latter approach, you focus everyone's attention, in a friendly way, on resolving a legitimate concern, not on the fact that it will cost the employer more money to do so. This approach takes advantage of the employer's general desire to be fair (see Commandment 6, "Understand the Role That Fairness Plays in the Process").

Avoiding Ultimatums

To be likable, avoid being adversarial and never force the other side "into a corner." Nobody likes a bully. As a rule, ultimatums are seldom effective. They certainly won't endear you to the person you are dealing with. Even if you have the bargaining power to force the other side to capitulate in the face of an ultimatum, there is rarely a need to do so. If your bargaining position is strong, you can get what you want, within reason, by simply maintaining a firm stance.

If you decide to extend an ultimatum, at least don't make it sound like one. Which of the following approaches do you think will be more effective?

1. "If you don't increase the salary being offered by $25,000 you can forget about my coming to work for you."
2. "I would really like to come to work for you, but it would not make sense for me to change jobs unless you could provide me with a substantial increase in salary, which I figure is about $25,000."

When you use your bargaining power in a way that embarrasses the other party, that person will insist on "winning" on some other issue. Most people share a basic desire for fairness, and when their sense of fairness has been violated, they seek to even the score. They may do it subtly, in a way you are never even aware of. If you are dealing with the vice president of human resources, for instance, that individual may at some future date tip the balance in favor of promoting someone else rather than you. You never know when the person you are bargaining with today will be in a position to help you or to cause you problems down the road.

I am reminded of an individual I worked with when I first started out my career as a lawyer. We were both associates at the same firm, and he obviously felt that we were competing for a limited number of partnership opportunities. So he did what he could to improve his position at my expense and at the expense of the other associates with whom we worked. In the end, though, he left the firm and I became a partner. Years later, when I was at Macy's, I bumped into him again. He was now a partner at another firm. He asked me to introduce him to the appropriate people at Macy's so that he could make a pitch to do some of their legal work. Somehow I never was able to find the time to do that for him. There is a saying in Hollywood: "Be careful how you treat people on your way up because you will certainly see the same people on the way down." You would do well to adopt a similar philosophy in your own business dealings.

Making It Personal

Try to connect with the employer's negotiator on a personal level. Don't be afraid to express your feelings about how the negotiations are going. You can even allow yourself to show some emotion, thereby encouraging the person you are dealing with to discuss his or her feelings as well. As long as you do not engage in personal attacks, this type of exchange can create a mutual bond that helps facilitate the negotiations. For example, if you are meeting resistance on a particular point that's important to you, try saying something like: "I really want to come to work here, but I am a little disappointed in the organization's response on this issue. I don't feel that management really understands how important this is to me. Maybe you could find a way to convey my feelings to them." Describing how you feel about an issue personalizes it. Once you have done that, it becomes difficult for the negotiator not to try to accommodate your request.

Negotiators generally prize "winning," but in employment negotiations they understand that it is more important that the person being hired feel that he or she has been well treated. Most employers seek to do what's fair. The people you are dealing with usually are employers first and negotiators second. That is why employment negotiations are different from most other types of negotiations.

Keeping the Tone Positive

Strive to always keep the tone of the discussions positive. It is generally better to say yes than no. For instance, if you concur with some elements of a proposal but can't agree to everything, emphasize the areas of agreement. As previously discussed, it is also ordinarily best to start with the easy issues (see Strategy 8). Reaching agreement on some issues quickly will enable you to develop a relationship with the employer's negotiator before the discussions get heated. The goodwill that is generated during the early stages of the negotiations will serve you well when you have to resolve the inevitable points of real contention.

Being likable doesn't, however, mean giving in just to avoid an argument. Never be apologetic about what you are seeking, unless you are asking for something at the behest of someone else (see Strategy 16). After all, if you can't justify the positions you are taking, you shouldn't be taking them in the first place. Don't be afraid to stand up for what you believe is right. If you do that in a nonadversarial way, you will gain the respect of the people you are dealing with. Just bear in mind that very few issues arise during employment negotiations that involve matters of principle. Most issues come down to money. Those types of interests can usually be satisfied in a variety of ways (see Strategy 10). If the employer is unwilling or unable to do something, it can, if it wants to, usually find some other way to provide you with what you are seeking or give you something of equal value.

Employment negotiations are no place for Rambo-style tactics, at least not by you (see Strategy 16). Nonetheless, disagreements are part of the process. Therefore, how you disagree is important. I recommend the following rules of negotiating etiquette:

1. When disagreements arise, focus on the issues, not on the person you are negotiating with, so that the disagreements don't get personal.
2. Always show respect for the other person even when you are disagreeing.
3. Never interrupt, no matter how wrong the other person is. Let the negotiator have his or her say.
4. Avoid unnecessary confrontation.
5. Argue your position rather than attacking the employer's. Attacking the negotiator's position will only force him or her to defend it.
6. Acknowledge that you understand why the negotiator is taking a position even while you disagree with it.
7. Explain your reasons for disagreeing and why you are asking for what you want.
8. Ask for the negotiator's help in resolving problems.
9. Present facts to support your position.

Remember, your objective is not to win debating points. It is to get the employer to agree to what you want. To do that, you first need to get the other person to see things from your point of view.

Have you ever been in an argument with someone who refuses to fight back? It is very hard to continue to argue. Soon you begin to feel very foolish. You disarm your adversaries by acknowledging their position. It is completely unexpected. They automatically feel the need to respond in kind. For example, if your future boss tells you that the most it can pay is $60,000 because paying more would have an impact on others in the organization, indicate that you recognize how that might be a problem. Acknowledging those concerns does not mean accepting a lower salary than you feel is appropriate. It merely sets the stage for you to begin exploring ways to resolve the problem, such as through granting a signing bonus or additional stock.

Few offers are ever withdrawn because of the actual substance of what is being asked for. However, I do know of a number that were withdrawn because of the way a candidate negotiated. One such situation that stands out in my mind involved a high-level executive being recruited by Macy's. I was negotiating the terms of employment with him. Throughout our discussions, it was "I have to have this" and "I absolutely will not agree to that." Everything was an ultimatum. After about a week of this, I sat down with my boss and described how the discussions had proceeded and where we were at the moment. His response was, "You know I really did not like him that much anyway. Why don't you just tell him it's not going to work out?" I certainly made no effort to convince my boss otherwise. The funny thing is that had the candidate approached the negotiations differently, we probably would have agreed to most of what he was asking for.

Remember, nobody wants to work with a jerk. Job candidates who are obnoxious negotiators not only are going to find themselves getting less but they may very well find themselves getting nothing at all.

In the end, you and the person you are negotiating with should have, at the very least, developed a mutual respect for each other if not a genuine friendship. Not only will developing a positive relationship improve the ultimate outcome for you but it will also serve you well in your new position later on. That goes without saying if you are negotiating with your new boss. However, even if you are negotiating with someone else, what that person thinks of you may have a direct impact on your career. Moreover, if you develop a good relationship with that person, you will have created a potential ally for the future. If this strategy accomplishes nothing else, that, in and of itself, would be worthwhile. Being likable will usually yield dividends in the employment package you are able to negotiate as well.

SUMMARY OF NEGOTIATING POINTS

▶ Remember that it's a lot harder to say no to someone you like.

▶ Get to know the employer's negotiator.

▶ Ask questions.

▶ Personalize the negotiations.

▶ Disagree without being disagreeable.

▶ Show respect for the person you are dealing with.

▶ Don't allow disagreements to become personal; focus on the issues.

▶ Build trust.

▶ Develop a relationship.

STRATEGY

10

Being Flexible

CONSIDERING THE POSSIBILITIES

When you can't change the direction of the wind, adjust your sails.

—H. JACKSON BROWN, JR.

Which is better: a signing bonus or a restricted stock grant? Your answer will depend on how you assess a company's growth prospects. It will also depend on your financial situation and personal preferences. Your answer might change, however, if the company increased the amount of stock it was willing to offer.

Employment negotiations typically involve a multitude of issues: salary, bonuses, title, stock options, benefits, and perks. In this context, much of what constitutes the art of negotiating is recognizing opportunities to improve upon what is being proposed by offering to trade one item for a different one. For a variety of reasons, an employer may be more willing to provide compensation in one form rather than another. One employer may favor providing incentives to its employees by granting stock options, whereas a different employer may prefer using performance bonuses.

Start-up companies usually cannot afford to pay large salaries but are often willing to give stock options to employees at various levels. Large publicly traded companies generally pay higher salaries; however, they usually do not provide the large equity stakes that smaller technology companies routinely offer. Wall Street firms typically award large year-end bonuses, frequently more than an employee's base salary. Sales-oriented companies, on the other hand, like to pay their employees on a commission basis. An employer's preference for certain methods of compensating its employees may be the result of time-honored practices, organizational structure, custom in the industry, or the organization's financial needs at a given time. Determining what those preferences are will enable you to craft a compensation package that maximizes what you receive.

After researching a prospective employer, you should have a general understanding of the types of compensation typically provided to employees at various levels. In developing your negotiating strategy, you may choose to start with what I would refer to as a "contrarian approach." That is, you might suggest a form of compensation or a benefit that the employer may find difficult to provide. For example, if an employer does not usually give signing bonuses, you may want to ask for one, particularly when you have a plausible reason for doing so. If you have to relocate, you might base your request on the need for a down payment on a new house. Any such request should be made in a manner that is not threatening and that makes clear that your accepting the job does not depend on it. Usually it is safe simply to inquire if the employer would consider providing the benefit in question.

This strategy also works well if you are currently being compensated in the manner you are requesting or receiving the type of benefit you are seeking. Similarly, if other employers you are speaking with provide the type of compensation or benefit you are seeking, it is appropriate for you to make such a request. Although asking for something that the employer is unlikely to agree to may seem counterproductive, it virtually assures that there will be a discussion about various compensation options. You will then have a chance to explore what is possible.

Your purpose is to listen. If you listen carefully, you will gather important information. You will learn about the employer's compensation philosophy, if one exists. You are also likely to receive signals as to where there may be room to improve the compensation package.

In response to the signing bonus request mentioned above, the employer's negotiator might directly address the problem you raise by suggesting, for example, the possibility of a no-interest home loan. Perhaps you will be told that the organization has an arrangement with a bank to provide employees with home loans at preferential rates. More likely, the negotiator will focus on benefits of the package that is being offered. If the discussion turns to the stock options you are being offered, explore the possibility of getting more. If the emphasis is on your annual bonus, discuss the criteria used to determine the amount of that bonus or a guaranteed bonus in the first year. Ask about the target and maximum bonuses. Find out if bonuses are determined by a set formula or if it is possible to make individual arrangements. If you discover that the only way you can get a substantially larger bonus is by increasing your base salary, focus your efforts on doing that. If the employer is unwilling to pay you more money up front, perhaps they will agree to a salary review after six months and again after a year. Listen carefully and remain flexible.

Another approach is to offer the employer a choice of alternatives. If you have no particular preference, allow the employer to decide among them. This demonstrates your willingness to be flexible and calls for a corresponding gesture on the part of the employer. It serves the added purpose of bringing the negotiator into the decision-making process. For instance, you might suggest getting either a signing bonus or a guarantee of a portion of your first-year bonus. Some organizations will not provide a signing bonus but are open to the idea of a guaranteed bonus, whereas others would rather provide a signing bonus and maintain a uniform bonus program without any guarantees. Letting the employer choose from among acceptable options will enable you to achieve your objectives and at the same time allow the employer to feel that it has gotten something as well.

I began this book by emphasizing the importance of preparation. An essential part of that preparation is determining your priorities. Being able to make trade-offs requires knowing what your goals are. Be careful, however, to remain flexible. Sometimes when you put a substantial amount of time and energy into preparation, you become blind to opportunities that arise during the course of the negotiations. The problem with a plan, particularly a well-thought-out plan, is that you tend to stick with it even when things don't turn out exactly as you anticipated. In employment negotiations, as in other types of negotiations, you need to be open to the opportunities that present themselves.

Young lawyers spend a lot of time preparing. They are hardworking by nature and never want to look as if they don't know what they are doing. So when they prepare for a deposition, they carefully plan what they are going to ask and meticulously write out all the questions. The only problem with that approach is that they cannot always anticipate what answers they will receive. What sometimes happens is that they continue to ask the questions they prepared, failing to follow up on the answers that are given.

Let me give you an actual example of one such deposition:

YOUNG LAWYER: What did you do on Christmas Eve, the date of the 7-Eleven robbery?

WITNESS:	I was home wrapping packages all evening.
YOUNG LAWYER:	All evening?
WITNESS:	All evening.
YOUNG LAWYER:	Did you see anyone else that night?
WITNESS:	Only my mother, who was home with me all night, and my friend Jay, who works at the 7-Eleven.
YOUNG LAWYER:	Your mother would do anything to keep you out of jail, wouldn't she?
WITNESS:	Yes.
YOUNG LAWYER:	Even lie for you?
WITNESS:	I guess.

The young lawyer is so focused on undermining the credibility of the alibi that she fails to hear, let alone follow up on, how the witness came to see his friend who happens to work at the 7-Eleven that evening. So it is, at times, in negotiations. We become so focused on our plan that we miss obvious opportunities.

Before you react to an unanticipated proposal, ask yourself what you might achieve by agreeing to it. Compare the possible financial rewards of the employer's proposal with what you could expect if the employer agreed to what you were considering. Remain flexible. Negotiating is a dynamic process. Opportunities will arise during the course of the negotiations. All you need to do is recognize, and take advantage of, the ones that are presented. As long as you keep your overall objectives firmly in mind, you will be able to seize opportunities as they arise.

Flexibility coupled with a little creativity allowed a friend of mine to take a job that she really wanted even though the initial offer was less than she was willing to accept. Sally was being considered for a position as the director of training at a midsized company. The last person to hold the position had not done a particularly good job and had been encouraged by his boss to leave. The employer was able to manage reasonably well for several months without filling the position. Although the president and the vice president of human resources understood the value of having a strong person in the position, others in top management, including the CEO, did not see why the human resources vice president couldn't handle training in addition to her other duties.

The interviewing process took several months. Sally met several times with most of the key members of the management team, including the president and the vice president of human resources. They obviously liked her.

She was very interested in the job. Finally she got a call to come in and meet with the two of them. She assumed she would be getting an offer and painstakingly prepared for the meeting. Unfortunately, the negotiations did not proceed as she anticipated.

The president told her that she was the top candidate for the position. However, he explained that they had originally not been looking for someone quite as experienced and they had a number of good candidates who were earning substantially less than she was. In light of what the former director of training had been earning, the most they could pay her was $60,000. The president told her that the company was considering instituting a bonus program, but it did not currently have one in place. They talked about the potential to grow in the position and to increase her salary once she proved her value. Although she was earning only $55,000 in her current position, she expected to receive a $10,000 performance bonus in her current position at the end of the year.

Unlike their previous meetings, this one was awkward. Sally expressed her interest in the job but indicated that she was disappointed in the offer. The president told her that under the circumstances there was nothing more he could do with the salary, but if she had any ideas about other ways to make the offer more attractive, he would be glad to entertain them. At that moment she really didn't have any so she decided not to say anything (see Strategy 23). Sally thanked the president and the human resources vice president and said she'd get back to them.

It was clear that Sally really wanted the job. She also believed that there was the possibility of advancement and more money down the road. However, she was not willing to accept less money than she was currently earning. The company's president seemed to be open to improving the offer, but he felt constrained by the way the position was viewed by the rest of the organization. Sally couldn't easily get the employer to increase the salary offer. She needed to be flexible and creative. She had several options. She could ask the employer to provide her with a car allowance and try to justify it in terms of her need to travel to the company's various facilities, although a car allowance would be unusual for someone at her level. She could seek a salary review in six months, after she had the opportunity to demonstrate what she could do. Another possibility might be asking for a signing bonus.

Sally decided to ask for a signing bonus to make up for the bonus she would be losing by leaving her current employer. The bonus would not affect the employer's salary structure. The company's president seemed to be open to improving the offer if he could do so without causing problems with the other managers or with the CEO. In addition, Sally asked to be reviewed after six months, by which time she would have proved her value. As it turned out, the president agreed to the signing bonus and to a six-month performance review. The last I heard, Sally was enjoying her job and doing well.

Most aspects of any employment arrangement are economic. Whether you get paid in the form of a bonus or stock options doesn't matter, provided that you have correctly calculated what each will be worth in the end. The negotiating process involves determining available alternatives. Once you know what your options are, you can determine their value as well as your comfort level with the risks entailed. Once you have done that, you can determine what trade-offs are possible. That is what effective negotiating is all about.

SUMMARY OF NEGOTIATING POINTS

▶ Listen.
▶ Be flexible.
▶ Be creative.
▶ Identify available options.
▶ Evaluate the economic value and the risks involved with each of the various alternatives.
▶ Determine your comfort level with each option.
▶ Be prepared to make trade-offs.

11

Patience, Persistence, and Timing

OUTMANEUVERING OR OUTLASTING YOUR OPPONENT

*Nothing in the world can take the place of persistence. Talent will
not; nothing is more common than unsuccessful men with talent.
Genius will not; unrewarded genius is almost a proverb. Education
will not; the world is full of educated failures. Persistence and determination alone are omnipotent.*

—CALVIN COOLIDGE

Not long ago I represented the senior vice president for sales and marketing at a large professional services organization. He was being recruited for
a similar position at a new media company. Because of the new employer's
compensation system, typical for that industry, the offer provided for a lower
base salary but a higher potential bonus than my client was receiving in his
current position. As a total package, this arrangement was acceptable to my
client. However, because the employer was in a turnaround situation, the
severance package was a very real issue. My client was justifiably concerned
about the proposed terms of his severance arrangement. The severance
package he had been offered consisted of one year's base salary and the continuation of benefits for one year after termination.

My client discussed his concerns with his prospective boss, the company's president. The president was sympathetic, but he deferred to the
employer's attorney on the issue. When I discussed the severance arrangement with the attorney, I proposed that my client's targeted bonus be

included as part of the severance calculation. The attorney was adamant that the employer could not agree to that proposal. She informed me that no other executives in the organization had a severance arrangement that took their bonus into account for the purpose of calculating the amount of severance.

The president was pressing my client to tell his current employer that he was resigning because he wanted to make a public announcement. My client was thinking about acquiescing just to be able to reach an agreement quickly. He wanted to try to accommodate the president, who would be his new boss. However, I persuaded him to call the recruiter who was handling the search and express his reservations about the severance proposal. I then called the employer's attorney again. I suggested that if the company could not include my client's bonus in determining the severance amount, it should at least provide a severance amount equal to his current base salary. After all, I argued, it was only fair to do so because my client was taking a cut in base salary in order to accommodate the company's salary structure. The attorney reacted negatively to the idea, but she agreed to present the proposal to the president. It was a fair solution to the problem.

Even though the lawyer did not like it, my client's situation was unusual enough that it did not set a generally applicable precedent. It certainly would not cause the problems that might have resulted if my client were the only executive to have his bonus included in determining the amount of the severance payment. Ultimately the company's president agreed to the proposal, although I am sure over the strong objections of the company's attorney. Even though the whole negotiating process took only one week, by being patient and persistent, we were able to greatly increase the amount of my client's severance package.

Two of the most important skills a negotiator can possess are the ability to wait and the ability to say no. In employment negotiations, the ability to say no without angering an adversary is invaluable. If you have ever been in an argument with a determined three-year-old, you understand the power of persistence. Children simply wear you down until eventually you give in. The same principle applies in employment negotiations, although you need to say no with a great deal more finesse than your average three-year-old uses.

It is not how quickly you reach an agreement that matters. It is what you end up with that counts. Patience and persistence are often the keys to getting a better deal. Patience is particularly effective during employment negotiations because time normally works to the employee's advantage. By the time you begin discussing the terms of employment, the employer has already made a significant investment in determining whom to hire. With that decision made, the employer will generally be anxious to conclude the negotiations and move on to other things.

When I say that time normally works in the employee's favor, I am talking about a few days or at most a few weeks. Sometimes the negotiations will consist of only one or two discussions; at other times they may involve a series of conversations occurring over a period of weeks. Understanding that we are not talking about extended periods of time, the longer the negotiations last, up to a point, the greater the stake the employer has in ensuring that a successful conclusion is reached (see Strategy 8).

If something is important to you, refuse to concede the issue. Even as you emphasize areas of agreement, continue to be firm on those aspects of the offer that are not acceptable. Be polite. Use phrases like, "I am very concerned about . . ." But if the issue is critical, keep saying no. Explain the reasons for your position. Explore alternative ways of satisfying your needs. Do not give in just to conclude the deal.

Sometimes you can achieve your objectives a little at a time. There is a saying: If you want to get a salami from someone who does not want to give it up, don't ask for the whole thing. Try to get it a slice at a time: one slice now, another later, and ultimately you will have the whole salami. That technique applies in employment negotiations as well.

If you are not making progress, change the subject; come back to the difficult issues later. If you still can't resolve a problem, move on to something else. Return to critical issues as often as necessary. At the same time, listen to the employer's objections. Consider those concerns and keep suggesting different options that will not only satisfy your needs but might also be more acceptable to the employer. If you continue to raise the issue periodically, the employer will recognize that it is important to you. As the negotiations draw to a conclusion, the employer may eventually give in on the issue just to complete the deal (see Strategy 24). If the employer cannot agree to what you want because of organizational concerns or provide you with an acceptable alternative, that will generally become clear and you will then have to decide whether or not to turn down the offer.

Patience will increase your bargaining leverage even more if the employer is working under a deadline. I recall one instance when I was negotiating on behalf of a retail executive. The discussions seemed to go on interminably through no fault of either party. Initially it took days for the employer's attorney to get back to me with responses. At some point the situation changed. The attorney started to return my calls the same day. The employer obviously was putting pressure on him to get the deal done. The negotiations began to move more quickly. Suddenly the employer's attorney conceded on some of the key points that remained open. Recognizing what was going on, I simply gave him the opportunity to concede on the issues of importance to my client without losing face and at the same time suggesting that if he couldn't agree I would consider his position with my client and get back to him next week. We were able to conclude the agreement on terms favorable to my client that afternoon.

In addition to patience and persistence, timing is crucial. When you say something during negotiations can be as important as what you say. Focus on the easy issues first. Ask for something you want after you have made a concession. Don't make all your concessions at once. Consider timing as a key part of your strategy when you are preparing for the negotiations.

Timing the start of compensation discussions, for instance, can have a major impact on how successful you are. It is universally agreed that the best time to begin discussing money is after you have been offered the position. The employer has decided that you are the best candidate for the job. Your future boss wants to hire you and to close the deal quickly. At that point, you are in the best position to begin bargaining.

Linda Seale, former head of human resources at MTV and an executive coach in New York City, relayed a story to me about one of her clients that illustrates the importance of timing. When Sandy was first interviewed for a top executive position, the chief executive officer asked almost immediately, "What are you currently earning?" and "What are you looking for?" Adeptly she responded, "I know salary is important, but to me the challenge and the mandate of the position are more important. I'm happy to discuss compensation, but I would rather focus on your needs and how I might be able to add value to the organization before we discuss money. Can we get back to that at the end of the interview?"

For the next two hours the discussion focused on the job and what needed to be accomplished. Sandy offered insights and ideas on how she might achieve those objectives. She sold her past accomplishments. The chemistry was excellent between the two of them. Near the end of the interview her future boss returned to the issue of compensation. Although the recruiter had indicated that he thought they probably would not pay more than $100,000 for the position, Sandy told him that her total compensation was currently in excess of $100,000 and she was looking for a position in the $125,000 range. After he got to know her and understood what she could do for him, salary was not even an issue. The chief executive officer asked her if she would be able to meet with some of the other key executives the following week. She was offered the job at a salary that more than met her expectations.

Similarly the vice chairman of a Fortune 1000 company used timing to great advantage in negotiating his employment agreement. On the day the company announced that it was filing for bankruptcy, he informed the board of directors that he would be leaving to become vice chairman of a competitor. Because of the critical role he was expected to play for the organization at that moment, he was able to negotiate an agreement that virtually guaranteed that he would become the next chief executive officer of the company. He was also able to negotiate a substantial salary increase. When the chief executive left the company a few months later, the vice chairman was elevated to that position. Even though he probably would have become chief executive officer anyway, his deft use of timing ensured that result.

Patience, persistence, and timing will help you achieve your objectives. You cannot achieve those goals, however, unless you know what you want. By the time you begin to negotiate, have your goals and priorities clearly defined (see the chapter "Beyond Research: Preparing to Negotiate"). Stay focused on your goals. Periodically review the list of priorities you made when you were preparing to negotiate.

Some aspects of a job are negotiable; others are not. What the employer offers with regard to the latter will either be acceptable to you or not, but they are not amenable to negotiation. Determine early on which items are so important to you that the employer's refusal to include them as part of the deal will lead you to decline the offer. Sometimes you will have no choice but to say no (see Strategy 25). However, if you are patient and persistent, yet open to different ways of satisfying your objectives, you will generally be able to reach an agreement that meets everyone's needs.

SUMMARY OF NEGOTIATING POINTS

► Know your objectives as well as your bottom line.
► Consider timing when you are preparing to negotiate.
► Start with the easy issues.
► Be persistent.
► Be prepared to say no if necessary.
► Always say no nicely.
► When you reach an impasse on a key issue, change the subject and return to the issue later.
► Listen and be flexible.
► Be patient.
► Don't agree just to conclude the negotiations quickly.

12

Taking Stock in Your Situation

WHEN AND HOW TO ASK FOR EQUITY

Because that's where the money is.

—WILLIE SUTTON WHEN ASKED
WHY HE ROBBED BANKS

In the movie *The Graduate* a guest at his graduation party says to Dustin Hoffman: "I have one word for you: plastics." What plastics was in the 1960s, paper is today. By "paper" I am referring to stock. Typically a key element in an executive's compensation package today is some form of equity, generally stock options. In 2008, CEOs earned on average $3.3 million in annual salary and bonus. Not a bad payday, but it pales in comparison to their potential for gains through stock options and other forms of equity. During that same time period, CEOs averaged almost three times as much in compensation other than salary; most of that compensation consisted of exercising stock options as well as restricted and performance stocks, resulting in an average total annual compensation of $12.8 million.

The highest-paid chief executive officers in 2008, as in previous years, all received the largest portion of their compensation from exercising stock options or from some other type of equity arrangement. Larry J. Ellison of Oracle drew just a $1 million salary, but he realized $182 million from the exercise of vested stock options. The next four top-paid chief executives also earned most of their pay from exercising stock options: Frederic M. Poses of Trane earned $127 million in total compensation of which $119 million was from stock options; Aubrey K. McClendon of Chesapeake

Energy earned $117 million of which $103 million was from stock options; Angelo R. Mozilo of Countrywide Financial earned $103 million of which $72 million was from stock options; and Howard D. Schultz of Starbucks earned $99 million of which $97 million was from stock options.

These trends have been consistent over time. In both good markets and bad, employees have made money, in many cases a lot of money, with stock options. Over the past five years Larry Ellison, for example, who became a billionaire from equity in Oracle, realized $429 million in compensation mostly as a result of the miracle of stock options. Over the past 40 years executives at all levels, not only CEOs, have been able to use stock options and other forms of equity included in their compensation packages to build substantial wealth in ways they never could have through salary and bonuses alone.

Stock Options

When I talk about stock options to my business school classes, I refer to them as "the best thing that can ever happen to an employee." Bob Corno, a financial adviser at the Mason Companies in Reston, Virginia, once described them to me as "an investment you make with perfect hindsight, offering an infinite return and requiring no investment of money until after the profit is ensured." A stock option grant gives the employee the right to purchase a certain number of shares of the company's stock at a fixed price, usually the market price on the day of the grant. If the price of the stock goes up, the employee gets the value of that appreciation. There is no cost to the employee when the options are granted.

Stock options are no-risk investments. If the price of the underlying stock increases, the employee stands to make a lot of money. If it goes down, the employee does not lose any money if he or she has not yet exercised the options. Moreover, when the price of the underlying stock increases, the employee does not have to pay taxes on the options until he or she has exercised the right to purchase the stock. For certain types of options known as "incentive stock options" (ISOs), no taxes are due until the stock obtained by exercising the options is actually sold. Even then, the employee's profit may be taxable at the lower capital gains rate. It would be hard to design an arrangement that is more favorable for an employee.

Stock Appreciation Rights

Compensation specialists nonetheless continue to come up with new and better ways to use equity to reward key employees. Another type of equity benefit that can be provided to employees involves stock appreciation rights (SARs). SARs provide an employee with the right to receive the increase in value of the employer's stock that occurs between the date the SARs are granted and the date they are exercised. SARs are similar to stock options except that employees don't have to actually pay any money to exercise them. SARs are often granted along with stock options. Sometimes SARs can be exercised only in lieu of the stock options (tandem SARs), giving employees the choice of which to exercise. Employers can also grant SARs that are exercisable together with stock options (nontandem SARs). In this case, employees can use the proceeds from the exercise of nontandem SARs to pay the exercise price for the related stock options and the required withholding taxes as well.

Restricted Stock

Employers may also grant restricted stock to key employees. This type of stock is given to the employee outright if certain conditions are met. For example, employees may be conditionally granted restricted stock which they will earn if they remain with the company for a specified period of time. Awards of restricted stock are often conditioned on meeting certain performance goals. Like stock options, restricted stock is issued at no cost. But unlike stock options, which provide the right to purchase the stock at a fixed price, shares of restricted stock are simply given to the employee once the conditions are met. The employee gets the full value of the restricted stock, not just the appreciation following the date of the grant.

Phantom Stock

Another form of equity that can be used to reward employees is phantom stock. Phantom stock can be converted into an equal number of shares of the company's stock or into their cash value at a specified future date. Phantom stock usually can be converted only after the employee has remained with the company for a certain number of years. An award of phantom stock may also be conditioned on meeting certain performance goals. Phantom stock entitles the employee not only to the value of the stock but also to the dividends paid on the actual shares. Normally the dividends are paid at the same time the phantom stock is converted. As with restricted stock, the executive gets the full value of the shares, and the value of the phantom stock is not taxed until the employee has the right to convert it.

Stock Purchase Requirements

A number of companies now require high-level executives to purchase a certain amount of the company's stock with their own money. The rationale for requiring stock ownership is to better align the executives' interests with those of the stockholders. The theory is that when executives have their own money at risk, they will focus on increasing shareholder value. If your employment agreement includes a requirement of this type, the employer will normally offer you a loan to facilitate the purchase as part of your compensation package. At the very least, you ought to seek an interest-free loan to finance the stock purchase. It is better, however, if you can get a signing bonus to cover the cost of the stock. Some companies use stock as a way to motivate lower-level employees by providing incentives for them to purchase and hold company stock.

Equity Packages

There are other ways for companies to provide equity to their employees. No doubt creative lawyers and accountants will devise new methods in the future. Providing equity to key employees benefits the company because ownership encourages those employees to remain with the company and to find ways to increase the value of the company's stock. For an employee, getting stock from a new employer, in whatever form, is ordinarily one of the quickest routes to financial well-being. Negotiating about stock is not limited to high-level employees. Particularly in technology companies, as well as other types of start-up ventures, stock and stock options are available to lower-level employees.

Over the years, much of my effort on behalf of executives has been spent negotiating over the amount of equity they will receive and under what conditions they will get to keep it. In many instances, executives earning substantial salaries and bonuses have left large companies because they were eager to receive a greater portion of their compensation in the form of stock or options. A major element of negotiating these deals is to determine how much stock, and in what form, an executive should be provided in light of what he or she is giving up.

I recall one agreement I negotiated on behalf of an executive who had been receiving large annual cash bonuses from his employer. His prospective employer, a small high-tech company, was in no position to provide bonuses of that magnitude. What it could provide was a substantial amount of equity. So that was what we sought.

The first thing we did was make sure that my client received his most recent bonus before leaving his current employer (see Strategy 6). Next we attempted to value the stock of his prospective employer. We looked at the company's earnings history and projected an annual growth rate of about 5 percent. On the basis of that projection, we sought a grant of a certain amount of restricted stock that, in accordance with the company's practice, would vest over a four-year period. Additional restricted stock would be granted a year later, when my client was to be promoted. We also sought and received the company's agreement to provide grants of a fixed number of stock options each year during the term of the agreement. The amount of these grants would increase if certain performance targets were reached.

The primary focus of the bargaining was to maximize the amount of equity my client received. Whenever the employer balked at a request, we returned to how much my client was giving up in cash bonuses by leaving his current employer, a strategy that can be used by most employees leaving large companies to join smaller start-ups. We emphasized that any increase in the value of the company's stock would be, at least in part, a result of my client's efforts. If he did not do a good job and the company did not prosper, he would not reap any benefit. Moreover, because he was accepting equity in lieu of cash bonuses, regardless of how well he performed, a major part of his compensation would now be subject to the vagaries of the stock market. In the end, we were able to obtain sufficient stock so that within four years, if our projections were met or exceeded, my client would be significantly better off with the new company's stock than he would have been with the bonuses from his prior employer. An added benefit of structuring a compensation package to include a greater proportion of equity is the tax advantages that stock and stock options provide.

The above example is a typical equity package that an executive might obtain from a company that either does not want to or is not in a position to match the employee's current cash compensation. Under these circumstances, a highly sought after executive will almost always be able to obtain an equity stake in the company. How large an equity position you receive will depend on how much the company wants to recruit you and how well you negotiate. A common tactic is to constantly remind the company of how much you are giving up by accepting the job, in order to persuade the employer to increase the amount of equity in the deal.

Unfortunately, unless you are a high-level executive, there is no guaranteed method to get a prospective employer to give you stock and/or options when you change jobs. For most of us, getting an equity stake in a company depends more on the company we join than on our negotiating prowess. Most large publicly traded companies have stock option plans, but participation tends to be limited to executives above a certain level. Therefore, your eligibility to participate in the program will depend on your position within the organization (see Strategy 4). Most employees have access only to stock purchase plans. These plans allow them to purchase a certain amount of company stock at a discount each year. Although eligibility to participate in a stock purchase plan can be an extremely valuable benefit that you should generally take full advantage of in a company that demonstrates good growth potential, you are unlikely to find yourself lunching with Warren Buffett as a result of your participation in the plan.

When can an employee who is not a senior-level executive expect to negotiate an employment deal that includes stock or stock options? When the employee chooses the right company. Large publicly traded companies don't offer stock options to most of their employees. Family-owned companies are even less likely to offer stock to employees who are not family members. However, many start-up companies, particularly high-tech companies, will offer stock options to employees with critical skills. Typically these companies can't afford to pay top dollar to hire the employees they want. They are often strapped for cash. In order to attract the talent they need, start-up companies regularly offer stock options to new hires. Ask the secretaries or programmers who started with Microsoft 30 years ago whether taking a lower salary in return for stock options was a good decision. Today many of them are millionaires.

If you choose the right company, you may be able to negotiate a compensation package that includes stock or stock options. If so, you can use the negotiating strategies described in this book to increase the amount of stock that you are offered. For employees with needed skills, a small start-up company is likely to be flexible in what it is willing to do to make up for the employees' having to accept a lower salary. Taking that route may turn out to be a good decision for you financially, provided that you can afford to take a cut in salary. The key is to select a company that will grow and be able to go public within a reasonable period of time. If the company you join is successful, those stock options may prove to be very valuable.

Keep in mind, however, that although equity offers the potential for large financial rewards, there is no guarantee of riches. Sometimes companies don't do well and your options expire worthless. As many of us have learned from personal experience, even good companies can end up in bankruptcy. Notwithstanding the fact that you have negotiated brilliantly and have received a substantial equity stake, the value of that stock will depend on how well the company does. Even if the company prospers, its stock price may be affected by gyrations in the stock market totally unrelated to how well the particular business is being run. Timing and luck will also generally play a role in the value of the stock you receive.

When you are considering taking some form of equity instead of salary or bonuses, you need to consider not only what you are able to get the company to agree to but also your current financial needs and your tolerance for risk. Evaluate the potential appreciation of that stock as if you were purchasing it, because when you accept equity as part of your compensation package it is usually in lieu of other compensation, so in a very real sense you are purchasing it.

SUMMARY OF NEGOTIATING POINTS

► Determine how much of your compensation you feel comfortable taking in the form of equity.
► If equity is important to you, look for companies that offer stock to employees at your level.
► Carefully evaluate the financial prospects of the company.
► Determine the types of equity plans available to employees at various levels.
► Negotiate participation in the best plan for which you could be eligible (or negotiate a higher-level position).
► Consider the possibility of trading salary for equity.
► Don't become enamored with the idea of getting stock and give up too much in order to get it. If you are paid enough money, you can always buy the company's stock.
► Remember that when you accept equity as part of your compensation package, it is usually in lieu of some other form of compensation. So evaluate the potential appreciation of that stock as if you were purchasing it, because in a very real sense you are.

STRATEGY

13

Using Another Offer Even When You Don't Have One

Of the things you have, select the best; and then reflect how eagerly
they would have been sought if you did not have them.

—MARCUS AURELIUS

If you have ever been to an auction, you know that the best thing that can happen to a seller is to have two bidders become emotionally involved in the bidding. The bidders soon care more about winning than they do about the prize. Inevitably the winner pays more for the item being auctioned than it is worth. If you can replicate these conditions in the employment context, you are certain to maximize your compensation.

This type of strategy needs to be pursued carefully, especially if you are using it with your current employer. Although organizations value employees whose talents are sought after by others, they also value loyalty. If your employer finds out that you are seeking employment elsewhere, particularly with a competitor, you may promptly be shown the door. Just as often, however, your employer will try to convince you to stay by outbidding the other employer. Ordinarily though, along with the counteroffer, your employer will begin the search for a potential replacement. After all, if you've threatened to leave once for more money, sooner or later you can be expected to do so again.

Using Another Offer with Your Current Employer

What good is getting another offer though, if using it to improve your current compensation will cause your employer to consider you disloyal? If you understand how to use it, you are always in a better position for having received another offer. In the first place, you may decide to accept the offer. Moreover, at the very least, it tells you something about your market value. If your current employer has consistently paid you less than you could command elsewhere, you may want to consider a move even if this is not the one. Finally, used properly an offer can improve your current situation without resulting in your being considered disloyal. In fact, it is possible to both demonstrate your loyalty and get your present employer to give you a raise at the same time.

Consider the following situation. Tom had just been offered a position as the chief operating officer at a consumer products company. At the time he was the chief operating officer at one of the company's competitors. Tom liked the company he was working for and was in line to become its chief executive officer, but the company would not commit to giving him the job when it became available. The offer he received from the competitor was for a lot more money than he was then making. More important, it offered him the opportunity to become the chief executive officer within a few years.

At this point Tom brought me into the negotiations. We were quickly able to reach agreement with the new employer on salary and bonus. After some hard bargaining, we were also able to agree on a very generous package of restricted stock and stock options. Details of his move were worked out, and I thought we would soon have a deal. Then we started discussing protections in the event things didn't work out: severance package, reasons for which he could be discharged, rights in the event of a takeover, and most important to my client, a commitment and timetable for him to become chief executive officer. Despite a great deal of effort, we were unable to get the company to provide sufficient guarantees for Tom to feel comfortable leaving his current position.

As sometimes happens when an employer bargains too long and too hard over the wrong issues, my client soured on the deal. Tom thanked me for my help and told me that even if we were able to work out adequate protections, he was no longer interested. He was prepared to stay in his current job and wait for his shot at being made chief executive officer. If that didn't happen, perhaps a better offer would come along in the interim.

I suggested another option. He could tell his current employer about the offer and use it as leverage to improve his situation there. Taking that advice, Tom told his boss, the current chief executive officer, that he had received an offer to be chief operating officer at one of their competitors, and he spelled out the terms of the deal we had negotiated. He also told his boss, who intended to retire some time during the next few years, that he was not going to accept the offer. Tom informed him that the only reason he had even considered it was that the board of directors had declined to make any commitments about his future with the company. He then asked his boss if he would be willing to try to get the board of directors to do something about that.

Tom did two things that enabled him to make use of a competing offer without jeopardizing his current position. First, he informed his boss that he was not going to accept the offer, thereby avoiding the perception that the company was being presented with an ultimatum. Second, he explained why he was tempted by the offer and enlisted his boss's help in trying to resolve his concerns. By so doing, he reaffirmed his loyalty to the employer and made his boss an ally in helping him get the commitment he sought. He also avoided creating an adversarial situation that would require his current employer to respond to a competing bid for his services. Telling his boss about the offer provided the ammunition that was needed to get the board of directors to take action. Although the directors would not give him any guarantees about being promoted to chief executive officer, they did indicate that he was their number 1 candidate at the moment. They also agreed, as part of an extension of his employment contract, to match the offer he had received. In addition, they agreed that if he was not made chief executive officer within a specified amount of time, he could leave with a generous severance package. Within two years Tom was promoted to chief executive officer.

Not everyone is a potential chief executive officer. Nor can we all expect to regularly get unsolicited offers from prospective employers. However, if you determine that you are being paid less than the current market rate for what you do, you can use that knowledge to remedy the situation. The first step is to find out what others are getting paid in comparable jobs. There are various ways to get that information [see the chapter "Everything You Need to Know about Using the Internet (and Other Sources of Information) to Help You Negotiate"]. In addition, keep your ear to the ground. When you hear about a job that interests you, contact the organization. If you decide the job is not right for you, casually let your boss know that another employer had expressed interest in hiring you for a better-paying job, even though you were not interested.

A word of caution is necessary here. Even if you have a firm offer in hand, don't make your employer feel that you are presenting an ultimatum. If you do, you had better be prepared to accept the offer because there is a good chance that your employer will immediately escort you out. Even if you aren't let go, you are likely never to be completely trusted again. Your employer will always be wondering when you are going to level another ultimatum.

Using Another Offer When Two Potential Employers Are Interested in You

Using another offer with your present employer is one thing. Using a second offer with an employer that is trying to recruit you is a wholly different matter. This is the best negotiating situation you can ever find yourself in. Here there is no issue of loyalty. You are free to create a bidding war if you can. Still, you need to proceed with caution. Someone that is seeking to recruit you may resent it if you appear to be playing one employer against the other. People do not like to feel that they are being manipulated. Go out of your way to avoid making the people you are negotiating with feel that way.

If two employers are trying to hire you, all things being equal, you will likely choose to go with the highest bidder. In real life, unfortunately, all things are rarely ever equal. We almost always prefer one organization or one boss over another. One employer will offer more opportunity for growth or more stability. The key, then, is to use the interest of the other employer to improve the offer from the employer you favor.

How do you accomplish that? I recommend that you refer to Commandment 5, "Never Lie, but Use the Truth to Your Advantage." If you have two offers, first try to get the less desirable employer to improve its offer. Since going there is not your first choice, you will be able to push hard to get its offer improved. In the end, it won't really matter whether you reach an agreement. After all, your objective is to use the discussions to improve your bargaining position with the other potential employer.

Once you have gotten as much as you can from the first employer, you can then go to your prospective boss at your employer of choice and honestly say: "I have this very generous offer from another employer, but the truth is I'd much rather work for you. However, I just can't ignore the gap between what they are offering and what you are offering. If you could just put together a package that is in the same ballpark, I would start tomorrow." Having other good job possibilities will provide the confidence needed to insist on getting what you are worth. It will also give you the courage to walk away if you don't. Moreover, the fact that someone else may enter into the bidding will pressure your employer of choice to complete the negotiations quickly and give you its best offer. This tactic will work even if you are the one that initiated the discussions with the other employer and even if you don't actually have another offer yet. You don't have to inform your prospective boss of the exact nature of the discussions—only that you are having discussions with another employer.

Some experts would suggest that you "accidentally" let the employer find out that you are talking to someone else. You might casually let people there see something from the other organization, such as a business card or an annual report. Alternatively, you could ask a secretary to place a call to the other employer for you while you are there. The problem with this approach is that you can never be sure if the appropriate people have actually found out what you want them to know. I prefer being more direct. Simply tell people that, although you would really like to work for them, you are also talking to a competitor and you don't want them to find that out from someone else. Your candor will not only improve your bargaining position but it will also enhance your credibility as well.

In short, you will get a better deal any time someone with whom you are negotiating knows you have other options. Whenever possible, therefore, you should create those options for yourself or, at least, create the illusion that they exist. Once you have done that, be sure that the appropriate people know about it.

SUMMARY OF NEGOTIATING POINTS

- ▶ Having another offer will almost always improve your bargaining position.
- ▶ Be careful how you use other offers.
- ▶ Talking to a competitor may be considered an act of disloyalty by your current employer.
- ▶ Let your current employer know about a competing offer by announcing that you are not going to accept it.
- ▶ Inform your boss of the reasons you were willing to consider the offer and ask for help in addressing your concerns.

► Don't make an employer feel that you are presenting an ultimatum.

► Create other potential offers for yourself by talking to employers that might be interested in you.

► If you have two offers, before using the offer from your second choice as leverage, try to get them to improve it.

► Even if you don't actually have another offer, it is helpful (at an appropriate time) to let your first-choice employer know that you are talking to someone else.

14

Not Negotiating as a Strategy

It is noble to spare the vanquished.

—STATIUS

The toughest time to negotiate is when you have little or no bargaining power and the other side knows it. Under those circumstances the best thing to do is to use the techniques discussed in this book to give the illusion that your bargaining position is better than it actually is (see Strategy 13). There will be times, however, when you are not in a position to do even that. One of those times is when you are willing to accept the job offer without regard to the financial arrangements because you are reluctant to take any risk that might cause the deal to fall through. Generally it is not a good idea to allow yourself psychologically to be in that position because the employer will recognize it and will use it to your disadvantage.

Unless you are willing to accept some risk, you cannot negotiate effectively. You will usually end up just accepting whatever the employer initially offers. Unfortunately, the first offer is ordinarily not the employer's best offer. Nonetheless, there may be any number of reasons why you may not want to negotiate. You may be out of work (see the chapter "When You're Unemployed: How to Gain Bargaining Leverage Even If You Think You Have None"). You may view this job as a once-in-a-lifetime opportunity or a way to gain critical experience. You may simply not want to take any chances with the offer. In such cases, there is little you can do to improve the offer other than to employ a strategy based on not negotiating—that is a strategy designed to avoid any possibility of jeopardizing the offer. If you are willing to take some risk, however, some of the other strategies discussed in this book will likely produce greater gains.

One occasion when not negotiating as a deliberate strategy may be the best approach is when you are just starting out in your career. As a recent graduate, you generally will not have any unique skills or experience that qualify you for the position you are seeking. Often you have been selected for the position not because of what you can actually do for the employer but rather on the basis of your potential. If you are hired, the employer will have to spend time and money training you. Moreover, ordinarily when you apply for a job right out of school, you are one of many candidates, all of whom could be trained to do the job. Unless you graduated from an especially prestigious university, have an outstanding academic record, possess some unique talent, or are lucky enough to graduate at a time when labor is in short supply, you will have little bargaining power. Under these circumstances there is not that much you can do to improve your negotiating position. That is when the only viable strategy is not negotiating.

A friend once asked me if I would talk to his son Sean about a job offer he was considering. Sean was a recent college graduate who had majored in business administration. He had sought out a position with a real estate developer in Los Angeles because of the company's excellent reputation. Sean considered it to be an excellent opportunity to learn the business, and he convinced the company to offer him a job even though he had no experience. His only concern was the salary. Since his parents lived in New Jersey, he could not do what many recent graduates do and get by on a relatively low salary by living at home. He was worried about being able to live in Los Angeles on the salary being offered. Although Sean had other job possibilities, none offered him the chance to gain the type of experience he was looking for. The Los Angeles position would be a chance for him to do something that he really wanted to do. It was very clear that, for Sean, salary was not the most important issue.

In light of all these factors, not negotiating was the most appropriate approach for Sean to use. In fact, under the circumstances it may have been the only plausible strategy that he could employ to improve the offer. So we discussed how he could negotiate a better deal by not negotiating.

He called the person who offered him the job and for whom he would be working. The conversation went something like this:

SEAN: I'm really excited about the position and I am going to accept it. I'm looking forward to working with you at Big California Realty Developer. Although I have other job offers that pay more, this is where I want to work. Would it be possible, however, to consider increasing the starting salary? I think it is low, and I know I will have a tough time living on that salary in Los Angeles. I want you to understand that if you can't do anything about the salary, I still want the job. However, I would appreciate anything you could do for me.

FUTURE BOSS: I'll see what I can do.

In the end Sean was given a relocation bonus to help him make the move and get settled in Los Angeles, with the promise of a raise in six months if he did a good job.

Sean was able to improve the offer by not negotiating. After all, he really wasn't in much of a position to negotiate. He had no experience; there were probably hundreds of other students who would have jumped at the opportunity to take the job. He might have told his prospective boss that he had other job offers at higher salaries and was considering accepting one of them if the employer wasn't able to improve its offer. His prospective boss would probably have responded by telling him to go ahead. Instead, Sean accepted the job unconditionally and asked for help so that he could afford to move to Los Angeles.

I cannot emphasize enough the importance of recognizing the role that fairness plays in employment negotiations. Fairness is paramount. It is the guiding principle that determines what an employer will and won't do. If you can convince an employer that what you are seeking is fair, you have a good chance of getting it. In order to do that, you need to have facts to support your request. If an offer is below the market rate for the position, be able to demonstrate that the salary being offered is too low. If you are relying on your personal situation to support a particular request, describe your needs in a way that will evoke sympathetic understanding.

Always bear in mind that employers want to make the people they are trying to recruit feel good about accepting their offer. At this stage, the organization is still in the courtship phase of its relationship with you. It will be very open to any reasonable request. A strategy of not negotiating recognizes, and takes advantage of, these basic principles. It also takes a realistic view of the relative bargaining positions of the parties. This approach employs the classic negotiating technique of taking a weakness and turning it into a strength.

As a child, you were instilled with a sense of fair play. When you win a game, you are suppose to be gracious. When the game is, for all intents and purposes, over, you don't run up the score. You are expected to help those who are weaker and who need your assistance. Seek the "help" of the employer's negotiator. Appeal to his or her sense of fairness.

This tactic works more often than you might imagine. Moreover, it is a very low-risk strategy. After all, you have nothing to lose. You should, however, employ this strategy only when you are willing to accept an offer even if the employer refuses to change it. In fact, the strategy begins by your accepting the offer that has been made. Then, and only then, do you try to convince your future employer that fairness calls for a modification of that offer. If you utilize this strategy effectively, the employer will resolve your concerns even though it knows that it doesn't have to.

SUMMARY OF NEGOTIATING POINTS

- ▶ Understand when not to negotiate.
- ▶ Accept the offer.
- ▶ Ask for help.
- ▶ Be able to support your request with facts.
- ▶ Appeal to fairness.
- ▶ Play on the employer's sympathy.

15

Creating Red Herring Issues

Appearances often are deceiving.

—AESOP

When herring are smoked and salted, they turn a brownish-red color. The British refer to these smoked fish as "red herring." In addition to being a delicacy, these fish have a distinct smell. In eighteenth-century England, opponents of fox hunting were able to put these fish to good use in furthering their cause. Animal rights activists of their day did whatever they could to prevent the hunts from proceeding. One of the ways they disrupted the hunts was to drag a red herring across the hunting trail. The smell of the herring would confuse the hunting dogs and prevent them from picking up the scent of the fox. This practice gave rise to using the phrase "red herring" to refer to a distraction from the real issues. In basketball, we refer to this as a "fake," as in "fake left, go right." In negotiating, a red herring issue is one that you don't really care about but introduce in order to be able to withdraw it later in return for some concession.

Creating red herring issues is a common practice used in negotiating collective bargaining agreements. Union negotiations, which typically involve a large negotiating committee, require a visible display of the process of give-and-take. Lots of requests are made by the union negotiators. Everyone knows that there is no real possibility that many of these issues will actually be agreed to. Similarly employers will ask for things that they know the union will not say yes to. Discussing a multitude of issues, many of which will be withdrawn in return for agreement on those issues each side considers most important to it, allows both sides, when the negotiations are over, to feel that they obtained the best possible deal.

The red herring tactic is less commonly used when negotiating employment agreements, and when it is, no one admits to it. In fact, some consider using red herrings to be unethical. Nonetheless, the need for some give-and-take is just as important in employment negotiations as it is in other types of negotiations.

If you insist on getting everything that you ask for before accepting an employment offer, you are likely to remain in your current job, or unemployed, for a very long time. Even if you do reach an agreement on that basis, it will probably be at the expense of the employer's goodwill; your future employer will likely feel that you have driven too hard a bargain. Maintaining some bargaining issues that you are willing to compromise on will make it much easier to reach an agreement and have everyone walk away feeling good about it. Creating red herring issues will allow you to make some compromises but hopefully prevent you from having to give in on those concerns that are most important to you.

The process sounds easier than it actually is. In the collective bargaining process, everyone recognizes from the start that some of the issues raised are red herrings. That is not the case when you are negotiating the terms of your employment. Your prospective employer would balk at the idea that you were raising issues that you really do not care about in order to gain bargaining leverage. Therefore, in this context, red herring issues should be reasonable requests for things that you would like but that you really don't expect your prospective employer to agree to. These issues will afford you room to negotiate. It would be nice if you could get the employer to agree to some of these points, but their principal value is that they can be traded away for other items that are of importance to you.

Let's assume, for example, that you have received an offer to be director of marketing for a new restaurant venture, Planet Poughkeepsie. You like the company. You like the way the job is set up. The salary and benefits look good, but you haven't been offered any stock options. You believe that the company will soon go public and that stock options would be very valuable. What should you do?

You could simply ask for the options. The employer might give them to you. On the other hand, the restaurant might say that it has already offered you a generous salary and will consider giving you options only after you prove yourself. Alternatively, you could not only ask for the options but also note that in your current job you have a company car, another feature lacking in the restaurant's offer. Alternatively, you could ask if the position could be restructured at the vice president level. It would be great if you could get a car and a better title, but what you really want are the stock options. You know, because of the impact these changes would have on the organization (other executives at your level are not given cars or the title of vice president), that the easiest of the three requests for the employer to grant is the stock options. By asking about the car and the title, you have created red herring issues that you will be willing to forgo if the employer grants you the stock options you really want.

You can also raise red herring issues by refusing to readily agree to something that you recognize the employer wants. Let's assume that you are being recruited by Mega Corp and know that every executive there has to sign a noncompete agreement, the basic form of which never varies. Although you would like fewer restrictions on where you can work after you leave Mega Corp, this issue is of much less concern to you than the criteria that will be used to determine your bonus. How can you use your knowledge that every new employee signs the same noncompete agreement to your advantage? Consider the following approach:

YOU:	I was speaking to my lawyer about that noncompete agreement you told me I would have to sign.
NEGOTIATOR:	And?
YOU:	He has some concerns.
NEGOTIATOR:	Really it's no big deal. Everyone signs it.
YOU:	If it's no big deal, why don't we just make the changes he is suggesting and move on.
NEGOTIATOR:	I can't do that.
YOU:	Well, I don't know anything about agreements not to compete. But if my lawyer is telling me I should be concerned, I guess I need to be concerned. I'll talk to him. If we can resolve my problems with the bonus criteria, I'm sure that we will be able to work out something on the noncompete as well.

Your concerns are real since your lawyer will no doubt have misgivings about any noncompete agreement you are being asked to sign. However, what you have done is create a red herring issue involving the employer's demand that you sign its standard noncompete agreement. You have made one issue conditional upon the other. Your willingness to accept the noncompete agreement will depend on the employer offering you more favorable bonus criteria. If the employer's negotiator has any leeway at all, the bonus criteria will be modified to incorporate any reasonable suggestions you make. Moreover, you have the added benefit of blaming your concerns with the noncompete agreement on your lawyer. Whenever possible, that is a good thing to do (see Strategy 16).

As previously discussed, the key to successfully negotiating terms of employment is convincing your prospective employer that what you are seeking is fair. Anything you ask for should be reasonable and defensible. Similarly, if you are not willing to agree to something, be certain that you can articulate a rationale for your position. Otherwise your credibility will be damaged. By the same token, you cannot expect to get everything you ask for. As a result, the discriminating use of red herring issues can be a very effective strategy.

Summary of Negotiating Points

- ▶ Negotiating calls for give-and-take.
- ▶ Don't expect to get everything you ask for.
- ▶ Red herring issues should be reasonable requests for improvements in the offer that you would like, but don't necessarily expect, the employer to agree to.
- ▶ Raise red herring issues so that you have something to trade at key points during the negotiations.
- ▶ In order to increase your bargaining leverage, you can create red herring issues by refusing to agree to something the employer wants.
- ▶ Be very careful how you use red herrings, if you choose to use them at all.

16

Blaming the Lawyers, Accountants, and Others

It's not whether you win or lose but how you place the blame.

—ANONYMOUS

Before we discuss how to blame the lawyers, let me offer some advice on how to use your lawyer. Lawyers, accountants, and other advisors can serve an important, and helpful, function during the negotiating process beyond just being useful targets at which to direct blame. If they are experienced and knowledgeable, they can be a valuable source of information and advice. They can anticipate problems and help you avoid them. They can assist you in developing negotiating strategies. They can even help you decide what is really important to you. They are not however, nor should they be, the ones making critical decisions. When advisors take on that role, the negotiations often turn into a contest between them, and you invariably are the loser. Their primary focus will be on winning. Your goal, however, is not to win but rather to get what is most important to you and to start off your career with your new employer on a positive note.

Executives who are otherwise decisive suddenly become insecure when they are negotiating about their own future. I have seen executives who regularly negotiate deals worth millions of dollars defer completely to the advice of their lawyers when it comes to negotiating their own compensation. Only you know what is important to you. When the negotiations are over, your lawyer will go back to working with other clients. You, on the other hand, will have to work alongside the people with whom you just finished negotiating.

Choose knowledgeable lawyers, accountants, and advisors. Listen to their advice, but make up your own mind. Lawyers, accountants, and other advisors are trained to identify risks and to try to protect against them. You have to decide how much risk you are comfortable taking. Although advisors can help you develop strategies to achieve your goals, ultimately you have to determine what those goals are. An accountant can value stock options, but only you can decide if you are willing to accept a lower salary in return for stock options.

Generally I advise against having your lawyer, accountant, or advisor directly involved in the negotiations, at least initially. You can generally achieve better results by directly negotiating as much of the deal as you can yourself, seeking advice along the way as necessary. You will generally be best served by keeping your advisors in a behind-the-scenes role.

Unless I am representing very high-level executives, who customarily have lawyers negotiate their employment contracts, I almost never negotiate directly on behalf of a client until after the employer's attorney becomes involved. Normally the person you negotiate with is your future boss or the human resources executive responsible for filling the position; that individual has a personal stake in seeing that you accept the offer. As a result, he or she will almost always be more generous than the employer's lawyer, who normally has an agenda of his or her own. Having someone else, particularly a lawyer, negotiate on your behalf is also likely to result in the employer bringing its lawyer into the process. That will generally not help you gain a more favorable agreement. Attorneys will almost always slow down the negotiations and will frequently make them more difficult.

Inevitably the agenda of the employer's attorney has little to do with satisfying your needs. It usually has more to do with impressing the client and limiting risk. Moreover, lawyers will generally be very concerned with setting precedents that might cause problems in the future. The lawyer for the employer will seek to give away as little as possible while still getting you to accept the position. That is how a lawyer determines success. Your future boss, on the other hand, is more likely to judge the success of the negotiations by whether the agreement is fair and whether you feel good about it.

Unless you are talking about technical legal issues that only lawyers understand, you are almost always better off dealing directly with someone involved in the hiring process, preferably your future boss. Even when the lawyers are negotiating between themselves, if there are major points of contention, it is often better for you to go back to the individual doing the hiring and resolve the issues directly with him or her. Unless the employer's attorney is already playing an active role in the negotiations, it is usually best not to bring your lawyer into the picture until it serves some tactical purpose. The same advice applies to using an accountant or anyone else acting on your behalf.

Gaining Credibility and Expertise

When does it make sense to use someone else to negotiate for you? There are a number of situations in which you might want to do so. First, you may simply not be a good negotiator. This is unusual for executives since negotiating is ordinarily an important part of their job. However, sometimes people are successful because of their technical expertise or their ability to inspire and motivate others or for some other reason that has nothing to do with being a good negotiator. In that case, it might be appropriate to have someone else handle the negotiations. But even then you may get better results dealing directly with the employer while seeking advice as needed.

Another instance in which you should consider bringing in your lawyer is when the employer's attorney is already actively involved and you need to "even up the sides." Doing so will prevent the employer's attorney from taking advantage of you by getting you to agree to something, the implications of which you don't fully understand. It will also prevent the employer from trying to use its lawyer's "expertise" to intimidate you. When the company's lawyer says to you "That is the way we always do it," you want to have your own lawyer who can respond that he or she always does it some other way.

Bringing in your own attorney will enable you to avoid appearing intransigent by refusing to agree to something that the employer's attorney claims is not only reasonable but customary. Moreover, most people feel more secure having their own lawyer present when they are negotiating with another lawyer. Finally, if the negotiations become difficult, having your lawyer along provides you with a means of taking the employer's attorney out of the picture. When the time is right, you can simply suggest that the parties sit down "without the lawyers" and try to work something out.

You may also want to use your lawyer or another advisor as an "expert," to lend credibility to your positions. If the facts support your point of view, having an expert present them can add weight to your position. If, for example, the salary being offered is below what other organizations are paying for similar positions, you might have your lawyer or accountant present the comparison information. If the negotiations are not at a level where it would make sense to bring your lawyer or accountant to the table, you can simply invoke his or her expertise when you present the information (that is, you could say, "According to my financial advisor . . .").

Injecting Someone Else into the Negotiations

Most often, however, you will bring someone else into the negotiations because you need to raise an issue that might upset your future employer. Using a lawyer enables you to take positions you would not otherwise be able to take. In addition, your attorney will only have limited authority and can make use of that fact. This allows your lawyer to seek concessions without being able to make them.

One way to take advantage of these dynamics is to have your lawyer deal with the employer's lawyer on technical or drafting issues while you continue to discuss substantive issues with the employer directly. For example, I was representing the senior vice president of human resources at a publishing company who was being recruited for a similar position by another publisher. As is frequently the case these days, the amount of severance pay he would receive was an issue. The employer had offered him a severance of six months' salary continuation minus any salary earned from other employment during that period. We were seeking one year's severance pay without regard to any income earned elsewhere. Therefore, not only was the amount of severance pay at issue but also whether it would be reduced by the income earned from other employment during the severance period.

The prospective employer was seen as a possible takeover target. Since my client had two children in college, he was especially concerned about job security over the next two years. He wanted a severance package that was sufficient in light of his situation, for him to be able to make monthly tuition payments for his children. He discussed those concerns with his future boss. At the same time, I began talks with the employer's attorney about a number of other issues. When we got around to the severance issue, I sought one year's salary to be paid in a lump sum at the time of termination. The employer's attorney was not willing to offer more than six months' severance and insisted that it be paid as salary continuation. She was also adamant that the employer could not agree to our proposal because every other executive participated in a severance plan that provided for a maximum of six months' severance to be paid as salary continuation.

After talking to my client, I suggested that he again discuss his concerns with his future boss, the company's president. He told the president that I had suggested that the company give him a signing bonus if the severance package could not be improved. I made the same proposal to the company's attorney. After all, I argued, it was only fair since my client was giving up a relatively secure job to join a company that could be taken over in the near future. By giving my client a bonus rather than changing the structure of its severance plan, the company could avoid stirring up problems with its other executives. However, in the event my client lost his job because of a takeover, he would have the bonus money available to pay his children's tuition. Ultimately, the company agreed to this arrangement, probably against the advice of its attorney.

The company's lawyer could not intimidate me by seeking to invoke her expertise to support her claim that the company could not agree to enhance the severance package because of the precedent it would set. I was able to make a strong argument based on fairness. I was also able to propose an alternative solution, which the employer could not reject on the grounds of setting a precedent. I could do the things that my client needed done but could not do for himself. He could not argue this point as forcefully as I could. It would have been much harder for him to suggest a signing bonus than it was for me. Most important, even though I don't know if he would have walked away from the deal over this issue, he was never put in a position where he might have had to make that decision. Because it was my proposal, if the company's president had reacted badly to it, my client could still have accepted the offer without losing credibility with his future boss.

Tackling the Difficult Issues

Lawyers, accountants, and other intermediaries can do things you cannot do. They can take more aggressive positions than you might feel comfortable taking yourself. They can argue much more forcefully than you could, particularly when they are dealing with the employer's attorneys. They can float "trial balloons" to see what kind of reaction they get, making clear that the proposals are their ideas, not yours. If the employer reacts negatively to the positions being taken by a professional on your behalf, you are free to disavow them. If someone gets angry over the way your lawyer is negotiating, you can apologize for his or her behavior and resolve the issue yourself. In the worst case, if the deal is about to fall apart, you can always blame it all on your lawyer and smooth matters over directly with your future boss. This is what spies refer to as maintaining "plausible deniability."

You may also be able to ask for things on behalf of your spouse or your children, even though those things "cost" the employer money. When you are changing jobs, other people's needs have to be considered. Your spouse or significant other and your children all will have something to say about your accepting a new position.

Typically family issues come to the forefront when a move is involved. Concerns about housing, schools, and the careers of trailing spouses are common. In recent years we have seen a substantial increase in the number of requests for help in finding jobs for spouses, help with getting children into the right schools, and assistance in finding care facilities for elderly parents. Any experienced recruiter knows that the wishes of family members will often determine whether or not someone accepts a job offer. Most employers will be sympathetic to your need to make your family happy or to address the concerns of a working spouse. As a result, employers are generally receptive to reasonable requests necessary to accommodate the needs of your family members.

Sometimes these issues, particularly second-career issues, can be dealt with through resources readily available to the employer. A few calls from a well-connected executive to contacts at other employers in town can often open doors for job interviews. Relationships with executive recruiters can also be called upon. Potential job openings within the organization itself can also be considered. Other issues can be solved only by giving you more money. To get a spouse to leave a house that he or she has just completely redecorated may require you to purchase an even bigger home in your new community and to have the funds available to redecorate it. In order to do that, you may need to ask for a signing bonus. When you give a readily understandable reason for seeking the bonus instead of simply asking for one, your request is more likely to be sympathetically received.

Since you will ultimately have to work with the people you are bargaining with, a lawyer, accountant, or other intermediary can be especially valuable when you have to deal with difficult issues. An intermediary can do those things that are sometimes strategically necessary but which you could do only at the cost of damaging your future career. Rather than not doing them, you can have them done by a surrogate. After all, no one is likely to hold an intermediary's actions against you, particularly if the intermediary is your lawyer. Similarly, when a request is based on the need to get your spouse or significant other to agree to a move, it is likely to be viewed sympathetically. Even if it is not granted, at least you are not likely to be seen less favorably for having made the request.

SUMMARY OF NEGOTIATING POINTS

▶ Treat lawyers, accountants, and others as advisors; don't let them make your decisions for you.

▶ Negotiate as much of the package as possible yourself before getting lawyers or other advisors directly involved.

▶ Call upon lawyers and accountants to lend credibility to your positions or to neutralize an expert put forward by the employer.

▶ Use others to press positions you would not want to have to argue yourself.

▶ Use others to take difficult positions so you can disavow them if the employer reacts negatively.

▶ Place the responsibility on others (particularly family members) when you are asking for something that benefits them.

17

Add-Ons

JUST ONE LAST THING

Many things which cannot be overcome when they are together, yield themselves up when taken little by little.

—PLUTARCH

I had just finished negotiating a labor agreement with a union in Pennsylvania. I was representing a company that needed to get certain concessions from its union in order to survive. Most of its competitors were nonunion companies that paid their employees lower salaries and provided fewer benefits. The negotiations were long and contentious. We argued about the cost of benefits. We fought over scheduling issues. We discussed the number of sick days employees received. And we disagreed about pay. Medical benefits, however, were the major stumbling block.

After almost six months of negotiating with very little progress, we called in a federal mediator. At about the point when I thought we would never reach an agreement, I met privately with the president of the union and the mediator. With a little creativity we were finally able to come up with a way to resolve the benefits issue. The other issues began to fall into place. As the day went on, we drew close to reaching an agreement. Only two issues remained.

The union wanted us to schedule employees strictly on the basis of seniority, and it also wanted more shop stewards. We could not agree to contractually restrict the employer's scheduling flexibility. So we offered to compromise on the number of stewards and agreed to instruct our managers to "consider" seniority when determining schedules. The union representatives considered our proposal for about half an hour. When they returned, their chief negotiator informed us that the union would agree to the deal if the company gave each employee two T-shirts. The employer was already providing its employees with workshirts, but the union wanted T-shirts for the summer months. In six months of negotiating the union had never once mentioned T-shirts. Now, at the last minute, it was asking for them in order to close the deal. The company's director of human resources did not want to give the employees T-shirts. Frankly, I didn't want to give them the T-shirts either.

We had already obtained most of what we needed. The company would be able to remain competitive. Under the circumstances, the union had received a fair deal. The request for T-shirts, at most, would cost the company a few hundred dollars. We knew we could probably get the same deal without the T-shirts, although it might take another negotiating session. In light of how close we were to a final agreement and everything we had accomplished, was it worth risking it all over a few hundred dollars' worth of T-shirts? Clearly it wasn't worth jeopardizing a deal that had taken over six arduous months to complete. The union knew it and so did we. In the end we gave the union the T-shirts.

There are several lessons to be learned from this story. First, you can usually get the other side to sweeten the deal a little bit as you near the end of the negotiations. If you are not careful, however, that little sweetener can leave a bitter taste in the mouth of your future employer. Thus, although this strategy almost always works, it should be used sparingly. In most cases, it is better not to use it at all. Since this tactic comes into play only as the negotiations are about to be concluded, it should only be employed for something that can be reasonably justified so late in the process. Moreover, this strategy will usually be successful only if the request is neither particularly costly nor problematic for the employer.

If you request something you have never previously discussed, your future employer may feel it is being taken advantage of, even if it ultimately acquiesces to your demands. Unless a recent development has forced you to raise a new issue at the last minute (perhaps the issue has just arisen or you honestly forgot about it), it is not a good idea to bring up as an "add-on" something that has never even been mentioned before. Rather, add-ons are better used as a way of seeking to improve upon something you have already been discussing but have yet to finally agree upon.

Let's assume that a prospective employer has offered you its standard relocation package. That relocation policy provides for one trip for you and your spouse to look for a house. Your spouse thinks you will need at least two house-hunting trips. You want the employer to pay for a second trip. In response to an offer from the employer that resolves most of the outstanding issues, you might say: "I think I could live with that, but I've discussed the move at home and my spouse thinks that we will need at least two house-hunting trips since we don't know the area at all. Would that be okay?" Presented that way, the employer will usually agree to the add-on (see Strategy 16).

A variation of the add-on technique is to seek a minor change in a non-monetary issue that has not yet been finally resolved. For instance, your prospective employer wants you to sign an "agreement not to compete" in the event you leave. You accept the fact that the employer will be giving you access to confidential information that it legitimately would not want to fall into the hands of a competitor. By the same token, you want to be able to find another job using your skills if you leave. As a practical matter, your skills are marketable only to a limited number of organizations. Your new employer is going to want the agreement not to compete to be written very broadly so that it covers every possible competitor. You, of course, are going to want to narrow the restrictions. If you are not able to resolve this issue to your satisfaction during the negotiations, as you near a conclusion, you could condition your acceptance of the offer on the employer agreeing to a more focused definition of whom it considers to be "a competitor." That definition, for example, could be limited to the employer's primary competitors, excluding those that don't compete in its principal areas of business. Or it could be reduced to a short list of the competing companies that your employer is most concerned with.

As you get close to an overall agreement, you will need to resolve any remaining issues. When you get what appears to be the employer's final offer covering all the outstanding issues, you can usually persuade the employer to agree to one or two additional items provided that they are not major.

An add-on strategy works because once people have invested a substantial amount of time and energy in something, they have a psychological need to bring it to a successful conclusion. The longer the parties have been negotiating, the more effective this strategy will be (see Strategy 8). The greater the psychological investment, the more likely people are to agree to a final concession in order to close the deal. Unless you appear to be taking undue advantage, if the concession you are seeking is relatively small, the negotiator almost instinctively will say yes to it. That way the agreement can be concluded without wasting any more time. Even if it is clear that you are trying to take advantage, you may still get what you want. However, in that case the agreement may be achieved at the cost of damaging your future relationship with the negotiator and with your new employer.

As I have stressed throughout this book, honesty is critical to successful negotiations. Unlike most other negotiating techniques, an add-on strategy rarely works well if it is planned ahead of time. If at the beginning of negotiations you tell yourself that you are going to use an add-on technique to try to upgrade the standard company car, the employer will recognize what you are doing. Even if you get what you are seeking, the ploy may work to your disadvantage in the long run. Add-ons generally cannot be scripted in advance. Rather, opportunities to request add-ons need to be recognized. If you understand the technique, as the negotiations draw to a close, you will be able to ask for add-ons in a way that does not appear to be manipulative.

Another word of caution: Don't try to reopen an issue as an add-on that the negotiator considers settled. If you've already agreed on a relocation package, don't at the last minute seek to get one more house-hunting trip. It will reflect badly on your integrity. It could even result in the employer having second thoughts about the offer. If during the negotiations you are not certain that you want to accept a particular term exactly as it is being proposed, be sure that you keep the issue open for further discussion. A statement such as "I need to think about that" (you anticipate significant changes) or "That generally seems okay but I need to review it further" (you anticipate requesting minor changes) will serve that purpose. Keeping an issue open in this manner enables you to move the negotiations forward but at the same time allows you to come back to it later without causing the other side to feel that you cannot be trusted.

What types of issues merit use of the add-on technique? Only those that will not make your future employer think you are being greedy. Considering whether your request can be justified as job related is a good test. For instance, any item that will help you do your job better and can be supported on that basis is a good candidate for an add-on. Getting a new computer, bringing along your current secretary, or being given a certain size expense account (if your job requires entertaining clients) could all be justified as last-minute add-ons. Issues needed to satisfy a spouse, such as those related to moving or to finding your spouse a job, are also good candidates to be treated as add-ons. After all, an employer will not blame you for issues that your spouse raises at the last minute, particularly if you have previously indicated that your spouse has some reservations concerning, for instance, relocation. Trying to upgrade the company car that is offered to you at the last minute, on the other hand, would generally not be appropriate. Other issues that might be suitable subjects to request as add-ons will become apparent during the negotiating process.

Asking for add-ons is much riskier in employment negotiations than it is, for example, when you are purchasing a car. After all, you don't care what the car dealer thinks of you when you insist that floor mats be thrown into the deal, just as long as you get the floor mats. Not so when you are being hired for a new job. Although the add-on strategy is as effective in employment negotiations as in other types of negotiations, it needs to be used more selectively. Whenever you are tempted to use the strategy, think carefully about how your employer will perceive your request. Is it reasonable? Can you justify it, or will the request be viewed as nothing more than an attempt to squeeze a little bit more out of the employer? If the employer would view such a request as taking advantage, don't ask. You can ill afford to have your new employer view you in that light.

SUMMARY OF NEGOTIATING POINTS

▶ You can usually get a prospective employer to improve its offer as the negotiations draw to a close.

▶ Don't ask for too much.

▶ Don't ask for something you have not previously discussed unless you have a good reason for bringing it up at the last minute.

▶ Be reasonable.

▶ Do not make the negotiator feel manipulated.

▶ Take advantage of the fact that the negotiator will ordinarily want to conclude the deal promptly.

▶ Be careful what add-ons you seek and how you ask for them.

▶ If you have any doubts, don't ask for an add-on.

▶ Keep in mind that how you negotiate can affect your career.

18

Looking for Exceptions

Any fool can keep a rule. God gave him a brain to know
when to break the rule.

—GENERAL WINFIELD SCOTT

A manufacturing executive hired me to represent him in negotiations with an employer that was recruiting him to be its chief financial officer. After finding out what was important to him, I checked the company's proxy statement. A proxy statement is a report sent annually by every public company to its shareholders before they elect the board of directors. The proxy statement must contain certain information, including a compensation summary for the company's five highest-paid executives, and it must be filed annually with the Securities and Exchange Commission. This particular proxy statement included the following footnote in the compensation summary:

> Includes a payment of $45,000 to Mr. Jones to compensate for benefits forgone in connection with his resigning from his prior employer and a payment of $9,480 to provide 401(k) plan equivalent benefits for the period prior to Mr. Jones's plan eligibility.

With this information, how difficult do you think it was to get the employer to compensate my client for the bonus he was losing by changing jobs and to give him 401(k) equivalent benefits until he became eligible to participate in the employer's plan? That is an example of looking for exceptions.

Fairness and competitiveness in the job market are the guiding principles that most employers use in determining whether to provide a certain type of compensation or grant a benefit that is not ordinarily afforded to an employee. Understanding how to use fairness is an essential tool in your negotiating arsenal (see the chapter "Principles for Negotiating: The 11 Commandments of Employment Negotiations"). For example, when I suggested that my client be compensated for the money he would lose during the required waiting period before he became eligible to participate in the company's 401(k) plan, the employer readily agreed. I met little resistance because of the way I made the request. I made sure the company was aware that I knew others had been afforded this benefit. I then pointed out the additional benefits, including his annual bonus, that my client was losing because the company wanted him to start as soon as possible. To compensate him for the benefits he had to forgo as a result of leaving his current employer, the company agreed to a signing bonus.

Once you have determined that an exception has been made for someone else, generally you can expect to be afforded similar treatment if you ask. The employer's sense of fairness will ordinarily result in its acquiescence to your request. If that doesn't work, you can tactfully indicate to the prospective employer that you know others have received the requested benefit. A sense of guilt at being caught trying to get away with treating you differently will typically ensure a quick capitulation on the issue.

Be careful how you convey that information. You don't want to be accusatory or to back the person with whom you are dealing into a corner. If you do, that person may feel a need to justify his or her previous denial of your request. The negotiator may then take the position that your circumstances differ from those in which the organization has granted similar benefits in the past.

One way to avoid causing the negotiator to become defensive is by asking a question (see Strategy 3). For instance, you might say, "I have heard that others have been given signing bonuses in the past. Could you check into that? After all, I will be giving up my year-end bonus if I take the job now."

The opposite is also true. If an employer has never compensated new hires for the loss of 401(k) benefits during the waiting period before they become eligible to participate in the plan, it will be exceedingly difficult to convince the company to do so for you. The company will not want to set a precedent that might require that those benefits be granted to future new hires.

When you ask for anything that is not a standard company benefit, you may be confronted with "We can't do that; it would be contrary to company policy." That type of response would be typical of someone not very high up in the organization's hierarchy. An employee at that level may not even be aware that an exception could be made. Alternatively, the employee may not feel comfortable seeking the authority to do so. Higher-level employees may invoke "company policy" simply because it is convenient or because they are looking for a reason to deny your request.

If the person you are dealing with doesn't have the authority to make an exception or to change a policy, it is usually best to move directly to someone who does (see Strategy 21). This strategy is particularly effective if the person with the requisite authority is your new boss.

On the other hand, if "company policy" is invoked because the negotiator wants to avoid dealing with the issue or cannot think of any other reason to justify denying your request, you may want to try convincing this person that it would be inequitable to apply the policy in your situation. Policies are ordinarily promulgated for good reasons. When those reasons don't make sense under the particular circumstances, exceptions can be, and frequently are, made. A policy can also be changed if the rationale for it no longer makes sense or if the circumstances you are faced with were not contemplated when the policy was created.

Don't let yourself be intimidated by someone who responds to a legitimate request by pointing to "company policy" as if it were a sacred commandment handed down from on high. Ask if the organization has ever made an exception to that policy. Suggest that the policy obviously was not meant to apply in these circumstances. Argue that it would be unfair to apply the policy. If all else fails, raise the issue with someone at a higher level.

Relocation is one area in which employers are often willing to make exceptions to their standard policies. Typically, relocation policies provide different benefits depending on the employee's level. They may include the costs of the physical move (that is, the costs of the moving company) and the closing costs on the purchase of a new home, up to a specified limit. More often than not, an employer will agree to a request for a lump-sum payment in lieu of reimbursement for actual relocation expenses provided that the payment is less than the maximum allowed under the relocation policy. A lump-sum payment may be preferable if you don't have much to move and are able to handle the relocation yourself. Alternatively, rather than seeking reimbursement under the employer's relocation policy for expenses incurred in connection with the purchase of a new home, you might ask the employer to pay for a rental for a period of time. This approach makes sense for both you and for the employer if you are likely to be transferred in a year or two. Other exceptions to the standard relocation package that employers commonly agree to are interest rate subsidies (if interest rates are high), loans that become forgivable after an employee has been with the employer for a certain period of time, tax and estate planning advice for employees relocating overseas, temporary living allowances, and the purchase of an employee's current home if it cannot be sold within a specified period of time.

Keep in mind that you are not likely to be offered the same relocation package as the employer's chief executive officer. However, depending on your circumstances, you may be able to obtain some of those same benefits. For instance, if interest rates are high and you currently have a mortgage with a low interest rate, it is reasonable to ask for an interest rate subsidy for a period of time or for the employer to pay "points" in order to reduce the amount you will have to pay in monthly mortgage payments. Sometimes employers will pay from one to three points, depending on local custom and practice. The fact that the organization recently provided similar benefits to another employee, even if that employee was at a higher level, can still be used to your advantage. In all probability, the reason they agreed to provide those benefits applies equally to your situation, even if the overall amount is scaled down to reflect the level of your job. If you are dealing with a benefit such as an interest subsidy or points, the lower cost of that benefit will usually already reflect the salary and level of your new position, because the cost to the employer will be based on the price of the home being purchased.

Exceptions are also commonly made in relation to medical benefits. Employers today often require a waiting period before an employee is eligible to participate in the company's medical plan. During this waiting period, most employees exercise their COBRA rights and pay the required premiums to remain in their prior employer's medical plan. You can often get a company to agree to reimburse you for those premium payments.

Where can you find out if certain benefits have been afforded to other employees? As mentioned earlier, the proxy statement of a public corporation will contain a great deal of useful information. This is a public document that can be obtained from the Securities and Exchange Commission and that is now readily available on the Internet as well [see the chapter "Everything You Need to Know about Using the Internet (and Other Sources of Information) to Help You Negotiate"].

The idea is to learn everything you can about any special deals that have been made in the past. Current and former employees may also be knowledgeable about what the employer has previously done in order to recruit new employees. If all else fails, you can always ask your prospective employer directly whether others have been provided the benefit you are seeking.

Once you determine what special treatment has been afforded to others, you will be in a better position to obtain those same benefits by making the case that your situation is similar. Identifying the exceptions that have been made for others in the organization will give you a critical negotiating advantage.

SUMMARY OF NEGOTIATING POINTS

► Try to find out what special arrangements have been made for new hires in the past.

► Seek those same benefits to the extent that they are appropriate to your circumstances.

► Issues related to relocation are particularly susceptible to special arrangements.

► Seek reimbursement for COBRA payments you will have to make to your current employer if your new employer's medical plan has a waiting period.

► Bear in mind that your prospective employer will be guided by fairness and market conditions.

► The level of the position you are being hired for will likely have an impact on what exceptions the employer is willing to make.

► Don't be intimidated by someone who responds to a legitimate request by invoking "company policy."

► Policies can be changed and exceptions can be made.

19

Using Headhunters When You Negotiate

Filling jobs is the objective; accommodating executives is not.

—JOHN LUCHT, SPEAKING
ABOUT EXECUTIVE RECRUITERS

Larry had been working with an executive search firm that was conducting a search for a vice president of operations. He had completed the interview process, and he had emerged as the employer's top candidate. Late one Monday afternoon the recruiter called Larry to inform him of that fact and to set up a meeting with the company. She now began to question Larry about the details of his current compensation, a subject he had managed to deal with in generalities up to this point. Larry continued to avoid directly answering her questions (see Strategy 1). Instead, he asked the recruiter what the employer was thinking about in terms of compensation. She responded that she didn't exactly know but that the company had mentioned a salary in the $75,000 to $100,000 range. Larry told her that he was expecting something in the $100,000 range. (Moments earlier, he had been thinking that an $85,000 salary would be acceptable!) Then he thanked the recruiter for all her help, and he set up an appointment for the next day to meet with his prospective boss.

Larry was able to use the headhunter both to get information and to send a message to a prospective employer about his salary expectations. Those are two ways you can make use of a recruiter during the negotiating process. Keep in mind, however, that the executive recruiter is being paid by the employer. The employer will probably be trying to use the recruiter in the same ways. The company will seek to have the recruiter get information from you about both your current compensation and your salary expectations. The employer will also be using the recruiter to get feedback about its proposals. As a result, generally you will not get any information from the recruiter that the employer does not want you to have.

If you are using the recruiter to channel information to the employer and it is using the recruiter to channel information to you, why not simply talk directly to each other? In the first place, sometimes one party to the negotiations, usually the job candidate, does not understand the role the recruiter is playing in the process, and the other party gains a significant advantage as a result. If, for example, a recruiter is able to get you to provide a detailed breakdown of your current compensation and benefit package, the employer will know exactly what it needs to pay in order to put together an offer that should be attractive to you. Similarly, once you tell the recruiter what you are looking for, you can be certain that a prospective employer will not offer you more than that, regardless of what they might have offered in the absence of that information.

Even if each side understands the role recruiters play in the process, the recruiters can still serve a useful purpose. A recruiter can be used to feel the other side out on various issues. By raising an issue through the recruiter, you can avoid locking yourself into a fixed position that would be difficult to back down from. This is often the most important role a recruiter can play in the negotiating process.

Maxine Hartley, a highly regarded executive coach in New York, advises candidates who work with recruiters to negotiate through them. According to Maxine, "Because ego is frequently involved during the negotiation of sensitive issues such as compensation, title, and responsibilities, rarely should a candidate negotiate directly with the employer if a recruiter is involved. Once an ill-conceived comment or request has been made by the candidate, it cannot be undone. The candidate is damaged, sometimes irreparably. The headhunter can effectively serve as a lightning rod, advocating the candidate's position without jeopardizing his or her candidacy."

A recruiter can also strengthen your bargaining position by letting a prospective employer know that you are also having discussions with other employers. A recruiter can do this more easily and with greater credibility than you can.

One of my clients, whom I will call Amanda, was being considered for a position as executive vice president for a publishing company. The publisher had used a recruiter to conduct the search. Now that Amanda had been selected for the position, the recruiter was seeking to get information for the publisher about her salary expectations. After some small talk, the conversation with the recruiter went something like this:

RECRUITER: What would it take for them to convince you to join the company?

AMANDA: I would want a base of between $100,000 and $125,000, depending on what the company is offering in terms of stock options and bonuses.

RECRUITER: I think $125,000 is a little high for them.

AMANDA: Then we should probably discuss bonuses and stock options. Do they have a bonus plan for executives at my level?

RECRUITER: I don't know. Why don't you ask them when you meet with them on Thursday?

AMANDA: I'd appreciate it if you could get me that information before the meeting so that I can be prepared to discuss it intelligently.

Amanda used the recruiter very effectively. First, by giving a range in response to the recruiter's question about her expectations and explaining under what circumstances she might consider a salary not at the upper end of that range, she presented the employer with some general parameters but retained a great deal of negotiating flexibility. She was also able to gain some insight from the recruiter as to what the employer was thinking.

By providing a salary range, she also was able to suggest where the bidding should start. Normally an employer will offer a salary in the lower half of any range a candidate suggests in order to leave itself room to negotiate. It can then gauge the candidate's reaction to what it is offering and respond accordingly. Therefore, if you suggest a range of acceptable salaries, make sure you are comfortable with the lowest salary you suggest. You may ultimately be able to get the employer to offer you more, but that is always difficult. Moreover, if the employer does subsequently increase its salary offer, it will usually be at the expense of something else you want.

However, by specifically conditioning her willingness to accept a certain salary on the number of stock options being offered and her potential bonus, Amanda left open the option of asking for additional salary, a larger bonus, more stock options, or some combination thereof. This approach sets the stage for further discussions once the employer makes its initial proposal.

The discussions will focus on possible trade-offs between base salary, bonuses, and stock options (see Strategy 10). Unfortunately, the bonus and particularly the stock options that were actually offered to Amanda were less than she had hoped for. Even after persuading the employer to increase its salary offer to $110,000, Amanda felt she should be able to get more.

Amanda then switched to a strategy that is very effective when negotiating through a recruiter. She floated several "trial balloons." She indicated that she was very interested in the job but was disappointed with the stock option package being offered. She asked if there was any way the company could increase the number of options. After speaking with the company, the recruiter informed her that it couldn't. She then asked if, in light of that, the recruiter thought it would be reasonable for her to ask for a signing bonus. After all, by leaving her current employer before year-end, Amanda was giving up her bonus and the company match to her 401(k) plan. The recruiter acknowledged that the request was not unreasonable, but she did not know if the publisher would agree to it. She offered to find out. In the end, the publisher did agree to a signing bonus, and Amanda accepted the job.

Floating trial balloons is another way you can use a recruiter. You can explore various options through the recruiter without committing yourself to any specific proposal and without losing credibility if the employer is not willing to consider what you are suggesting. You can also try to enlist the recruiter as your advocate. A good way to test the waters is to first raise an issue with the recruiter and see what kind of reaction you receive: "The company's offer provides for six months' severance pay. I am concerned about the possibility that the company may be taken over, and I feel that a year's severance pay would be appropriate. Do you think the company would agree to that?" By working through the recruiter, you leave yourself room to back away from a particular position if the employer does not respond positively.

In addition to floating trial balloons, you can also use the recruiter as an outlet for expressing your concern or displeasure with a particular employer proposal. Those concerns will be viewed very differently if they are raised by the recruiter than if you make them directly to the employer. You might even suggest to the recruiter that, unless a particular issue is resolved to your satisfaction, you cannot see any way to accept the offer. You would almost never make such a comment directly to a prospective employer.

Finally, you can always ask for the recruiter's help, particularly when you have reached an impasse on a difficult issue. Describe the problem to the recruiter, and solicit ideas as to how it might be resolved. After all, the recruiter knows the employer better than you do and should have a good idea of what is possible. A recruiter can explore various alternatives with the employer in a way that you could not. When the recruiter discusses an idea with the employer, it is not a proposal from a candidate it is negotiating with. It is a suggestion from someone who is working for them. Moreover, if the recruiter is the one suggesting the solution, he or she will generally work hard to convince the employer to accept it. The fact that it comes from the recruiter, rather than from you, also makes it more likely that the employer will accept the proposal.

Recruiters have a significant incentive to ensure the successful completion of the negotiations. They have a major stake in the outcome. If they are hired on a contingency fee basis, they get paid only if their candidate accepts the job. Even if a recruiter is hired on a retainer basis and gets paid regardless of whether any particular candidate accepts the job, if you turn the position down, the recruiter has to spend time and effort finding another candidate acceptable to the employer. In either case, the recruiter has an incentive to help the parties reach an agreement. Knowing that, you can use the recruiter to advance your negotiating agenda.

SUMMARY OF NEGOTIATING POINTS

▶ Use the recruiter to get information.

▶ Assume that any information you get from the recruiter is information that the employer wants you to have.

▶ Provide information to the recruiter that you would like conveyed to a prospective employer.

▶ Use the recruiter to float trial balloons.

▶ The recruiter can serve as a means to express your unhappiness with a proposal from the employer.

▶ Ask the recruiter for help when you have reached an impasse.

▶ Never forget that the recruiter is being paid by the employer.

▲
20

Making the Employer's Negotiator Look Good

The deepest principle of human nature is the craving
to be appreciated.

—WILLIAM JAMES

Several years ago, an executive hired me to handle the negotiations when he was being recruited to become chief operating officer of a fast-growing technology company. The employer was being represented by its regular outside corporate counsel. The negotiations were extremely difficult. We went back and forth on almost every point. Mostly we negotiated with each other by phone, exchanging written proposals by fax and calling our clients as necessary to seek their guidance. Sometimes more than a week would go by before the employer's attorney would get back to me on a particular point.

The company's lawyer was a very good negotiator and clearly understood the significance of every word and comma that we agreed upon. However, I thought he frequently missed chances to put his client at an advantage. He was so focused on ensuring that the agreed-upon contract language was exactly the way he wanted it that substantively he often gave up more than he needed to. He obviously was proud of his skills as a contract writer. Frequently, I was able to get significant concessions by agreeing to the language he was proposing on issues that were not of major concern to my client. As you can imagine, this was a long and painstaking process.

Suddenly, however, my adversary seemed to become more accommodating. We quickly reached agreement on a number of outstanding issues. I knew that I would be able to get most of what my client wanted on the remaining issues. Up to that point I had been getting my way by allowing the employer's counsel to determine how certain contract language would be written. I now recognized that his agenda had changed. He obviously had been told to get the deal done. When he learned that I was going away on Friday morning for a long weekend, the pace quickened further. When by the end of the business day Thursday we still had not finished and I suggested we talk again on Monday, he clearly seemed concerned. He asked if we could try to wrap things up that night. I knew that if I agreed, it would increase my bargaining leverage because I could always threaten to break off the negotiations and get back to him when I returned the following week. Also, I had grown to like this fellow and understood that if I took off for the weekend before we concluded, he would have a problem with his client. So we kept working until we finished.

My client was happy, and I think the employer's counsel and the employer were also happy. By understanding the counsel's need to wrap up the negotiations and allowing him to look good with his client, I got the best deal possible for mine. Later I found out that the reason for the sudden urgency was that the employer was eager to announce my client's appointment as its new chief operating officer. In fact, the employer's lawyer had been told to get the deal done so the announcement could be made on Monday.

As I discuss in my book *UP: Influence, Power and the U Perspective—The Art of Getting What You Want*, the best way to be successful in your negotiations is to understand the motivations of the person you are dealing with. Bear in mind that the negotiator's interests may not be the same as those of the employer. She may want to conclude the negotiations quickly because of another project that needs attention. Or the negotiator may be under instructions to make sure that you accept the job offer. Alternatively, she may be under strict budgetary constraints, limiting what can be offered. Whatever the negotiator's agenda, you will be more successful if you understand it.

Letting the negotiator look good in ways that do not cost you much also will facilitate the process. How do you find out what someone's agenda is? Usually all you have to do is listen carefully to what is being said. Get the negotiator to talk about herself. Watch the body language. An experienced negotiator will not reveal the employer's bottom line. She is, however, likely to provide subtle signals as to the employer's priorities. In addition, negotiators will generally freely discuss the things that are going on in their life since they do not have a direct impact on the negotiations. These topics may, however, give you some indication of the negotiator's personal priorities.

Identifying the people to whom this person must answer may also give you some insight into what the negotiator needs to do to look good in their eyes. For example, if the negotiator reports to the chief financial officer, the total cost of the package may be a primary concern. On the other hand, if your future boss is the head of sales and marketing, getting you on board quickly may be of paramount importance. If the negotiator works in human resources or the legal department, her boss may be most interested in the impact the deal will have on others in the organization.

The people you are negotiating with also want you to think well of them. This is particularly true if you are dealing with your future boss. You can take advantage of how that person sees himself. A boss who fancies herself a mentor will want to help you negotiate a good deal. Seek her help. Someone who views himself as a teacher will want to share knowledge about the organization. Encourage him to do so. If you are negotiating with a long-tenured employee, she will probably want to demonstrate to you what a good place to work this is. Ask about all the good things the employer does for its employees and try to use them to enhance your package.

For the most part, people consider themselves to be fair. Appeals to fairness, therefore, will be effective with most of the people you negotiate with in the employment context—with one notable exception. A good number of lawyers and business executives are competitive. Some, however, carry this trait to an extreme. Appeals to fairness will generally be less effective with these individuals. It is more important to let them believe that they have "outnegotiated" you.

The lawyer who represented the technology company during the negotiations described above fell neatly into this last category. He not only considered himself a craftsperson but also needed to "win" points during the negotiations. You need to allow these individuals to "win." But to do so, you don't have to give up things that are important to you (see Strategy 15). Let them win on the issues you select. Reluctantly give in on points you don't consider of major import. By understanding what your goals are, you will know which issues to concede on. Periodically referring to the list of goals created in preparation for the negotiations will keep you on track when you are tempted to concede on an important point without receiving something of equal value in return (see Strategy 11).

Understanding and helping your adversary obtain her objectives while at the same time achieving your own goals will generally enable you to negotiate a better deal (see Strategy 5). The more successful you are, the more important it is to make sure the person you are bargaining with feels good about the outcome. This is particularly true if you are negotiating with your future boss. When the negotiations are over, compliment the other person on the way the process was handled. Say nice things about the employer's negotiator to someone who will tell her what you said. Let her boss know how professionally the negotiations were handled.

Finally, you should make it easy for the negotiator to agree with you. Sometimes the negotiator will want to agree but won't want to look like he is giving in. He may be under pressure to agree in order to complete the negotiations quickly and may resent that fact. Let him save face. Don't box her into a corner. Concede on some minor points. Agree reluctantly. Let him choose among options that are equally favorable to you (see Strategy 10). Make sure that the negotiator believes he got the best deal possible under the circumstances.

Summary of Negotiating Points

- ▶ Understand the agendas of the people you are dealing with.
- ▶ Remember that the negotiator may have an agenda that differs from that of the employer.
- ▶ Try to find out to whom the negotiator must answer, and help that individual look good in their eyes.
- ▶ Take advantage of the negotiator's self-image.
- ▶ Make it easy for the negotiator to agree with you.
- ▶ Make sure the people you are dealing with feel good about the outcome of the negotiations.

21

Bypassing the Negotiator
(Unless It's Your Future Boss)

*I don't want to talk to Jerry Mahoney; I want to
talk to Paul Winchell.*

—HOWARD STERN, REFERRING TO A
VENTRILOQUIST AND HIS STAGE DUMMY

Since I graduated from law school, I have purchased four new cars and
leased one. Except for the car I bought for my 18-year-old son, I negotiated
very good deals on each of those purchases. (You lose all bargaining leverage if you make the mistake of bringing an 18-year-old buying his first car
along with you.) I learned something from each of these negotiations.

One important lesson I learned is to try to avoid negotiating with anyone who does not have the authority to give you what you want. As Lisa
Gersh, former president of the Oxygen Network said to me, "Never take no
for an answer from someone who cannot say yes."

Typically when you buy a new car, the salesperson has no authority to
agree to anything. The salesperson negotiates with you and then announces,
"I have to take what we just agreed to back to my sales manager for
approval." Then the sales manager comes out and tries to renegotiate everything you have just agreed upon. This can be a very effective negotiating
tactic. If you don't know it is going to happen, you will have already given
away too much before the real bargaining begins. You will also have the disadvantage of having a psychological stake in reaching an agreement after
you have invested time and energy in bargaining with the salesperson (see
Strategy 8). The sales manager, on the other hand, who has just come into

the process, knows exactly what he or she is doing and will, if you allow this to occur, have a strong bargaining position. You need to be aware that most car dealers will try to use this tactic on you and be prepared for it. If the sales manager tries this, don't start negotiating all over again. Simply insist on the deal that has been agreed to or go to another dealer.

When you are engaged in employment negotiations, you want to make sure that you are bargaining with someone who has sufficient authority because you can't simply just go to another employer if the negotiator cannot deliver. Sometimes, however, ensuring that the negotiator has appropriate authority can be problematic. If attempting to bypass a lower-level negotiator will damage relationships that may be important to your future career, it may be better to work through that person even if it means that the negotiations will be more difficult.

There are three basic situations, however, in which you should consider trying to bypass the negotiator: (1) when the negotiator has no authority, (2) when the negotiator is using lack of authority as a negotiating tactic, and (3) when the negotiator has the authority to agree but is not willing to do so. Your response to each of these situations will vary. However, your goal in each instance will be to negotiate with someone other than the person you find yourself dealing with. As the title of this strategy indicates, if you are bargaining with your future boss, it will be hard, and probably ill advised, to try to end-run that individual in order to negotiate with someone else. Attempting to do so probably will be futile; it will also likely hurt your relationship with your future boss and most likely your career as well.

After you have successfully completed the interview process, normally someone from human resources will get back to you with a formal offer. That person will often be the recruiter who first contacted you about the position. (In smaller companies the human resources director or your future boss may handle the follow-up directly.) If you are offered the job by someone other than your future boss or the head of human resources, that person will be limited to conveying the terms of the offer, explaining available benefits, and answering any questions you may have. Typically that individual will not have the authority to negotiate further or significantly modify the terms of the offer. The response you will likely receive is, "I am not in a position to do anything about that" or "Let me get back to you." Often some reference will be made to "company policy" or to how "we don't do that here."

Once you have determined that the person you are speaking with has no ability to agree to anything of importance, you have several options.

First, you can try to find out who has the necessary authority and speak to that person directly. Second, you can seek assistance from your new boss. Finally, if you choose to ,or you have no choice but to, you can work through the lower-level person and make concessions sparingly, understanding that whatever you agree to may be subject to renegotiation by someone else.

When you are dealing with someone who lacks authority, discuss the less important issues first in order to get a feel for how best to negotiate with this person. Preliminary discussions may also provide you with an excuse to deal with someone else. If, for example, you are told that the something that you thought the negotiator had previously agreed to was disapproved, find out who was responsible for that decision. Then try to speak directly with that person or ask your future boss to intervene.

Another approach when dealing with someone lacking in authority is to request that he or she offer solutions to the issues you raise. It is exceedingly difficult for people to claim that they cannot agree to something if they are the ones who propose it. Finally, you can make your proposals tentative as well. For example, you might use a what-if approach and make it clear that what you are suggesting may need to be modified after you have had the opportunity to review it with your lawyer, accountant, or spouse (see Strategy 16).

You can use the same responses if you are dealing with someone who you believe actually has authority to reach a final agreement, at least within certain limits, but purports to need someone else's approval for whatever is agreed upon. This is a position that lawyers often take. Lawyers understand how to use a claim of lack of authority to their clients' advantage. They typically are given sufficient authority to reach an agreement, or at least they have a very good understanding of what their clients are willing to agree to. To be able to claim a lack of authority, many lawyers will actually ask their clients not to give them certain authority. That way they can truthfully state that they need to discuss any proposals with their clients before they can agree to anything.

There are several other ways to respond to a feigned claim of lack of authority. One is to embarrass the negotiator into "getting" the appropriate authority by suggesting that it might be easier if you dealt directly with the person making the decisions. Another way to level the playing field, particularly if it is the employer's attorney who is claiming a lack of authority, is for you to introduce your own attorney into the process. Your lawyer will, of course, be equally limited in authority. Alternatively, you can try to negotiate the substantive aspects of the agreement directly with your future boss or with someone else in the organization who has sufficient authority, leaving the "drafting of the agreement" to the lawyers.

When the employer's lawyer is involved, it is relatively easy to take the position that you do not feel comfortable without your own attorney being present. You can then suggest to the employer that it might be better, in the interest of time, for you to speak directly with him or her. In the unusual situation in which your future employer still wants its lawyer to handle the discussions, it is not unreasonable to ask that the employer pay your attorney's fees. Finally, when you have to deal with someone who uses lack of authority as a negotiating tactic, be wary of agreeing to any major concessions before you have obtained a firm commitment from the employer as to what it is willing to do in return.

The most difficult and possibly most beneficial situation in which to bypass the person you are negotiating with arises when that person actually has the necessary authority but is not willing to agree to what you want. When this occurs, you have to find a way to raise the issue with someone at a higher level without unnecessarily antagonizing the person you are negotiating with. Even if the second person is not at a higher level, he or she may still have sufficient influence to change the negotiator's position. If you are negotiating with people from human resources or the legal department, for instance, they will generally be very solicitous of the wishes of line managers for fear of being accused of being insensitive to the needs of the business.

Typically, the individual you will seek out in attempting to bypass the negotiator is your future boss. That is the person who has the most at stake in your accepting the offer and is the logical individual to champion your cause. It is only natural to discuss a problem that might prevent you from accepting the offer with the individual who is hiring you. However, even if your future boss is at a higher level than the original negotiator, you need to approach the situation carefully. If you ask your prospective boss to overrule the negotiator, even if your boss is in a position to do so, he or she may choose not to do so. Your new boss may believe it is not the right thing to do or may want to avoid causing internal problems. Similarly, the person being overruled may seek support from his or her boss or may otherwise attempt to sabotage the deal. Even if the original negotiator is forced to agree, you could be creating an enemy who is in a position to damage your career at some future date. Therefore, it is better to seek help in getting someone to influence the negotiator rather than try to overrule him or her.

One possible approach is to describe the problem to your prospective boss and seek advice on how to handle the situation. Ask if there is anything the boss can do to help. Once your future boss agrees to get involved, the issue is likely to be resolved in your favor.

What should you do if your future boss is the one making the offer and doesn't have sufficient authority, pretends not to have the authority, or has the authority to agree but won't? Do the best you can and negotiate anyway, unless you can get your future boss to suggest you speak with someone else. Although there is no surefire way to get your boss to do that, there are ways you can encourage it. For example, if your prospective boss blames an impasse on "company policy," ask if there is anyone you could talk to who would be able to make an exception to the policy. If the boss does not refer you elsewhere, you will just have to live with what is being offered or not accept the job (see Strategy 25).

It would be a Pyrrhic victory to get what you want by making your new boss feel that you went over his or her head to get it. It is unlikely that the boss will ever trust you. That is clearly not the way to start off a new relationship.

SUMMARY OF NEGOTIATING POINTS

▶ If possible, avoid negotiating with anyone who doesn't have authority to agree to what you want.

▶ If you have to negotiate with someone who doesn't have sufficient authority, make concessions sparingly.

▶ If you are negotiating with someone who lacks sufficient authority, get him or her to propose ways to resolve your concerns.

▶ If the person you are dealing with is using a lack of authority as a negotiating tactic, consider having someone else negotiate for you.

▶ If you need to bypass the negotiator, seek help from your future boss.

▶ Be careful how you handle someone with the authority to agree to what you want but who won't do so. Seek to influence rather than overrule.

▶ If your future boss is doing the negotiating, don't go over his or her head without getting permission from him or her first.

22

Using Information

FACTS, FIGURES, AND COMPARISONS

The facts ma'am. Just the facts.

—JACK WEBB IN THE TV
SERIES *DRAGNET*

Ken was in a tough position. He wanted the job, but he felt that he was worth more than was being offered. An expert in distribution, he had worked his way up to be transportation manager in charge of distribution for a large manufacturing company. Because he had been with this employer for virtually his whole career, his salary had not kept pace with that of his peers elsewhere. Complicating his situation, in his initial discussions with the recruiter, he had made the mistake of telling the recruiter exactly what he was earning (see Strategy 1). The offer Ken received was just enough more than he was making for it to be worthwhile for him to move, but it was still substantially less than the market rate for comparable positions.

Ken told the person extending the offer how interested he was in the job and how excited he was about the possibility of joining the company. He thanked him for the offer but expressed disappointment about the salary. Ken stated that he thought the salary being offered was low in light of what others in similar positions were earning, and he offered to provide salary survey data showing what comparably sized companies were paying their transportation managers. In addition, Ken explained how much money he had been able to save his current employer by making the distribution system faster, more efficient, and less costly. In the end, he was able to get the employer to agree to a salary and bonus structure more in line with what he considered to be his true market worth.

There are two types of information you can use to negotiate your compensation: information about the market value of the position and information about the particular value you bring to the position. If people in similar positions at comparable organizations earn more than you are being offered, or if they participate in a stock option plan and you won't, you can present that information to your prospective employer. This data will be very useful if the organization is unaware of market conditions. That is frequently the case when the person you are replacing had been with the employer for a long time and, as a result, was being paid a below market salary. Perhaps that is the reason your predecessor left. Moreover, to the extent that you can demonstrate your market value because you have another offer, you can usually get the employer to improve its offer (see Strategy 13).

Often, however, an employer that is offering a salary below the market rate is aware of that fact and is doing so intentionally. Sometimes the company will include something else of equal value—for example, stock—as part of its proposal. At other times an employer will offer less than the market rate because it cannot afford to pay more or because paying more would upset its internal salary structure. In that case providing facts about the overall job market will do little to improve your bargaining position.

Under those circumstances, rely on facts and figures to sell what you can do for the employer. How much did you increase sales in your unit last year? How much did you reduce distribution costs? Demonstrate in concrete financial terms to your prospective employer what you have been accomplishing in your current job. Showing the value you can bring to the employer will place you in a better position to get paid more. After all, if you can demonstrate that you will be able to save a half-a-million dollars by improving inventory controls as you did for your current employer, it is unlikely that a prospective employer will balk at paying you the extra $10,000 a year you are seeking.

Providing objective, verifiable information to support your position serves other purposes as well. It tends to depersonalize disagreements. Objective data can refocus the parties on the fairness of the proposal. Most important, providing information that supports your position affords the employer's negotiator a graceful way to give in without losing face (see Strategy 20).

Often during negotiations one party will argue so strongly for a position that it is difficult to modify that position even after it becomes clear that there is a need to do so. New information allows the negotiator to change his or her stance without appearing to concede. Often that is enough to resolve what appears to be a serious impasse.

Market data can also be effective when you are starting from an otherwise weak bargaining position. If, like Ken, you really want the job and are willing to accept the position even though the compensation being offered is not what you expected, providing the prospective employer with objective data showing the value of the position offers you the best chance of getting the employer to improve its proposal. Employers, no matter how strong their bargaining position, still want to appear to be fair (see Commandment 6, "Understand the Role That Fairness Plays in the Process"). When you ask even the most ruthless negotiators about how they treat their own employees, they will almost always describe themselves as "tough but fair." Offering objective data to support your position appeals to a need to be fair. Moreover, the employer will want you to feel good about joining the company, and that will be hard to do if it ignores the information you have provided.

Facts, figures, and comparisons of both market data and the value you bring to the position can also be useful when you are negotiating with your current employer. Showing what you have accomplished for the company in terms of additional earnings or cost savings is helpful if you are attempting to justify why you deserve a raise. Market rates are also compelling when you are seeking a salary increase from your current employer. If you are being paid less than others in similar positions, fairness dictates that your employer adjust your salary accordingly. You should also be prepared to show, in concrete terms, how much it would take to train your replacement and how much productivity would be lost as a result.

If that does not do the trick, your employer either does not seriously believe that you might leave or does not care. In either case, you probably should look for another job, if for no other reason than to prove to yourself that you are marketable. Once you have another offer, you can use it to negotiate a salary increase if you still want to remain with your current employer (see Strategy 13).

Even information that arguably does not support your stance can be used to your advantage. If there is an obvious weakness in your position, address it. If you don't, the employer's negotiator certainly will. By bringing it up yourself, you will enhance your credibility. Candor can be disarming. When attorneys try cases, they always want to bring out any problems with their case before the other side does. That way it does not undermine their case. Nobody thinks that you have been caught trying to put something over on them.

For example, let's say the salary information you are using doesn't include the value of stock provided as part of the compensation package and your offer includes a small stock option grant. You should indicate your appreciation of that part of the offer, note that the value of equity is not included in your data although some of the employers included in the survey also offer employees stock options, and state that even considering the stock option grant, you still feel that the salary portion of the offer is low. Presented in that way, if you don't get the salary increase, you might be able to get the prospective employer to increase the size of the options grant instead.

Being forthright and addressing the issue will create trust while at the same time allowing you to place the adverse information in the most favorable light possible. It will also allow you to develop a relationship with the negotiator. When you do that, it will be much harder for the employer to be less than candid with you. The more of a personal relationship you develop with the negotiator, the better the deal you will be able to get.

This does not, of course, mean that you should make the employer's case for it. Your purpose is to argue forcefully for your proposals, which should be expansive but reasonable (see Strategy 2). Only when the employer is certain to raise an objection should you try to preempt it by bringing the issue up first.

Information is critical to the success of any negotiation. That is why preparation is so important [see the chapters "Beyond Research: Preparing to Negotiate" and "Everything You Need to Know about Using the Internet (and Other Sources of Information) to Help You Negotiate"]. You can use the information obtained about the prospective employer during your preparation, such as the employer's salary structure, to formulate your proposals, without ever revealing that you have this information. However, to support your positions, you should provide other types of verifiable data such as market surveys and descriptions of what you have accomplished for your current employer. Even more important, offering such information can provide the employer with a justification for changing its position, without having to appear simply to be caving in to your demands.

Summary of Negotiating Points

▶ There are two types of objective information that can be used when negotiating compensation: market data and the particular value you bring to the position.

▶ Both types of information can be used effectively even, or perhaps especially, if you have a weak bargaining position.

▶ Objective, verifiable data of either type can be used to support an appeal to fairness.

▶ Facts, figures, and comparisons are especially useful when you are negotiating with your current employer.

▶ Providing new information allows the employer's negotiator to give in without losing face.

▶ Even information that arguably does not support your position can be used to your advantage, provided that you bring it out first in order to preempt it from being raised by the other side.

23

Silence Is Golden

WHEN TO LET THE OTHER SIDE TALK

When you have nothing to say, say nothing.

—CHARLES CALEB COLTON

Sandy had been offered a position as advertising director for a specialty store chain. She and her future employer were readily able to agree on most of the employment terms. The one area in which they were having difficulty reaching agreement involved the severance package. Because of the number of retailers that had gone out of business or been taken over in recent years, Sandy was particularly concerned about the severance package. She had two problems with the employer's offer: the amount of the severance pay and the fact that the employer was insisting that its severance obligation be "mitigated" by any salary earned elsewhere during the severance period.

Mitigation is a legal concept that many employers seem to be incorporating into their severance policies. Under a severance arrangement that requires mitigation, the severance amount is paid in the form of salary continuation, with the employer reducing the amount of severance pay by any salary earned elsewhere during the period of continuation. The reason normally given for requiring mitigation is that the purpose of severance pay is to provide employees with financial protection until they find other jobs, not to provide them with a windfall. The problem with mitigation is that it reduces or eliminates the incentive to find another job, particularly if a new job involves accepting a reduced salary. Mitigation does not take into account the fact that if an employee has to accept a lower-level position, it may take years for the employee to return to the same salary level follow-ing his or her termination.

Sandy had asked for a severance of 12 months' salary to be paid in a lump sum if she was terminated without cause. The employer came back with an offer to guarantee her 6 months' salary continuation, mitigated by any salary she earned during this period. She felt that 6 months was not suf-ficient and that her severance amount should not be reduced if she found other employment. The employer responded that its severance policy applied to everyone, and it included a mitigation provision. She was then asked how much severance pay she would require if it included mitigation. Sandy did not know how to respond to this question. Had she answered, she would have been implicitly accepting the fact that her severance agree-ment would require mitigation and the employer would then begin negoti-ating the amount of that severance pay.

Instinctively Sandy understood that when you don't have a good response, don't respond. After pausing for a moment, she turned the ques-tion back to the employer: "I really had never considered that the sever-ance amount would require mitigation. Why don't you see how much severance pay you can provide without mitigation?" (see Strategy 3). About a day later she heard from the employer. Once more Sandy was told that the employer had to require mitigation because every other employee's sev-erance arrangement required mitigation. Then Sandy was again asked what she needed in terms of a severance package if it included mitigation. Sandy replied that she would think it over and get back to the employer.

Sandy was not happy with a severance package that required mitiga-tion, but she understood that if all the other employees, without exception, were required to accept this arrangement, she would probably have to accept it as well. Having reached that conclusion, she decided to take a different approach. She sought to protect herself from the possibility of a lengthy period of unemployment, or more likely underemployment, by getting more money up front in the form of a signing bonus (see Strategy 10). Sandy rec-ognized that making such a request this late in the negotiations could cause problems. She also knew that the employer was anxious to fill the position and that she was the only candidate the company was considering at that moment. So she simply waited.

After about a week she received a call from the recruiter who was han-dling the search. The recruiter wanted to know where things stood. Sandy responded that she didn't know where to go from there. She explained that she had not expected the employer to insist on mitigation and she was concerned that if she lost her job because of a takeover, her career might be significantly set back. She assumed that, in light of the way the employer's severance policy was structured, the most she could expect was a year's severance pay, and she felt, with mitigation, that amount did not provide her sufficient protection. Sandy then inquired as to whether the recruiter thought a signing bonus was possible (see Strategy 19). That way, in the event that she lost her job following a takeover, she at least would have the bonus money to help tide her over. The recruiter offered to find out. In the end, Sally agreed to 12 months' severance pay with mitigation along with a signing bonus.

No one can be certain that Sandy's not calling back for a week made the employer more receptive to her suggestion of a signing bonus than it would have been if she had immediately proposed that solution. However, silence can often work to your advantage during negotiations. Often, if you have stated your position clearly, or if you don't like the direction the negotiations are taking, it is best not to say anything more. Let the other side make the next move.

If you are being pressed during negotiations for a response and don't know what to do, find a reason to take a break. Go to the bathroom. Get a cup of coffee. Break for lunch. Indicate that you have to be somewhere and schedule another session. Use the time to regroup. Seek advice. Collect additional information to support your position. Rethink your stance. Develop a new game plan. Let the other side worry about what you are thinking. What is important is to regain control over the pace and the agenda.

One of the most difficult things to do is simply to keep quiet and wait. It takes a certain amount of self-assurance to make your point and remain silent until you get a response. We are trained from an early age to avoid lulls in a conversation. Good conversationalists keep the discussion going. Silence makes people uncomfortable. If you don't say anything, though, chances are that the person you are talking to will.

One of the tricks that lawyers use when questioning a witness is to just remain silent after the witness completes an answer rather than ask another question. This tactic typically causes the witness to continue speaking, which often yields more information than was initially provided. Try an experiment with a friend. Ask a general question. After your friend answers, remain silent, smile, and continue to look right at him or her. Even if it appears that the speaker has finished, after a brief pause, the speaker will inevitably continue answering. This technique works equally well during negotiations. Just as nature abhors a vacuum, people are uncomfortable with silence. They will seek to fill the void. In all probability the person you are dealing with will do something to try to move the negotiations forward.

A well-timed delay in getting back to the employer's negotiator can often work to your advantage, provided that you do not appear to be avoiding him or her. For the same reason that periods of silence during a conversation create discomfort, breaks in negotiations that last longer than expected, and during which there is no communication from the other side, can be unnerving. The employer will wonder whether you are still interested or if you have received another offer. Moreover, it may be under pressure to fill the position quickly. As long as you have not promised to respond by any specific time, you can delay getting back to the employer. That could be for a day, or it could be for a week, depending on the nature of the negotiations.

If you don't schedule a resumption in the bargaining relatively promptly, in all likelihood the employer's negotiator will contact you. How quickly the company does so will give you some indication as to how anxious it is to complete the negotiations and have you start work. If you are not contacted within a reasonable period of time, you can always call the employer's negotiator back yourself. If the negotiator asks you why you hadn't gotten back to him or her sooner, you can respond that you didn't have any good ideas as to how to resolve the issue. Usually this response not only will be truthful but it will also put the burden on the employer to try to come up with a solution.

How should you respond if someone uses silence with you? If, while you are in a discussion, the negotiator remains silent for a lengthy period of time after you have completed an answer, the best response is for you to pause long enough to make clear that you know what is going on and then ask: "Did that answer your question?" Similarly, if the employer's negotiator indicates that he or she will get back to you with a response, it is often best to simply wait until he or she does so.

If you can't wait, you can call the employer, reiterate that you are very interested in the job, and then try to create a sense of urgency. For example, you could state: "I need to get the matter resolved quickly because I have some projects at my current job that it would not be fair for me to start if I plan to leave." Or you could ask for a prompt response because you "are also talking to another employer" (see Strategy 13). If a headhunter is involved, you can contact that person to find out what the employer is thinking (see Strategy 19). As long as you understand that the delay may be a tactic to try to pressure you into conceding on a key point, your call to find out the status of the negotiations will not affect the way you bargain. Moreover, sometimes a delay in getting back to you may not be a tactic at all. Rather, the negotiator may have a legitimate reason for not calling—for example, he or she might need to get approval from someone who is unavailable or they might have personal issues at home.

It is important to understand the effect silence can have on the person you are bargaining with, and on you if you allow it to. As a rule, you want to control the pace of the negotiations as well as the agenda. Using silence to your advantage is one way to do that. Be careful, however, not to over-use this technique. Neither silence nor delay should be used to such an extent that the employer thinks you are unreliable or you don't care about the job. After all, your reliability and enthusiasm are part of the reason you were offered the job in the first place.

SUMMARY OF NEGOTIATING POINTS

► Use silence strategically.
► When you have made your point, remain silent until the other side responds.
► Often it is best to let the other side make the next move; silence will encourage the negotiator to do so.
► When you are not sure what to do, or when things are not going the way you want, find a reason to take a break.
► A well-timed delay in getting back to the employer can work to your advantage.
► Do not let someone use silence or delay to pressure you.
► Be careful not to use silence or delay to such an extent that the employer thinks that you are unreliable or you are not interested in the job.

24

How to Win by Conceding

There are occasions where it us undoubtedly better to incur loss than to make gain.

—Titus Maccius Plautus

In labor negotiations, it is considered to be bargaining in bad faith not to offer concessions. This method of negotiating is referred to as "Boulwarism," after one of the more famous practitioners of this approach. Lemuel Boulware was a vice president of labor relations at General Electric in the 1950s, and he believed that the way to negotiate with a union was to start out with a reasonable proposal and steadfastly refuse to change your position. The National Labor Relations Board, the government agency responsible for regulating labor relations, ruled that negotiating in this manner constituted illegal bad-faith bargaining. Failing to offer concessions, according to the National Labor Relations Board, was the equivalent of "not bargaining at all." Even when this technique is successful, it leaves the other side feeling taken advantage of. As a result, in most types of negotiating, the practice is frowned upon. This is particularly true in employment negotiations because how you handle yourself while bargaining will provide the basis for your new employer's first impression of you.

Giving in Order to Get

Our commonly shared understanding of fairness calls for a reciprocating gesture when someone gives us something. Cultural norms dictate that when one side makes a concession during negotiations, the other side should respond in kind. This is part of the etiquette of negotiating. When bargaining about the terms of your employment, take advantage of this need to reciprocate.

Often the best way to gain a concession is to give one. Tactically, it is best to seek concessions immediately after you have agreed to one. When it comes to negotiating, people have very short memories.

At the beginning of the negotiations, try to determine how the employer responds to concessions. When you raise a concern, does the negotiator react without the need to bargain (the "problem solver")? Or does the negotiator consider conceding too easily to be a sign of weakness (the "macho negotiator")? Is it sufficient to concede on a point and then follow up by asking for a concession later (the "fair trader")? Or is it necessary to make the quid pro quo explicit (the "horse trader")? This understanding will help you determine how to strategically use concessions.

When a horse trader, for example, asks you for a concession, you need to specifically condition your agreement on the employer consenting to one or more of your requests. Thus, instead of simply offering to forget about the no-interest home loan you had asked for and hoping that the employer will respond favorably, you need to request something in return. For instance, you might indicate that if the employer were willing to give you a signing bonus, it could avoid the problem it seemed to be having with your request for a no-interest home loan.

Unfortunately, most negotiators do not fall neatly into one category or another. Their responses will vary depending on the issue. You should do the same. It is usually best, at first, to try a problem-solving approach. If that doesn't work, use the horse trader approach for major concessions and a fair trader approach for minor ones.

Concessions can be used when the negotiations start to bog down or when you reach an impasse on a particular issue. Do not make a concession too readily, even if it is unimportant to you. The other side will not value what you are giving up if you do not act as though it is meaningful. Ordinarily, you should make only one concession at a time. Also, be able to provide plausible-sounding justifications for changes in your positions. Explanations can be based on your attempts to accommodate the employer's needs, concessions granted by the employer, new information you have obtained, or changes in your circumstances. Properly timed concessions will allow you to appear cooperative and should get the negotiations moving forward again on a positive note. The strategic use of concessions throughout the negotiations can help you achieve the objectives that are most important to you.

Use the early stages of the negotiations to explore the employer's positions on the issues. Go over each aspect of the offer. Seek clarification of anything you don't understand. Ask questions about why certain aspects of the proposals, such as the bonus criteria, are structured the way they are. Determine if there is flexibility on various items. In response to any proposal that appears to be unusual, question whether the employer has experienced problems in the past that have resulted in the need for that proposal. Gather as much information as possible (see Strategy 3).

Try to determine why the negotiator is taking certain stances. The negotiator may provide a sound justification for a position being taken or may simply fall back on "policy." Sometimes you will not be given any reason at all. It is possible that the negotiator simply does not have the authority to agree and may not want to go back to the employer to obtain it (see Strategy 21). One of your objectives during these early discussions is to determine what issues are important to the employer and where there is bargaining flexibility. Depending on the nature of the negotiations and the level of the employee involved, this part of the process may last less than an hour or it can extend over several days. It is also a good idea, after an initial session in which you have asked a lot of questions, to request a little time to digest the information you have received.

Timing Your Concessions

It is best not to concede issues too easily or too early. Thoroughly discussing issues will enable you to identify those areas where the employer is either not willing or not able to give in. Generally an employer will turn down a seemingly reasonable request out of concern for the impact that granting it might have on the organization. A prospective employer might willingly agree to something if you were the only person affected, but it is not likely to disrupt the whole organization just to hire you. If, for example, an employer provides all its sales representatives with a midsized American car, it is not going to agree to your request for a BMW, even if you offer to accept a lower salary in return. To do so would result in other sales representatives asking for BMWs. The fact that the employer was able to negotiate a lower salary in return will be lost on your peers. Similarly, an employer will ordinarily not risk upsetting its salary structure by paying you substantially more than others at your level.

Concessions can be effectively used to conclude the negotiations. If you have identified the right issue on which to concede, offering it as part of a package to resolve all the outstanding issues will maximize the impact of that concession and enable you to reach agreement. This technique is frequently used by car dealers. At the point where you have almost reached agreement on the price of the car, the salesperson says: "That is the best I can do on the price, but if we can reach an agreement today, I'll throw in the gold package at no extra charge." By this time, the salesperson has gotten you to the point where you can see yourself driving along the highway in that new red convertible. Now, with the chance to get the gold package for free, the deal becomes too good to pass up. Of course, in agreeing to the dealer's offer, you are giving up the possibility of getting any further price reduction. The desire to complete the deal coupled with the last-minute offer of the gold package is too much to resist (see Strategy 8). That is why using a concession to close the deal is so powerful.

In employment negotiations, this technique works basically the same way. After you have thoroughly explored the employer's position, you can begin to lay the groundwork. By this time you should have identified those issues that appear to be important to the employer. You will want to get as much as possible in return for acquiescing on those issues. To do that, understand that some issues are essentially nonnegotiable. Often the reason they are nonnegotiable, as discussed previously, is that agreeing to them would affect the rest of the organization. When you discuss these points during the negotiations, provide the employer with all the reasons that it should agree to your request. Be forceful in your arguments. Don't let the employer's negotiator pressure you into agreeing before you are ready.

Generally there will be a number of areas in the employer's initial offer that you will want to change. Some of them will be important to the employer; others won't. An important part of the negotiating process is to determine where there is room for give-and-take. As the discussions proceed, you will need to yield on some issues in return for other concessions. To be able to use a concession to close the deal, however, you must unyieldingly maintain your position on at least one issue of importance to the employer until the very end.

Once you get to the point where you have agreed on almost everything, you are ready to make the most of your final concession. Of the issues that remain, at least one must be an issue important to the employer. The more important this issue appears to be for you, the more valuable it will be when you concede it. In using a concession to close the deal, limit yourself to one or two things that you want but have not yet been able to get the employer to agree to. The magnitude of what you are seeking should be approximately equal to, or preferably less than, that of the concession you are about to make.

Offer to concede on the remaining key issue of concern to the employer in order to reach an agreement so that you can come to work for the employer. In return, ask the employer to acquiesce on the other outstanding issues. If more than one or two requests are still on the table or if other nonnegotiable issues remain, you will need to drop them as well. Provided that you have properly judged the importance of the issue you are conceding, the employer will likely agree to accept your position on the other issues in order to reach agreement.

Concluding the Negotiations

Let's look at how this works in a concrete situation. Assume you are negotiating with the technology company, described earlier, that requires all its employees to sign a standard agreement not to compete. Early on you identify the terms of the noncompete agreement as an issue that is not negotiable. Everyone without exception is required to sign it. You ask to limit the number of companies to which the noncompete restrictions would apply. The negotiator tells you that he cannot agree to that. You ask to reduce the period covered by the restrictions from two years to one year. That request is denied as well. Then you move on to discuss other issues. At this point most of the outstanding items are resolved. The only issue that remains—other than the agreement not to compete—is the severance package. Now is the time to offer a concession to get the technology company to agree to what you want in terms of the severance package.

The conclusion of the negotiations might go something like this:

You:	I understand that the agreement not to compete that you want me to sign is very important to the company. It creates a lot of problems for me though. But if you can't change it, I guess I'll agree to sign it in order to get this thing wrapped up.
Negotiator:	That's good.
You:	Since that noncompete will probably keep me from working, I'm sure you will agree to a one-year severance package.
Negotiator:	I don't know.
You:	I really could not possibly agree to the noncompete unless I had the security of a reasonable severance package in case things didn't work out.
Negotiator:	One year is a very large severance package.

YOU: Then why don't we make the noncompete for six
            months?
NEGOTIATOR: Okay, we have a deal.

It is important not to appear to be manipulative when you use concessions. No one wants to feel like he or she is being taken advantage of. To avoid giving that appearance, select an issue about which you have legitimate concerns. If an issue is of critical importance to the employer, it most likely involves your giving up something of real value. Properly done, the use of a concession to conclude the negotiations allows you to maximize what you get in return.

When you are granting concessions, trust your instincts. Generally it is a good idea to vary your approach. Sometimes you can simply concede on a point and follow up with a request for something else. At other times you will want to offer to trade one item directly for another. ("I'll forget about anything over and above your regular relocation policy if you'll give me a signing bonus that I can use to cover any additional moving expenses.") Occasionally you may concede without asking for anything in return simply to gain some goodwill. Remember, however, that your goal is not to win the company's "Congeniality Award." It is to get the best possible deal.

Always try to keep something in reserve in order to wrap up the negotiations. It might be something that you want but know the employer is not willing to agree to, or it might be something that the employer needs you to agree to. It could also be something important to you that you are willing to give up if the overall package is sufficiently attractive. On the other hand, it could be an issue that is actually less important to you than you have let on (see Strategy 15). Whatever issue you select, wait until the time is right and use it as leverage to reach a final agreement.

Throughout the negotiations, granting concessions strategically will enable you to get a better deal. As the process nears a conclusion, concessions can be used to maximum effect. Making a concession at the end of the negotiations may enable you to obtain something you could not have gotten the employer to agree to at an earlier stage. This is, in part, because by this time the employer already has a major stake in ensuring a successful outcome (see Strategy 8). It also allows the employer's negotiator to feel like a winner (see Strategy 20).

SUMMARY OF NEGOTIATING POINTS

▶ Don't concede on issues too easily or too early.

▶ Thoroughly discuss the employer's initial offer before you begin negotiating.

▶ Identify issues that are of critical importance to the employer.

▶ Agree to concessions strategically, and vary your approach in granting them.

▶ Generally follow a concession immediately with a request to reciprocate.

▶ Always try to keep in reserve an issue important to the employer that you can use to close the deal.

Walking Away

He has departed, withdrawn, gone away.

—CICERO

Of all the negotiations I have been involved in, the one that I am most proud of is one that did not end with my client accepting the job—at least not the job for which we were initially negotiating. My client was the president of a midsized company. He had been approached about joining its main competitor as president. The compensation package he was offered was significantly more than he was earning, including a substantial amount of stock. With a little effort we were even able to get the employer to improve the financial terms of the deal.

The only problem we encountered was getting the company to agree to a satisfactory severance package if things didn't work out. Although the severance package is always important, in this case I felt it was critical. The prospective employer was not doing well, and it was rumored that the parent company might sell it off. We asked for a severance package of 18 months' salary and benefits continuation, extended to two years in the event of a change of control (that is, a sale of the business). Equally important to my client was the accelerated vesting of the restricted stock and the stock options he was to be given in the event he lost his job.

Despite our best effort, we were not able to get the employer to agree to an acceptable severance package. In light of the company's situation, I counseled my client not to accept the job without a suitable severance package. Although I thought we might eventually reach a satisfactory resolution of the severance issue, my client decided he did not want to work for this company. He reasoned: "If it is this hard to get agreement on a reasonable severance package, what's it going to be like actually working for them?" So he walked away from the deal.

The story does not end there. We decided to use the offer to see if we could get his current employer to improve his compensation and to give him some assurances about being promoted to chief executive officer in the near future. To avoid the risk that he would be considered disloyal, we decided not to try to get his current employer to bid against the offer (see Strategy 13). My client told his boss, the current CEO, about the offer, and he made it clear that he was not going to accept it. He explained the reasons why he had considered the offer. He asked for help in resolving his concerns because he really wanted to stay there.

As it turned out, walking away was the right decision. My client was given a substantial raise, additional stock options, and a promise that he would be considered for the chief executive job within the next two years when the CEO expected to retire. He is now CEO of the company. As for the company that tried to recruit him, it was sold within six months, and its chief executive officer lost his job, presumably without the benefit of an adequate severance package.

The best way to ensure that you get a good deal is to be able to walk away. To do that, it helps if you are satisfied remaining in your current position or have another job possibility in the works. When you are not desperate to take a job, you will bargain with more confidence, knowing it will not be the end of the world if this particular deal does not go through. You will also be able to ask for more if you are not afraid of losing the opportunity. This is not a strategy; it is an attitude that applies to every negotiation.

It is also essential when you employ a walking-away strategy. By definition, walking away is a high-risk stratagem. As the name implies, there is always the possibility that you are saying goodbye to the offer. When you adopt a walking-away strategy, you have to be prepared for that possibility. And, of course, not taking a particular job sometimes can be the best thing to do. You will find that out, however, only in hindsight after you have obtained a better position, with a better compensation package elsewhere. At other times just showing that you are willing to walk away will greatly strengthen your bargaining position.

This is a sufficiently risky strategy, and you need to think it through carefully. It is best used when you are certain that there is no way you could accept the job unless the employer changed its position on certain key issues. In that case, you have nothing to lose by employing a walking-away strategy. Another instance where this approach can effectively be used is when a prospective employer really needs or wants to hire you. Be careful, however, because rarely do employers ever need or want employees so desperately. If you are relying on the employer crumbling at the very thought of not being able to hire you, you are very likely to be disappointed.

Your goal, when using this strategy, is to walk away without foreclosing the possibility that the employer will reconsider its position and make you a substantially better offer. How you do that is critical. You need to be gracious. Compliment the negotiator on how the negotiations were handled. Extend your thanks for all the negotiator's efforts. Place the blame for the failure to reach agreement on some objective impediment outside of the negotiator's contol. Employing traditional negotiating theory, you might describe the situation as one in which the circles simply do not overlap (see Strategy 5). While expressing your regrets about not being able to accept the offer, go over all the reasons why you were excited about the job in the first place. Finally, let the negotiator know that if another position becomes available that will satisfy your requirements or if there is some way to overcome whatever the stumbling blocks are, you remain interested.

By so doing, you are letting the negotiator know that the reason you are turning down the offer has nothing to do with the job or the employer or the way the negotiator handled the process. If you were declining the offer for any one of those reasons, there would be no room for the employer to come back to you with a new proposal. By focusing on objective impediments to the deal, you make it clear that if the employer can figure out a way to remove those obstacles, you will be happy to take the job. In that way the negotiator is not boxed into a corner and forced to try to justify how the negotiations were handled. If the negotiator's position on the thorny issues does not really constitute the employer's bottom line, then a resolution should be possible. If there are real obstacles to reaching an agreement, you have given the negotiator the opportunity to become a hero by figuring out how to overcome them. In any event, you have left the door open to further discussions.

Let's assume you are ready to walk away from a job offer over the issue of stock options. You have asked for a grant of a certain number of options immediately and additional options a year from now if you meet certain agreed-upon criteria. The employer does not want to give you any stock options until you have been on board a year and have proved yourself. It also wants any award of stock options to be discretionary. The negotiator appears to be unwilling to agree to specific criteria for the award of those options. You like the employer and are excited about the job being offered. However, without a guarantee of sufficient equity in the company, it does not make financial sense for you to accept the offer. How do you walk away and still leave the door open for further negotiations? Your conversation might go something like this:

YOU: Unfortunately, it doesn't look like this is going to work.

NEGOTIATOR: What do you mean?

YOU: I am really excited about the opportunity, but there is no way I could take it without getting a significant amount of equity. I would be giving up too much. I really appreciate your effort to put this deal together. It's too bad the company couldn't figure out a way to give me more stock.

NEGOTIATOR: I don't know if I can do anything, but let me talk to my boss again.

One twist to this approach is to let the negotiator know that you intend to drop a note to the hiring manager (assuming that manager is not the one negotiating with you) to say what a good job the negotiator did and how sorry you are that you could not accept the offer because of whatever it was that the company could not agree to. The possibility that you might write such a letter is likely to cause a negotiator who has room to improve an offer a great deal of discomfort. A person in that position might improve the offer simply to avoid being second-guessed as to why those improvements weren't made in the first place.

When you employ a walking-away strategy, you need to be prepared for the fact that the employer may not make you another offer. As long as you are willing to pass up the job, however, and you don't close the door to further discussions, you have accomplished your goal. You have strengthened your bargaining position by making it clear that you won't accept the job unless the employer can satisfy your needs. More important, you have not forced the employer into a corner by presenting an ultimatum. You have, regretfully, had to withdraw your candidacy, and you have done so in a way that indicates your motive has nothing to do with the employer, the job, or the negotiator. Taking that approach provides the opportunity to solve whatever problems are standing in the way of your accepting the position.

SUMMARY OF NEGOTIATING POINTS

- ▶ Be prepared psychologically to walk away from an offer.
- ▶ Try to have more than one job possibility in the works.
- ▶ Do not accept a position unless it meets your minimum criteria.
- ▶ Never frame requests as ultimatums.
- ▶ Explain why you are not accepting the offer.
- ▶ Reiterate all the reasons you would have liked to accept the job.
- ▶ Extend your thanks for the negotiator's efforts.
- ▶ Leave the door open to further negotiations.

Job Security

How to Ensure That You Get to Enjoy
the Fruits of Your Efforts

An oral contract is as good as the paper it is written on.

—Anonymous

After she was fired from her job, Janet received her severance package, but her employer refused to pay her the annual bonus she thought she had been guaranteed. She showed me her offer letter, which stated that she was guaranteed a bonus of at least $20,000. It was unclear from the letter how long the guarantee was to last, although Janet clearly understood at the time she was hired that a portion of her bonus was to be guaranteed each year. Unfortunately, the person who hired her and who sent her the letter was no longer there. As a result, the employer chose to interpret the guarantee language as covering only the first year of employment. Even though I thought Janet might prevail in court, we discussed the costs and the risks involved. We also spoke about the difficulties she would encounter finding a new job if potential employers found out she was suing her former employer.

When Janet informed higher-ups at the employer that her attorney thought she was entitled to the bonus, they made it very clear that, if they were sued, they would not do business with her in the future. Because she was considering becoming a consultant, she had to take that threat seriously. Despite her appeals to fairness, her employer refused to concede on this issue. Janet decided not to sue and walked away from the bonus she believed was owed to her.

Getting It in Writing

Because of greater employee mobility today, as well as the large number of mergers, acquisitions, and downsizings, even individuals who are performing well are likely to lose their jobs at some time during their career. When people change jobs, there are frequently mismatches in terms of personality, corporate culture, and job fit. As a result, issues surrounding termination have become more important today than ever before.

It will do you little good to have obtained, through your negotiating efforts, an excellent salary, generous stock options, lots of perks, and the job of your dreams if you can be summarily dismissed without a sufficient severance package. If you fail to satisfactorily negotiate the terms under which you can be terminated, you risk losing everything else you may have achieved.

While you are being recruited, the person seeking to hire you will likely make all sorts of promises and representations concerning job security. However, when you are being terminated, the employer will ordinarily disregard any promises you thought had been made to you, particularly if the person making them is no longer there. Instead, an employer will be guided by its regular severance policy unless you have a written agreement clearly stating that you are entitled to a better severance package.

Even though verbal promises, if you can prove that they were made, are enforceable in a court of law, more often than not it does not make sense to sue your former employer. To protect what you worked so hard to achieve through the negotiating process, the terms of employment should be spelled out in writing. This does not require a 20-page formal contract drafted by your lawyer. It can be a simple confirmation letter signed by a representative of the employer setting forth the basic terms that have been agreed upon. Not only is such a letter legally enforceable but if the terms are clearly set forth, it is also much less likely that a lawsuit will ever be necessary.

Even if you do not get everything you want, whatever you do get you should certainly be able to get in writing. At a minimum, two key issues need to be covered: compensation and termination. For the reasons discussed above, the conditions under which termination can occur and the severance package you will receive if you are terminated are probably most important to have in writing. Other important issues include the job description, the employer's right to transfer you, your reporting relationship, vesting of stock and options, applicable perks and benefits, and what happens in the event of death or disability.

If things go well, you will not need an agreement. Your employer will be happy with you and will want to make sure you are happy. However, if things don't go as planned—if there is a takeover, if you get a new boss, or if there is just not a good fit—then you are going to wish you had spelled out what was agreed to in writing; and as odd as this may sound, so will your employer. In light of the increased likelihood of employment litigation, employers also have an interest in entering into an agreement at the outset of the employment relationship that spells out under what circumstances you can be terminated and what you get in the event that you are.

Initially you need to determine whether the employer routinely provides new hires with employment contracts and, if so, at what levels (see the chapter "Beyond Research: Preparing to Negotiate"). If you happen to be at a level where contracts are routinely offered, then getting an employment contract won't be an issue. In most cases you will not be at that level. If you are not, you will probably want to use a "confirmation letter" rather than seek a formal employment contract. Approached properly, employers will rarely refuse to put in writing what they are offering you.

Even employers that, as a matter of policy, do not offer "employment contracts" usually send new hires "offer letters" setting forth the terms of employment. Those letters, if written correctly, will serve the same purpose as an employment contract and will most likely be enforceable in a court of law. You can send a confirmation letter that will not only serve the same purpose but will also allow you to determine how the agreed-upon terms are described. The difference between a confirmation letter and an offer letter is that the former is written by you and signed by a representative of the employer, whereas the latter is sent to you by the employer.

Once you have determined that you are not going to seek a formal employment contract, how should you go about getting what has been agreed to put in writing? At the conclusion of the negotiations, you can state, "In order to make sure there are no misunderstandings, I will confirm my understanding of what has been agreed upon in a letter." Particularly if you have been using memos and/or e-mails throughout the negotiations, this suggestion will seem routine and will not likely engender any opposition (see Strategy 7). The agreements spelled out in those memos or e-mails can simply be incorporated into the final confirmation letter. At the end of the confirmation letter, you can either request the employer to sign indicating that the letter accurately reflects the terms of the job offer or, alternatively, ask the employer to incorporate those terms into an offer letter.

On occasion, the person you are dealing with might respond to your suggestion of sending a confirmation letter with: "What do you need a letter for? Don't you trust me?" If you are negotiating with your future boss, a reaction of that type is particularly problematic. When that occurs, you need to depersonalize the situation and answer along the following lines: "This has nothing to do with you personally. In fact, if I were certain that you would always be here, I would be perfectly happy just to rely on your word. However, tomorrow you might get hit by a bus or leave the organization. In light of that possibility, I think it would be helpful, to avoid any possible future misunderstandings, if we put down in writing what has been agreed upon."

Termination

You must resolve two basic questions about termination when negotiating the terms of your employment: (1) Under what circumstances can you be terminated? and (2) What will you receive if you are terminated? Many employers have policies that state that they are "employers at will." An "at-will" employer retains the right to fire an employee "for any reason or no reason" without any further obligation. Sometimes employers will specifically include at-will language in their offer letters. More often, if nothing is agreed to about the employer's right to terminate you, the employer will state in its offer letter that you are being hired "subject to all the employer's policies." Even if that is all that is said, you are likely to be an at-will employee unless the offer letter otherwise specifically deals with the issue of termination because the employer probably has a policy saying that all employees, unless specifically agreed otherwise, are at-will employees.

If at all possible, you do not want to agree to be an at-will employee. You want your employer to guarantee your employment for a certain term or else limit its right to terminate you to instances of serious misconduct. Most employment arrangements that are not at will, even those for a specified term, provide that an employee can be terminated "for cause" or "for good cause." In addition, they typically allow for termination "without cause" provided that the employer makes certain specified severance payments and provides agreed-upon benefits. What is typically at stake, therefore, in the determination of whether a discharge is "for cause" is your right to receive severance pay, bonuses, benefits continuation, outplacement, and/or accelerated vesting of your stock or options.

Employers today are insisting that most employees below a certain level be treated as employees at will. If you are being hired by such an employer, instead of trying to limit its right to terminate your employment—a limit that will prove difficult, if not impossible, to obtain—you can achieve the same results by acknowledging that you are an employee at will but getting the employer to agree to severance pay in the event you are terminated without cause. The definition of "cause" is important. As part of that severance package, in addition to a lump-sum severance payment or salary continuation for a specified period, you will want to include payment of current-year bonuses (on a pro rata basis if necessary), benefits continuation, outplacement, and/or accelerated vesting of restricted stock and options.

Strategically, the issue of severance terms should be depersonalized and dealt with as an issue that needs to be covered in the event that the person you are dealing with leaves the organization, the same way you approached the need to have the terms of employment spelled out in writing. If you have a strong bargaining position, you may want to include a definition of "cause," which you will want to define narrowly, spelling out the types of conduct that will constitute cause. Ideally you want "cause" to be defined as "serious misconduct or a willful failure to do the job." Otherwise, as is more typically the case, it is generally best simply to allow that the employer can terminate you "for cause without further obligation" and to allow that in addition, the employer can terminate you "without cause provided that . . ." and then spelling out what you get in the event that termination is not done "for cause."

If you are seeking to get the employer's agreement to include a termination-for-cause provision as part of its offer, it is a good idea to emphasize that you are not seeking to prevent the employer from firing you if it is unhappy with your performance. Rather, you are merely trying to ensure that you are provided a sufficient severance amount to allow you to take care of your family (if you are not married, you can substitute your "aged mother," your "foster child in Guatemala," or yourself) until you find another job. In that context, it is only fair that you be given severance pay unless your termination is for cause.

You may also want to get your employer's agreement to provide you with written notice of any performance problems and a reasonable opportunity to correct them before you can be fired, or at least provide you with written notice of the specific reasons for termination if you are fired. When an employer is required to articulate in writing the reasons for discharge, that requirement, in and of itself, serves as a check against arbitrary terminations. Your employer will think carefully before terminating you for a reason that, once spelled out in writing, may have to be defended in court. Including a provision of that nature makes it much more likely that an employer will simply choose to give you severance pay rather than seek to invoke its right to fire you for cause.

After agreement is reached on when and for what reasons you can be terminated, you need to determine what you will receive if that occurs. The amount of severance pay is usually the first issue that must be resolved. Most severance policies are based on length of service. Ordinarily the longer you work for an employer, the more severance pay you receive. Anywhere from one week per year to one month per year of service is typical. However, since you are most at risk of losing your job in the first year of employment, it is important to seek a minimum amount of severance pay regardless of your length of service. You can expect to get agreement to a minimum severance of from two weeks to one year's salary, depending on the level of your position and the industry you are in.

In addition to the amount of severance pay, the employer may raise other related issues such as whether severance will be paid as salary continuation (most employees want it paid as a lump sum) and whether earnings from other employment will be used to offset the employer's severance obligations (referred to as mitigation). Often employers will set forth the manner in which the severance will be paid only after the amount of severance pay has been agreed upon, stating: "that is how severance is paid." You can preempt this negotiating tactic by including in your initial request a statement that severance will be paid "as a lump sum upon termination." Whether you agree to accept severance pay as salary continuation or to allow earnings from other employment to be used to offset the employer's severance obligations will depend on your bargaining position, the employer's past practices (see Strategy 18), and the total amount of the severance package being offered (see Strategy 10).

Don't forget to ask for continuation of your benefits as well. Although employers are required by law to offer you the option of continuing your *health* benefits *at your expense* (COBRA), you ought to be seeking to continue *all* your benefits *at the employer's expense* as if you remained employed. Medical benefits in particular are expensive. Moreover, once you agree on a severance amount, if you ask, most employers will agree, as part of the severance arrangement, to include continuation of benefits at their expense for the severance period following a termination without cause. Since the severance period is usually determined by the amount of time it should reasonably take someone at your level to find another job, if you encounter resistance to your request, you can persuasively argue that benefits should be continued for an equivalent period of time.

The other major termination issues that you need to concern yourself with are how your bonuses and any unvested stock or options will be treated. In the event that you are terminated without cause, your employer will ordinarily not pay you any bonuses unless the criteria for your receiving them have already been fully achieved. You may, however, be able to get the employer to agree to pay you a prorated portion of your targeted bonus, or the guaranteed portion of that bonus if there is any. With regard to stock or options, employers will sometimes agree to allow vesting on a prorated basis or even allow the stock or options to continue to vest during the severance period. For purposes of negotiating, you have a powerful argument as to why you should receive such benefits. These are benefits that are being offered to entice you to leave your current place of employment, where you are probably receiving similar benefits. All you are asking is that, in the event you are terminated without cause, these benefits be provided to you.

Diminution of Responsibilities and Transfers

Once you have dealt with the issues governing termination, you also need to protect yourself against certain methods that unscrupulous employers use to try to circumvent the protections you have negotiated. Even if the employer you are joining has an excellent reputation, it may be taken over by another company, and in that event, you will be glad you have these protections.

For instance, it is important to make certain that your duties and title are clearly spelled out in your offer letter and that they cannot be changed substantially without your agreement. Although your future employer will want some flexibility to change job responsibilities to meet changing needs, most employers will agree to include language such as the following: "You will be employed as vice president of marketing, with such duties, responsibilities, and authority as are consistent with that position." This type of language in an offer letter will prevent an employer from trying to force you to leave by changing your job responsibilities so that it won't have to fire you and give you severance pay or other termination benefits. Furthermore, employees who leave "of their own accord" are prevented from arguing that agreements not to compete should not be enforced because they were terminated without cause.

If your job duties are not spelled out in the confirmation letter, an employer could make your job sufficiently disagreeable or redefine it in a way that might hurt your marketability, in an effort to get you to resign.

Although an employer is generally required to act in good faith, it is also free, in the absence of an agreement to the contrary, to change an employee's job duties. Therefore, if you have not protected yourself and the employer is not too blatant in its efforts to force you out, you may have to suffer those new responsibilities or forfeit your severance package.

You may also want to spell out your reporting relationship. Even though you have defined your job duties, employers can effectively diminish your status by making you report to someone at your level or, depending on how those duties are defined, by removing your operating responsibilities and assigning you to "special projects." If you fail to protect against this, you leave yourself open to efforts intended to force you to resign and thereby deprive you of severance benefits.

Similarly, you need to protect against being transferred without your consent. For example, you might seek inclusion of a statement in your offer letter that you "will be based in New York City or within a reasonable commute from there (not to exceed 30 miles), unless you agree otherwise." This gives the employer reasonable flexibility to move its offices but at the same time prevents it from forcing you to move in order to keep your job. It also protects you against an employer using the threat of a transfer to force you to resign without having to give you severance pay and other termination benefits. Unless you are amenable to the idea of heading the employer's new Anchorage, Alaska, facility, you will be glad that you restricted its ability to transfer you without your consent. As a practical matter, you cannot prevent an employer from transferring your job responsibilities to another location for legitimate business reasons. You can, however, ensure that you have the option of moving to that new location or receiving the severance pay and other termination benefits that were agreed upon if you elect not to move.

Death or Disability

You also need to cover what happens in the event of your death or disability. Many employers offer their employees the opportunity to purchase long-term disability insurance, usually with the employees paying the premiums. Most long-term disability plans, however, require that disabled employees be out of work for a specified time period, ordinarily six months, before they become eligible to receive disability benefits. Therefore, you will want to get your prospective employer to agree to continue to pay your salary in the event you are unable to work because of a disability until you are eligible to begin receiving long-term disability benefits.

Typically an employer will not agree to pay you severance benefits in the event of your death or a termination due to disability because presumably that has been covered through the life and long-term disability insurance provided by the employer. You still, however, need to deal with the issue of bonuses and the vesting of stock and options in the event of termination due to death or disability. You can seek the full value of any bonuses that you would have earned during the final year of your employment and the vesting of all unvested stock or options in the event of your death or disability termination. An employer, however, is more likely to agree to provide those benefits on a prorated basis. Carefully review the applicable option and bonus plans before spending time and effort, and negotiating capital, on these issues. Ordinarily stock and stock option plans, but not bonus plans, deal with what happens in the event of death or disability, and you are unlikely to get the employer to change those provisions. You may also seek to have your employer continue providing benefits to your surviving dependents for a period of time after your death.

Agreements Not to Compete

Employers today often ask their employees to sign agreements not to compete. These agreements generally provide that, during the employee's tenure with the employer and for one or two years after termination, the employee will not go to work for a competitor. Although there are limits to the enforceability of these agreements, in most states they are enforceable as long as they are reasonable. Agreements not to compete need to be entered into cautiously because they can keep you from getting a job in the industry that you know best. Before you accept an offer of employment, ask if you will have to sign an agreement not to compete and, if so, request to see it.

Many employees do not worry about agreements not to compete because they believe either that it won't be enforceable or that the employer won't choose to enforce it. Notwithstanding that possibility, you should never sign anything that you would not want to be bound by on the hopes that it won't be enforced. Even if an agreement not to compete is unenforceable, another employer that might otherwise be interested in hiring you will be reluctant to do so if it means that a potential lawsuit comes along with doing so. In addition, some employers condition the payout of severance packages and bonuses or the vesting of stock and options on complying with noncompete agreements as a means of enforcing them without the necessity of going to court. An employee's violation of the noncompete agreement relieves the employer of having to pay the agreed-upon severance amounts and/or bonuses. Supplemental pensions are also sometimes conditioned on complying with noncompete agreements.

If you have to enter into an agreement not to compete, make sure that it is drawn narrowly. For example, instead of simply agreeing not to go to work for "a competitor," get the employer to define what it considers to be areas of competition. Better still, get your future employer to list the organizations it does not want you to work for when you leave. Limit as much as possible the length of time the agreement will be in force as well as the geographic scope of the agreement.

Another restriction employers often seek is an agreement not to disclose trade secrets or other confidential information you have access to during the course of their employment. In addition, when hiring individuals in creative fields, prospective employers typically seek ownership rights to any inventions or discoveries you make during the term of your employment. Finally, you may be asked to agree not to hire or solicit employees working for the employer after you leave. With any of these types of agreements, it is important to narrowly define what it is you are agreeing to and to protect your freedom of movement to the greatest extent possible. Seek legal advice before you sign any type of agreement that restricts your postemployment activities. Although you may have to agree to some restrictions on those activities, in return you ought to be able to improve your severance package by arguing that those restrictions will make it more difficult to find other employment.

SUMMARY OF KEY POINTS

▶ Have what is agreed upon spelled out in writing and signed by someone on behalf of the employer.

▶ Be certain to deal with the issues of when you can be terminated and what you will receive in the event you are terminated.

▶ Determine if employment contracts are generally given to employees at your level. If not, send a confirmation letter or ask for an offer letter that spells out in writing what has been agreed upon.

▶ If getting what has been agreed upon reduced to writing becomes an issue, depersonalize your reason for wanting a written confirmation of the offer terms.

▶ Protect yourself against the employer attempting to force you to resign in order to avoid giving you the agreed-upon severance package.

▶ If you have to enter into an agreement not to compete, negotiate the terms narrowly.

▶ Don't sign an agreement you would not want to be bound by in the belief that it is not enforceable or is not likely to be enforced.

▶ Seek legal advice when appropriate.

When You're Unemployed

How to Gain Bargaining Leverage Even
If You Think You Have None

*The greatest discovery of my generation is that a human being can
alter his life by altering his attitudes.*

—William James

Frank came to me seeking advice. He had been unemployed for nearly three
months. He didn't have a job offer yet. He was talking to several employers and wanted to be prepared in the event one of them decided to make
him an offer. We talked and got to know each other. Frank was a marketing executive with an impressive background. He had lost his position following a takeover. He was looking for a marketing position at a place where
he could possibly one day become president.

Frank was optimistic that any day he would be getting a job offer. Over
the next few weeks I spoke to Frank periodically to find out how things were
going. Every time we talked, he told me about the employers he was meeting with. Finally, after several months, he got an offer from an employer in
Boston. The offer was a good one. We did our research and developed a
negotiating strategy focused on getting additional equity and a commitment
to being promoted to a bigger job if he did well.

Frank didn't rush the negotiations. While we were negotiating, Frank
continued to meet with other employers. In fact, shortly thereafter he
received a second offer. In the end, we were able to get everything we
wanted from the employer in Boston, and he accepted that job.

Despite the fact that finding a job took longer than he expected, Frank exuded confidence throughout. I know there were times that privately he must have wondered whether he would ever again have a job as good as the one he had just left. Nonetheless, he didn't panic. He never showed doubts—not to me, and certainly not to any prospective employers. As a result, Frank ended up with two very good job offers and was able to negotiate an excellent package.

During my career I have known many people who have had to endure periods of unemployment—some of them were friends, some were clients, and some were people whom I personally had to lay off from their jobs. Being unemployed is always difficult, not only for the person without a job but for his or her family as well. The good news is that all of them found jobs that they liked at least as much as the ones they left. Although being unemployed is unsettling, with the benefit of hindsight and a new job, all of them were glad they had been forced to go through the process. Having grown comfortable in their jobs and with families to support, few would have ever considered leaving on their own to try something different. Being laid off required them to examine who they were and what they wanted to do with the rest of their lives. As a result, most are much happier in their new jobs, and they are excited by the fresh challenges they face daily.

Because of the large number of mergers, acquisitions, and downsizings that have occurred in recent years, being unemployed no longer carries the stigma that it once did. Employers know that good employees lose their jobs through no fault of their own. The ideal candidate is no longer someone who has been with one employer for an entire career. In fact, that is often viewed as a negative by recruiters when they are considering candidates. Today, the successful candidate is one who can handle change well. Individuals who have successfully worked at different organizations and in different industries are often better able to adapt. Employers and recruiters understand that.

In the context of employment negotiations, the only difference between a candidate who is employed and one who is unemployed is often confidence. If you believe in yourself and exhibit that confidence to the world, you will be able to employ all the strategies discussed in this book just as if you were employed. Of course, you still need to prepare thoroughly and be able to recognize when a particular strategy is appropriate. But how you negotiate when you are unemployed is primarily a matter of attitude.

Frank is a good example. Throughout his job search he maintained a positive attitude. He was confident he was going to be able to find a good job. He pursued his job search aggressively, treating it just as he would any other marketing campaign. He even came to me in advance of having received a job offer so that he would be prepared when one came. He continued to display that confidence even though the search took longer than he expected. That attitude explains why Frank has done so well in his career despite the occasional setback. As long as you maintain a positive attitude, you will be able to negotiate from a position of strength. Not only will you be able to negotiate better but you will also find that employers are more interested in hiring you.

Sometimes an employer thinks you will take less money because you are unemployed. If you allow employers to believe that, you not only will get less money but you will also make yourself a less attractive candidate. Convey, by the way you present yourself, that this is not the case. Employers are not looking for candidates who want to work for them because they can't find anything else. They are looking for people who really want the position and who won't leave as soon as something better comes along. As Ted Pilonero, a New York human resources consultant and the president of the Joseph Group, has pointed out: "If people act like they are desperate for a job, most employers will immediately lose interest." Never allow an employer to believe you don't have other options because if you are hired on that basis, you will be taken for granted for the remainder of your career with the organization.

If all else fails, and an employer is unwilling to pay you what you are worth, you can turn down the job offer, leaving the door open for the offer to be improved (see Strategy 25). Obviously you would do so only when other possible strategies have failed and you are not willing to accept the job on the terms being offered. This will be easier to do if you have continued to pursue other opportunities while negotiating. Turning down the offer can even be used to strengthen your bargaining position with other employers. You can strategically let other prospective employers know about the offer and that you turned it down.

It is easy to get discouraged when you are unemployed. How do you stay positive? There are several things you can do. First and foremost, take good care of yourself physically. Exercise regularly. Watch what you eat. Dress well. Buy some new clothes. The better you look and feel, the more confident you will be [see the chapter "Dressing the Part to Enhance Your Ability to Negotiate(and Your Career)"]. You should also get into a routine: exercise; make a certain number of calls each day to people who might be helpful with your job search; meet with those willing to meet with you; send follow-up letters; and plan your next day's activity. The busier you are, the better you will feel.

The best way to strengthen your negotiating position is to have options (see Strategy 13). Human nature is such that if you have two job offers, you will almost always bargain harder because if one deal doesn't work out, you always have the other to fall back on. Simply talking with a number of other employers, even if you don't actually have another offer, will have the same effect. That is why Frank kept meeting with other potential employers even though he was seriously negotiating with a company that he wanted to work for.

Probably the most important thing you can do to remain confident when you are unemployed is to find someone to talk with about what you are doing and how you are feeling. A spouse or significant other can satisfy that role, but it is usually better to find someone who is less personally involved and who understands what you are going through. An outplacement counselor or career coach will serve that purpose nicely. As part of any severance package, it is a good idea to try to get your employer to pay for outplacement. In addition, there are available support groups made up of people who are also unemployed. These groups meet regularly so that their members can help one another with their job searches, share information, and provide moral support. Some are affiliated with outplacement services; others can be found through church or community organizations. Ask people who have recently gone through the process.

There will be times when you are feeling down and things appear hopeless. Just knowing there are other people going through the same things and experiencing the same feelings can help you maintain a positive attitude. Often you will be able to keep things in perspective when you compare yourself with others who are worse off. In addition, every time a member of your support group finds a job, it renews your faith that things eventually will turn out all right. Those people will continue to be helpful to you in your job search as well. They may also be helpful to you later on in your career. Most important, some of them will become your friends.

Whether you are employed or unemployed, with the right attitude you can use the techniques described in this book to negotiate effectively. You will be able to start your new career knowing that you have gotten the best possible deal. From there, if you perform well, you should be able to continue to improve upon it.

SUMMARY OF KEY POINTS

▶ Always maintain a positive attitude.

▶ Demonstrate to the world that you have confidence in yourself and your abilities.

▶ Take pride in your appearance. Exercise regularly and dress well.

▶ Find a disinterested person you can talk to about what you are going through.

▶ Join a support group.

▶ Continue actively conducting your job search until you accept a new position; even if you are negotiating with one employer, always have other potential opportunities in the works.

▶ Remember that many others have gone through what you are going through and ended up better off than they were before.

Gender Differences in
Employment Negotiations

What is the best thing about having a woman boss?
You make more money than she does.

—Howard Stern

Howard Stern's humor notwithstanding, women, on average, still earn only 80 cents for every dollar a man earns, up only a few cents from 10 years ago. While some of that difference can be explained by differences in age, education, years on the job, time out of the workforce, hours worked, and choice of occupations, somewhere between 11 and 40 percent of the difference cannot be accounted for by those factors. Some part of that difference no doubt is still the result of discrimination. However, a significant portion of that disparity results from women either not negotiating or not asking for enough when they discuss compensation. I have been working in human resources for over 20 years, and during that time I have rarely encountered a man who did not negotiate some aspect of an initial offer of employment, whereas I have dealt with many women who simply accepted or occasionally rejected an offer without making any attempt to negotiate.

In my discussions with successful businesswomen, recruiters specializing in the placement of women, and career coaches that have worked extensively with women, the one thing they all agree on is that the dynamics of negotiating are different when women negotiate with men and even when women negotiate with other women than when men negotiate with men. Maxine Hartley, an executive coach with Right Associates who was previously an executive recruiter, summed it up nicely: "Men and women are different and they negotiate differently." Women who appreciate those differences are likely to be more successful.

One female labor negotiator I know has been very effective by being "one of the guys." She is loud. She can drink and swear with the best of them. Although on occasion she uses the fact that she is an attractive woman to her advantage, her negotiating style can be best described as "persistent and tough." She wears her opponents down. Most women, and many men, could not successfully employ this approach to negotiating. She tempers her aggressive style with a sense of humor and makes it work for her not only when she negotiates with unions but when she negotiates with her employer for her own compensation as well.

A good starting point for developing an effective negotiating style is to be yourself. To be successful, you have to be comfortable with the style that you adopt. Women who are successful with an aggressive, "competitive" style are able to do so because it comes naturally to them. They have also learned how to do what they do with grace and style. As Carolyn Wall, former publisher of *Newsweek* put it: "They can do it because they do it with charm. Charm is their secret weapon." Janice Reals Ellig, a partner in the executive search firm of Chaddick and Ellig and the author of *What Every Successful Woman Knows*, suggests that one way for a woman to avoid being seen as too aggressive is "not to keep pushing" when she is facing strong resistance. Instead, Ellig suggests "letting it go for a while and then coming back to it." Veteran broadcaster Jan Hopkins, former anchor of CNN's *Street Sweeps*, likens this approach to what she does when she is interviewing guests on her show who are not being responsive: "You come back to the same issue several different times and in several different ways."

It is important to be authentic because if you are not, people will know it and you will lose credibility. Some women, like my friend, can be successful with a negotiating style similar to the "competitive" style favored by many men. Women, however, should not necessarily mimic the negotiating styles that work for men; rather, they should take advantage of what works best for them. Since a confrontational style usually is not the best approach to take in employment negotiations even for men, women are generally well advised to adopt a more collaborative approach or at least to appear to be doing so (see Strategy 5). At the same time, women need to be firm in their resolve to achieve the objectives they set for themselves.

There is no one right way for women to negotiate. Each of the strategies set forth in this book can be used by women just as effectively as by men. Of course, implementing these strategies requires making adjustments to reflect each individual's personal style. Nevertheless, women frequently make a number of mistakes when they are negotiating their compensation. The purpose of this chapter is to help women avoid some of the most common mistakes.

The most serious mistake that women make is to ask for too little. Although doing so is a problem for some men as well, women almost uniformly underestimate their own worth (see Strategy 2). If men generally should ask for 10 percent more than they think they are worth, women should ask for 25 percent more.

Vivian Eyre, a New York career consultant who is president of Partners for Women's Growth, Inc., attributes the reason that women ask for too little to women visualizing the negotiation in their head beforehand and anticipating a negative reaction. As a result, they ask for too little or fail to ask for anything at all.

Vivian also highlights another phenomenon that holds back many women when they negotiate. In her view women can be too "rules oriented." She illustrates this problem with the following story about one of her clients. Suzanne had been hired by a publishing company to head a new publishing unit. When she took the job, she agreed to accept a higher base salary and a lower bonus because the employer's compensation policy provided for a greater portion of compensation to be in base salary and less in bonus than her prior employer.

Through her talent and hard work Suzanne was able to increase revenues in her first year on the job by more than 30 percent. She was recognized for her accomplishments by her peers and her boss. However, the closer it got to the time when bonuses were to be awarded, the more dissatisfied she became. When Suzanne first consulted Vivian, she was ready to leave her job because, in her view, the bonus amount she would receive was grossly unfair considering what she had accomplished over the past year. Vivian suggested that Suzanne explain to her boss how she felt and, in light of her performance, ask him to adjust the amount of the bonus. Suzanne responded that she couldn't because of the way the bonus plan was structured. So it took a little coaching to give her the confidence she needed to meet with her boss and negotiate a bigger bonus.

Suzanne was intimidated by what she understood the rules to be. Before talking with Vivian, she had never even seriously considered trying to renegotiate her bonus. Instead, she was ready to leave a job she liked and did very well. Women are socialized as young girls to follow the rules. They are rewarded for respecting authority. They don't have a lot of role models to show them how to get around the rules. As a result, they are more likely than men to be intimidated by the invocation of "company policy." Unfortunately, to succeed in negotiations you sometimes need to figure out ways to get around the rules.

Too often, women also allow their relationships to get in the way of their seeking to be compensated at the level they could otherwise command. Judge Kathleen Roberts, a professional mediator and former United States Magistrate, told me a story that I have heard many times before. She was advising a friend considering leaving government to go back into the private practice of law. Her friend was talking to a partner at a firm where she had previously worked about the possibility of returning to work there. Judge Roberts suggested that she also talk with some other firms. Her friend responded by saying that she would not consider doing that because she felt it would be "disloyal."

This is an example of how women allow relationships to hold them back when they are negotiating compensation. I don't know any man who would not have taken Judge Roberts' advice. The fact that she had worked at the firm previously, knows how the firm operates, and gets along well with the other members of the firm increases her value to them. Yet Judge Roberts' friend, instead of using her relationships to improve her bargaining position, allowed them to hold her back. This woman would certainly have been able to negotiate a higher salary if she had competing offers from other firms. Under the circumstances she could have been very open about the fact that, even though she really wanted to return to her old firm, she felt she owed it to herself to talk to other firms as well. No one at her old firm would have held that against her. They would, however, have offered her more money to make sure she returned to work for them.

From her years of experience as a recruiter placing women in high-level executive positions, Maxine Hartley concludes that "many women have a difficult time being direct when it comes to money, power, and titles. They want these things as much as men but frequently do not claim their right to them when negotiating." By placing too much importance on relationships, women often find it difficult to take firm negotiating stances. They agree in order to be liked, whereas they would get better results by firmly maintaining their position. Men, on the other hand, are more likely to remain focused on their goals. By the same token, this desire to avoid disagreements often results in women finding creative solutions to satisfy everyone's needs (see Strategy 5). Some of the best negotiators I know are women that understand the need to be firm in their resolve to achieve their goals but flexible in how they go about achieving them.

Women also tend to be more sensitive than men to issues of fairness. This can work to their advantage when negotiating compensation with a new employer where perceived fairness plays an important role in the process (see Commandment 6, "Understand the Role That Fairness Plays in the Process"). However, it also can work to their disadvantage because it frequently results in their being too accommodating to the positions taken by the other side during negotiations.

Focusing on fairness is particularly problematic when asking your current employer for more money. Time and again women base their requests for higher salaries on fairness rather than on their worth to the organization. When they seek raises, they justify their request by invoking fairness— the number of years they have been with the employer, the fact that they were the ones that trained their new boss, or how their salary is less than that of others in the organization. An appeal to fairness is less effective when you are negotiating with your current employer than when you are seeking a new job (see the chapter "Negotiating with Your Current Employer: You Don't Get What You Deserve; You Get What You Negotiate"). It puts your superiors on the defensive. You force them to justify their previous actions. If they agreed to give you what you are requesting on the basis of an appeal to fairness, they would be admitting that they had done something wrong. After all, they are the ones who are responsible for the actions that you are claiming are unfair. Instead of talking about fairness when seeking a raise, emphasize your contributions to the organization.

Carol Raphael is the chief executive officer of the Visiting Nurse Service of New York, the largest not-for-profit health-care organization in the United States with almost a billion dollars a year in revenue. Carol readily admitted that she could have gotten a better compensation package when she negotiated her employment contract. She didn't really negotiate. She just asked the board for what she thought was fair, and they agreed to give it to her. Asking for more, even though she could have gotten it, would have been, in her words, "unseemly." On the other hand, when she is negotiating on behalf of the Visiting Nurse Service, she always tries to get the best deal she can for the organization.

Like many women, Carol has a difficult time negotiating for herself. Notwithstanding that reluctance, she doesn't want to feel that she is being taken advantage of. So she would have "no problem" seeking a raise if she felt that she was being paid significantly less than her peers at similar institutions. While I don't advocate pushing to get every last penny you can get when you negotiate, there is nothing wrong with negotiating for yourself.

Dr. Patricia Farrell, a professor of clinical psychology at Walden University, notes: "Women find it much less difficult to negotiate on behalf of others. This places them in the role of caregiver, a role they feel very comfortable in. When it comes to negotiating for themselves, on the other hand, women often feel that they don't deserve what they are asking for." Moreover, because women tend to view things in the context of relationships, they "take things personally. Asking for things for themselves becomes more difficult because if they are turned down, it is seen as a rejection of them." As a result, women tend not to feel comfortable negotiating for themselves. Even women who are excellent negotiators for others often don't negotiate well on their own behalf.

As a parent, I have always tried to teach my daughters that there is nothing wrong with negotiating to get what you want. Recognize that your happiness and the things you want are just as important as the wants and needs of others. You cannot truly make the others around you happy unless you are happy yourself.

Sometimes just recognizing your tendency to put the needs of others ahead of your own is sufficient to cause you to change your behavior. Randy Kahn, a managing director at Citigroup's Salomon Smith Barney who negotiates multi-million-dollar real estate deals for a living, recognizes that when it comes to negotiating for herself, she has a hard time. So when she has to negotiate for something she wants, she keeps that in mind and compensates for it. She is "aware of what she has to do and is conscious of what it takes." She "forces herself to push just as hard or harder when she is negotiating for herself." As a result, Randy has been able to succeed in the very male dominated world of investment banking.

One way Dr. Farrell suggests that women can overcome a reluctance to ask for what they want is to see themselves "as negotiating for someone else." Ask yourself what you would do if you were advocating for someone else. How would you do it? Then do it. Before a woman begins to negotiate on her own behalf, Dr. Farrell advises that she "give herself a little pep talk." Sit down and make a list of all the reasons why you deserve what you are asking for.

You can never go wrong being guided by the maxim that it doesn't hurt to ask (see Strategy 2). Executive coach Maxine Hartley spoke of a friend that had been offered the executive director position at a nonprofit organization in New York City. She wanted the job, but she was unhappy with the salary being offered. Maxine had her put together a list of five things that would make the package more attractive to her. Her friend lived in New Jersey, so first on the list was to get the organization to pay for her commuting costs and parking. The nonprofit also owned an apartment in the city that she wanted to be able to use when she needed to stay over. A signing bonus was then added to the list. Rounding off her list was an early performance review to address the salary issue. Any one or two of these items would have more than offset the low salary she was being offered. She presented her list to the board of directors not as demands or as a threat that otherwise she wouldn't accept the position but as requests that she thought were reasonable in light of the position she was being offered. In the end, the nonprofit agreed to several of her requests and she accepted the job.

Compare the advice Maxine gave to her friend with what Maxine described as her own worst negotiation. She was a young human resources executive being interviewed for a job with an employer in Atlanta. She was flown down for several interviews. She liked the organization. And they wanted to hire her. She spent a lot of time talking with them about compensation. In the end, she didn't go to work for them because of the money. She was looking for a salary of at least $50,000 a year. Ultimately, they could offer her only $40,000. When they made her the offer, she didn't negotiate. She just turned down the offer. Today, she would have tried to bridge the gap by asking for any number of things such as a signing bonus or a raise once she achieved certain agreed-upon objectives. When she was asked why she didn't do that at the time, she replied, "It just never occurred to me to negotiate."

Failing to negotiate is not only a problem for young women seeking their first job. Cathy Black, president of Hearst Magazines, noted that even experienced businesswomen sometimes don't ask for commensurate compensation when they are given additional responsibilities or are promoted into a bigger job. When asked why, she responded by quoting something Gloria Steinem told her when they worked together at Ms. Magazine in the seventies: "Women have a terminal case of gratitude." They tend to be flattered by the offer. They are afraid to do anything that might jeopardize it. Often they don't even consider the possibility of asking for more. When they are really interested in a job, they usually accept it with little, if any, negotiating. While it is normal to appreciate being afforded an opportunity, you have a right to expect to be compensated appropriately. But you will usually still have to ask. If you don't, you probably won't be paid what you deserve.

Employers expect all but entry-level hires (and in recent years even those sometimes) to negotiate. Therefore, they almost never start with their best offer. If you do not negotiate, you will probably be accepting less than the employer was prepared to pay. As discussed earlier, this is not only a mistake but it is one that is compounded throughout the remainder of your career. Every raise and every bonus you receive will be smaller because they will normally be calculated as a percentage of your artificially low base salary. Even the number of stock options you are awarded will normally be based on your salary.

Often women think that they will accept a job, prove themselves, and then ask for a raise. Adopting this approach may result from not believing that you are in a position to negotiate, being afraid that if you ask for more you might lose the job offer, being uncomfortable negotiating, or simply from believing that it is the most effective approach. Whatever the reason, in most instances you will be wrong. Although it probably sometimes happens, I have never seen anyone lose a job offer because of what he or she asked for, only how he or she asked for it (see Strategy 9). Ordinarily once you prove yourself in a job, you will be able to get even more money, over and above what you negotiated at the time you were hired. By not negotiating in the first instance, you are not only forgoing the money you could have gotten at that time but also reducing the amount of the raise you will get after you prove yourself. Keep in mind that if you could have initially negotiated a salary that was $5,000 higher than the one you accepted without negotiating, when you get that 10 percent raise, it may not even make up for the $5,000 you could have gotten initially and that 10 percent will be $500 less than it would have been if you had negotiated in the first place.

Moreover, your employer may think less of you if you don't negotiate. The company may even become concerned that you will not be able to negotiate effectively with vendors and customers. When Davia Temin was offered the position of head of strategic marketing at General Electric Capital, she had very little experience negotiating compensation. While she had been extremely successful in her career and had negotiated lots of business deals, she really had never negotiated her own compensation. In the past when she was offered a new position, she saw it as a choice. If she liked the offer, she accepted it. If not, she turned it down.

This position at General Electric Capital, though, was at a whole different level. She would be on the management committee of one of the largest companies in the industry. She realized there were a lot of things that she could ask for and she really didn't know where to begin. So she sought advice from a friend who wrote a career column. He advised her to ask for more money, a signing bonus, stock options, and a contract. A part of her was afraid that the people she was dealing with "would be mad" at her for negotiating and they wouldn't "like" her. But she took her friend's advice. To her surprise, their reaction was just the exact opposite of what she had anticipated. They expected her to negotiate. The company's executives had all negotiated when they were hired. Further, they wanted to know that Davia was an effective negotiator because she would have to negotiate on their behalf once she was in the job. Davia not only got what she asked for but she also earned their respect in the process.

As discussed previously, the single most important factor in an employer's decision as to how much to offer a job candidate normally is the candidate's current salary (see Strategy 1). For women who are likely to be earning less than their male counterparts, disclosing details about current compensation is likely to have an even more negative impact on their salary than for men. If you have to provide information on your current salary, take pains to show that you understand that your salary is well below the market rate and that it is one of the reasons you are looking for another job. However, rather than having to justify why your current salary is not relevant, you are far better served by disclosing to a prospective employer as little information as possible about what you are currently earning. That way the company will have to base its offer on what it thinks the market is for someone with your skills and experience, not on your current salary.

In the end, regardless of whether you are negotiating with your current employer or with a prospective employer, the only way to be certain that you get what you deserve is to know your market worth and to be willing to walk away if you are not able to negotiate a compensation package that fairly reflects that market value. It is easier to do that if you either have another job offer or, at least, are in conversations with other potential employers. Even if you anticipate getting a good offer from an employer that you like, continue talking with other potential employers. Knowing you have other job opportunities will make you more confident and enable you to negotiate better. Moreover, if you get another job offer, you can use it as leverage to improve a pending offer (see Strategy 13). At the very least, having another offer will render your current salary irrelevant. If your current salary is well below the market rate, that could be a major factor in getting the higher salary you deserve.

SUMMARY OF KEY POINTS

▶ There is no one right way for women to negotiate.

▶ Be yourself and develop your own negotiating style.

▶ Don't be afraid to ask for more than you think you can get.

▶ Negotiate for yourself as if you were negotiating for someone else.

▶ Don't feel encumbered by what you consider to be the rules; sometimes you need to find a way to get around the rules.

▶ Avoid appeals to fairness when you are dealing with your current employer.

Negotiating When You Are Seeking Your First Job

Don't waste your time learning the "tricks of the trade."
Instead learn the trade.

—H. JACKSON BROWN, JR.

When I graduated from Harvard Law School, I had several job offers. One of the offers I was considering was from a very prestigious New York law firm for a lot of money, with the potential for even more money in terms of a year-end bonus. I ended up, though, accepting an offer from a smaller but well-regarded firm in Seattle for a great deal less money, even taking into account the lower cost of living there. I was inclined to go to work for the smaller firm because I felt I would get better experience, more quickly, there. What made up my mind was when I sought to negotiate about my initial assignment.

The New York firm was handling a massive antitrust case. While I wanted to be a litigator, I didn't want to spend my first few years working on a single case primarily reviewing documents. So I asked if there was any way the firm could guarantee that I would not end up working exclusively on that one case. The law firm said it would try to accommodate my interests, but it couldn't promise that I wouldn't end up assigned to that case. In contrast, the Seattle firm had one partner who was not only a well-known trial lawyer but also had a reputation for caring about training the associates assigned to him. So I asked if I could spend my first year at the firm working for him. The firm agreed and I accepted the offer. What I learned from that partner not only about law but about leadership, negotiating, and dealing with people, has proved invaluable in every aspect of my varied career since then.

Negotiating for your first job after you graduate should not be focused principally on money. In the first place, even the very best candidates are not all that different from other recent graduates. Therefore, most employers pay all their new hires in any given job at a particular location the same starting salary. Even when there is no set salary structure for recent graduates, there is not as much flexibility in negotiating salary. When it comes to negotiating salary, new graduates simply don't have that much bargaining power. Moreover, money is not the most important thing you can negotiate in your first job. That does not, however, mean you don't have any room to negotiate about money or that you shouldn't do so if the salary being offered is not competitive.

Training and development, on the other hand, are the most critical aspects of your first job because what you learn on that job forms the foundation upon which your career is built. The skills you learn and the experience you gain are what makes you valuable to future employers and allows you to negotiate for more money. Whom you work for and with, the types of projects you work on, the training and development opportunities you receive, the exposure you have to different people within the organization, and the availability of tuition reimbursement for graduate study are among the items that should be high on your priority list when it comes to your first job. And they are generally negotiable. All you usually have to do to get what you want when it comes to training and development opportunities is to ask (see Strategy 14).

The most important aspect of negotiating about your first job is to ask the right questions and to pick the right employer. I don't mean that you have to find a place of employment where you will be able to spend the rest of your career happily ever after. "Happily ever after" is normally reserved for fairy tales. You will probably have many jobs during your career, and you will likely have several different careers during your life as well. Once you actually start a job, you may decide that what you thought you wanted to do isn't really what you wanted after all. It may even take you several jobs before you find the right career for you. Each of the jobs you have along the way will be the right job if you are learning and developing expertise and honing your people skills.

To the extent that you have choices as to who your boss will be, that is often the most important factor in the experience you will gain in your first job. Your prospective boss's record for having his or her employees promoted to good positions both inside and outside the organization is a key indicator of how good that person is at developing people. Sometimes you can negotiate about who your boss will be, as I did in my first job. More often than not, getting the right boss comes not from negotiating but from selecting the right employer.

Here are a few tips that will help you make the most of that first job. Heeding this advice will allow you to build a solid career foundation that will facilitate your negotiating for more money, better benefits, and greater job security in every subsequent job you have during your career:

- Constantly seek out learning opportunities. Volunteer for assignments in which you will learn new skills. Take advantage of any training opportunities your organization offers. Take courses at local universities and online. Consider pursuing an advanced degree at night.

- Take responsibility for your own career. Often recent graduates find that the job they accepted isn't exactly the job they thought they were going into so they leave and look for another job. A better response might be to seek out additional responsibilities in your areas of interest and where you can add value. In that way you can create the job you want. Move on when there is no further opportunity to learn new skills or gain valuable experience.

- It is not enough just to keep your boss happy; you need to find the time to build relationships with others throughout the organization. Your future success requires the help and support of many individuals. Begin to build that network early.

- Technology is no substitute for spending time with people. Technology plays a critical role in today's workplace, and recent graduates are generally very comfortable using it. Technology doesn't, however, take the place of face-to-face interaction with others in the organization. Learn to become comfortable speaking and contributing at meetings. Management makes judgments about leadership potential based on how you present yourself. If you need a keyboard to communicate effectively, it will end up holding your career back.

- Develop interests and friends outside of work. In addition to building and nurturing a network within your organization, seek out and maintain a diverse set of friends outside of work. You never know where the next great opportunity will present itself or what information will prove critical to your future success.

- Help people even when there is nothing immediately in it for you. That way they will be more likely to think of you when opportunities arise in the future without your even having to ask them.

Bear in mind that negotiating on your first job doesn't stop once you have accepted the position. It is a continuous process. When you become aware of opportunities to gain valuable experience, seek to take advantage of them. When the employer runs training programs that will advance your career, ask to attend. When assignments come along that offer you the chance to learn new skills or gain exposure to people in the organization, volunteer for them. If you are willing to take on those assignments in addition to your other work, no one is likely to say no to you. Negotiate a development plan with your boss that provides for specific training opportunities when you get your first performance review.

Be proactive about your career, and gain the skills and experience that will propel it forward. Employers look for individuals who are adaptable, and they frequently hire and promote people not because they can do every aspect of a new job but rather because they believe that they can learn whatever they need to in order to do the job. Keeping up with trends in your field and continuously learning new skills will not only keep you marketable but will also make it easier for you to negotiate as you seek to advance your career.

SUMMARY OF KEY POINTS

▶ Training and development are the most critical aspects of your first job.
▶ Choose your employer based on what training and experience you will gain there.
▶ Make sure your boss has a good reputation for developing subordinates.
▶ Seek to influence the choice of whom you work for and with, the types of projects you work on, and the opportunities to gain exposure to key people within the organization.
▶ Ask lots of questions.
▶ Don't be afraid to ask for what you want.
▶ Consciously begin to build a network both inside and outside the organization.
▶ Continue to negotiate about training and development opportunities after you begin the job.

Negotiating with Your Current Employer

You Don't Get What You Deserve; You Get What You Negotiate

Regardless of what company you work for, never forget the most important product you're selling is yourself.

—H. Jackson Brown, Jr.

What do you have to do to get the raise you deserve? Start by understanding what will motivate your boss to want to give it to you. It could be appreciation for a job well done. But if that were the case, you would have probably already received a raise. More likely it will be something that your boss thinks you can do for him or her in the future and a desire to motivate you to do it. Alternatively it may be fear that if you don't get a raise, you will leave and your boss will have to find someone else to do whatever it is you do that is important to him or her.

Many of the strategies discussed in this book apply, or can be adapted, to negotiating with your current employer provided that you take into account the different dynamics involved. Unfortunately, most organizations tend to take their employees for granted. This is particularly true when the overall economy is weak. That is one reason employees who stay with the same employer for a long time tend to fall behind their more mobile peers in terms of compensation. By the same token, after being with the same employer for some period of time, employees get comfortable. They tend not to push as hard to improve their compensation as they do when they are changing jobs. Most significant increases in salary, moreover, when you are already with an organization result either from an increase in responsibilities, often in connection with a promotion, or from concerns that you might leave. Therefore, any strategy you use with your current employer should include an effort to gain more responsibility or make yourself so invaluable that the possibility of your leaving would cause immediate concern.

Doing a Good Job

The best way to improve your negotiating position with your current employer is to do an outstanding job. Hard work and good results matter. However, they are not enough by themselves. In addition, you need to convince your boss that you are important to the organization and would be difficult to replace. The way to do that is to make your boss look good.

We all tend to be motivated by our own self-interest. Your boss is probably no exception. Make your boss's priorities your priorities. Don't ignore the other things you do that are important to the success of the organization, but make sure that you give priority to the projects your boss considers most important. If your boss needs something, deliver it promptly and make sure it is correct. You want to be viewed as someone who can be counted on when your boss needs something important done. Athletes refer to this type of individual as the "go-to-guy or gal"—the person you want to get the ball to in the final seconds of the game when you need to score. Being that person for your boss will distinguish you from your coworkers. If you do that, your boss will work very hard to make sure you are happy with your compensation.

It is also a good idea to share the credit for your successes with your boss. (In addition, always share credit with the people who work with you and for you and with those who have helped you achieve those successes. If you don't, your successes will no doubt be fewer because those people will not continue to help you in the future.) The better you make your boss look to his or her superiors and peers, the more he or she will fight for you when it comes time to determine salary increases.

Attitude is also important. You are more likely to get raises and promotions if you are enthusiastic and have a can-do attitude (see Strategy 9).

Understanding How to Ask for a Raise

When seeking a raise, you need to find a reason for asking that will resonate with your boss. "I have not had a raise in a long time" is not a sufficient reason to ask for one. Neither is "My landlord just raised my rent." On the other hand, "I just completed my MBA," "I am your top producer," "I took on additional responsibilities when Sally left and have handled them without a problem," or "I have a job offer from a competitor" are all reasons that would justify your receiving an increase.

If you can't find a reason to justify your request, create one. For instance, you could offer to take on additional work if you are given a raise. Uyen Nguyen, a traffic assistant at KSTP-TV, describes how, in a prior job, he once received a $10,000 raise, as did others in his department, by proposing to his manager that they change the way their work was being done. He and his coworkers took on more work and responsibility. As a result, not only did his work become more satisfying but getting "a big raise wasn't bad either."

According to Ron McMillan, coauthor of *Crucial Conversations: Tools for Talking When Stakes Are High*, some people mistakenly treat seeking a raise as "asking for a favor" rather than as "conducting a business negotiation." In order to be successful, your request should be based on its merits. If you don't deserve a raise, you shouldn't ask for one. Show how you have gone above and beyond what was expected of you in terms of results or how you have "added value" by taking on additional responsibilities. You also need to determine what people doing similar work are earning elsewhere, information readily available on the Internet [see the chapter "Everything You Need to Know about Using the Internet (and Other Sources of Information) to Help You Negotiate"].

Regularly Communicating Your Accomplishments

Make sure your boss and other key people in the organization know what you are accomplishing. When you are interviewing with a new employer, you are always selling yourself. You need to do the same thing with your present employer—not just at review time but all year long. Without appearing to be self-promoting, make sure key people throughout the organization, especially your boss, know about your successes. Although we all assume that our bosses know what we are doing, most do not fully appreciate the accomplishments of their employees because they simply don't know what they've done or perhaps they even think someone else did it. If you want a raise, you have to make sure that your boss recognizes the contributions you have made to his or her success—not in a boastful way but in a factual manner.

It is essential to communicate your successes but to do it strategically. Keep your boss abreast of your achievements but in a way that does not appear to be bragging. When you are talking to your boss about other matters, casually mention your most recent accomplishments. Executive coaches teach their clients to work on developing a relationship with their boss that allows them just to call up or drop by and matter-of-factly deliver the news whenever something good happens. Linda Seale, an executive coach and the former head of human resources at MTV, describes this as "practicing being casual." Executives who are good at their jobs and master this technique can rise meteorically.

You should also send copies of relevant memos and e-mails to people who have an interest in projects you are working on. Take the opportunity to discuss what you are doing with employees in other areas that might be affected by your work, particularly if they are at higher levels than you. Similarly you should show an interest in what others are working on, offering assistance where appropriate. Seek out high-visibility projects where you can showcase your talents. Remember, if others in the organization speak highly of you and want to work with you, your value will soar in the eyes of your boss and others in positions to influence your compensation.

Build a case all year long for increasing your salary. Don't start thinking about it shortly before your annual performance review. By then it is too late. Decisions on salary increases have already been made. Keep an ongoing record of the things you are doing and your accomplishments throughout the year. Two to three months before your annual review, find a way to provide your boss with a summary of what you have accomplished over the past year. That is sufficient time prior to your review for the information to be able to have an impact on it, but not so proximate that it will appear that you are trying directly to affect the outcome.

Taking Timing into Consideration

By properly timing your request for more money, you maximize the likelihood that you will get it (see Strategy 11). In many organizations, raises and bonuses are given out once a year in conjunction with annual performance reviews. In smaller companies raises tend to be given out on an ad hoc basis. If salary increases occur at a set time each year, you need to keep that in mind; but you need not wait for your annual review before asking for a raise. Seeking a raise outside the review cycle can result on occasion in your getting two increases in a given year. You are always free to sit down with your boss to discuss compensation. If you need an excuse to do so, create one (see Strategy 13).

To the extent that you can control the timing of various projects you are working on, time the completion of high-visibility projects to coincide with your annual review. Most people have very short memories when it comes to the successes of others. Regardless of when it occurs, after you have achieved a major success is a good time to approach your boss to ask for additional responsibilities and/or more money (see Strategy 22). Particularly if your work has had a significant impact on the employer's bottom line, you may be in a position to seek a raise outside the normal review cycle. Even if you aren't given a raise at that time, you will no doubt be told that what you have accomplished will be taken into account at review time. You will be able to remind your boss of that promise prior to your next review.

If you have the choice between asking for more money or asking for additional responsibilities, it is usually best to seek the latter. Your request will be better received, and a salary increase will likely follow once you are given added responsibility. Another good time to ask for a raise is when you are in the middle of working on an important project that would suffer if you left the organization.

Taking on Additional Responsibilities and Learning New Skills

If you want to be paid more, you generally will have to do more. The mastering of new skills or the assumption of added job responsibilities can be used to justify a request for an increase in salary. Take every opportunity to learn new skills that are needed by the organization. Let people know that you have those skills and put them to use. If your employer does not give you a raise, you will be able to take those new skills and additional experience to another employer that will.

Presented properly though, your boss should appreciate that the new skills or additional work you are doing will redound to his or her credit. If your boss can achieve greater productivity through your efforts without hiring additional staff, he or she can champion a salary increase for you while still saving the organization money. This strategy works particularly well when times are tough. Be creative in suggesting additional responsibilities for yourself. When people leave the organization, consider ways that the important aspects of their work could be accomplished, in part by you or your team, without having to replace them.

Equally important, recognize when opportunities arise to take on more responsibility, and take advantage of them. I am reminded of one executive who did that with great success. Judith was the executive vice president in charge of finance for a restaurant chain. When the president of the chain abruptly resigned, she offered to take responsibility for several other departments. Although the position did not remain open long enough for her to establish herself as a contender for the president's job, when a new president was appointed, she continued to supervise two of the departments that had temporarily reported to her. As a result, she was given a significant salary increase and awarded a substantial number of additional stock options.

If you take on added responsibilities or learn new skills, use the opportunity to make a case for being promoted (see Strategy 4). Doing so creates a no-lose situation for you. If your case is strong enough, you are likely to get the promotion you are seeking. With the promotion will come a salary increase. If you are a valued employee but a promotion is not forthcoming, you are still likely to get a raise to assuage your feelings and to keep you from leaving. Moreover, you can always revisit the issue of a promotion at a later date. Even if you believe that a promotion is not possible at this particular time, making the case for one will increase the probability of your getting a salary increase and will pave the way for a possible promotion at a later time (see Strategy 15). That, of course, is your primary goal.

Even if accepting additional responsibilities does not immediately lead to a raise or a promotion, once you have demonstrated that you can do the job, you can ask for a raise or a promotion. Jerri DeVard, most recently senior vice president of brand management and marketing at Verizon Communications, described how she used that approach to get a promotion. She was the vice president for marketing at Pillsbury. At the time sales and marketing were separate departments. For business reasons it made sense to have sales and marketing together in one department. So she systematically went about trying to demonstrate that it would be more effective to combine the departments. She began to work more closely with the sales department, and she had her staff do so as well. By the time she actually went to her boss to suggest that the two departments be merged into one, there was little disagreement because the departments were already working so closely together. As a result she was promoted to vice president of sales and marketing to head the combined department, with a substantial increase in salary.

Being Aware of Your Market Value

Always be aware of your market value. Test the waters in the job market periodically, even if you are happy where you are. Stay visible in your industry. Play an active role in trade and professional associations. Go out of your way to meet and get to know executive recruiters, particularly when you are not looking for a job. Always return their phone calls. If you are not interested in a search they are handling, help them identify other potential candidates. That way they will be sure to call you the next time they have a search in which you might have an interest.

Constantly market yourself, both inside and outside your organization. Talk to any employer that shows an interest in you provided that you can do so discretely without your current employer finding out. Determine how marketable you are and what you could earn elsewhere. Then use that information to increase your compensation (see Strategy 13). If you have a realistic understanding of how marketable you are and the salary you can command elsewhere, you will be confident in your arguments when you are seeking a salary increase.

You should also try to determine what your current employer is paying new hires (see the chapter "Beyond Research: Preparing to Negotiate"). If you become aware that the organization is hiring at your level, comb the job boards on which it normally posts openings to see if salary information is provided. Periodically checking job postings in your industry is an excellent way to determine the current market value of your position.

The fact that an employer has to pay higher salaries to recruit from the outside can be used to demonstrate that your salary has gotten out of line with the market. You can use that information along with other compensation data to show that your salary is no longer competitive [see the chapter "Everything You Need to Know about Using the Internet (and Other Sources of Information) to Help You Negotiate"].

As previously discussed, comparing your salary to those of other employees working with you generally is not a very effective approach. Since those salaries were set by the employer, attacking their fairness will be viewed as an attack on the organization. By raising the issue in that way, you may actually reduce the likelihood that your salary will be adjusted because the employer will feel it needs to justify its earlier salary decisions (see the chapter "Gender Differences in Employment Negotiations").

Letting Your Boss Know You Are Interested in Being Promoted and Asking for Help

The easiest way to increase your salary significantly is to get promoted. Since the person selected for a promotion is usually the one who wants it the most, it is important to let your boss know that you want to be considered for promotion. By seeking your boss's advice as to what you need to do to be promoted, your boss becomes an ally in the process. If you follow the advice you receive and keep your boss informed of your efforts, when a promotional opportunity becomes available, you can usually count on your boss's support.

Peter Handal, chairman and CEO of Dale Carnegie Training, suggests that one way to get a promotion is to identify an individual that is being groomed for one and indicate that you would be interested in his or her job when he or she is in fact promoted. This approach can prove very effective and may even hasten the other person's promotion because often what is holding it up is the lack of a successor to fill that person's current position.

Be honest with yourself about the positions you seek to be promoted into. It does you little good to be promoted into a position that you won't be successful in. Just because it is a good job doesn't mean it is a good job for you.

If you want a raise, you would do well to heed the following advice offered by Ron McMillan: "Use the right words, couching your request as a good business decision rather than a favor. Demonstrate why you deserve a raise, remaining factual but explaining how you determined that a higher salary is warranted. If your boss says no, ask your boss to explain his or her point of view. If possible provide the boss with additional information or ask what you have to do going forward in order for the boss to reconsider." The easiest way to get a raise is to deserve one and to ask for it in the right way.

Using Another Job Offer to Get a Raise

Sometimes you need to have another job offer in order to get a substantial increase in salary. Another job offer forces the employer to recognize that you are undervalued in terms of what you could earn elsewhere. That usually results in a salary adjustment. However, if you use another offer as leverage to get a raise or a promotion, you have to be willing to leave if your employer does not respond with a counteroffer. You may even be asked to leave immediately once you inform your employer that you are considering another offer. That risk can be reduced if you approach the subject properly.

No matter what you say, implicit when you use another offer as leverage is the threat that you might leave. It is generally best, though, not to actually threaten to leave if you don't get the salary increase or promotion you are seeking. Most people do not respond well to threats. Instead, let your boss know that you have received another offer but that you do not intend to accept it. That way you avoid the perception that you are presenting your employer with an ultimatum. You can follow this up with a discussion as to why you even considered the offer and enlist your boss's help in bringing your compensation up to the market rate as evidenced by the offer. That way you reaffirm your loyalty while at the same time making your boss an ally in seeking to rectify the situation.

The same basic concepts apply whether you are asking for a raise, seeking a promotion, or negotiating with a prospective new employer. Know your worth, ask for what you want, and be willing to walk away if you don't get it. The primary difference is that it may take more time and be more difficult to get your salary increased significantly by your current employer. The longer you have been in the same position and the further your compensation is below the market rate, the harder it will be. Getting your salary increased to the appropriate level may have to be accomplished over time, and it may require several steps.

Sometimes the only way you are going to get a raise or be promoted is to indicate that you are planning to leave. David Gammel, president of High Context Consulting, once got a promotion because he went to his CEO and told him that he had decided to leave. He thanked him for all the opportunities he had been given at the company, and he let the CEO know that he was planning to move to Europe in a few months. When the CEO asked what would keep him around, he said he'd stick around if he was put in charge of international. A few days later his boss came by and said she didn't know what he had said to the CEO but he was now in charge of international issues for the organization. Although normally you would not go over your boss's head to seek a promotion unless you were seeking to be promoted to a position at his or her level, when you are resigning there is little harm in expressing your appreciation to higher-ups as long as you only say positive things about your boss and the organization as whole. This is not a time to share even truthful criticisms because you may need these relations going forward or may even end up returning in the future.

Telling your boss that you plan to leave unless you are promoted is an extremely risky strategy, even if you do so in a manner that is not threatening. There are times, however, when you have no other option. In that case, though, you had better have another job lined up and be prepared to take it because there is an equally good chance that rather than be promoted, you will be shown the door. Although sometimes the only way to get a substantial salary increase is to take a job with a new employer, your willingness and ability to leave will allow you to negotiate more confidently with your current employer and make it less likely that you will, in fact, have to do so.

Summary of Key Points

▶ Recognize that the dynamics of an ongoing employment relationship are different from those of negotiating with a new employer.

▶ Continuously market yourself both inside and outside your organization.

▶ Support your boss's priorities.

▶ Make your boss look good.

▶ Share credit for your successes.

▶ Communicate your successes to your boss and others on a regular basis.

▶ Several months before your annual review, find a way to outline for your boss what you have accomplished during the past year.

▶ Learn new skills that are needed by the organization.

▶ Seek out additional responsibilities.

▶ Understand how to ask for a raise or promotion.

▶ Be aware of your market value.

▶ If your current employer fails to recognize your true market value despite your best efforts, explore the possibility of changing employers.

Index

About the Author

Lee E. Miller is the cofounder of YourCareerDoctors.com and the managing director of NegotiationPlus.com. He also writes a career column for the *New Jersey Star Ledger*, the largest newspaper in New Jersey. A Harvard Law School graduate, he advises on careers, compensation, and negotiating. He is an adjunct professor of management at Seton Hall University, where he teaches MBA courses in influencing and negotiating, managerial decision making, and human resources management. He is also an adjunct professor at Columbia University.

Miller is the author of *UP: Influence, Power and the U Perspective—The Art of Getting What You Want*. He is a coauthor with his daughter, Jessica, of *A Woman's Guide to Successful Negotiating*, which was selected by *Atlanta Woman* magazine as one of the 50 best books for professional women and by the *Early Show* and *Good Morning America* as a featured book.

Previously he was the senior vice president of human resources at TV Guide Magazine, USA Networks, and Barneys New York; vice president of labor and employee relations at R.H. Macy & Co.; and a partner and cochair of the employment and labor group of one of the largest law firms in New Jersey. He is also the former chair of the International Association of Corporate and Professional Recruiters and secretary to the Union County Motion Picture Advisory Board.

He has extensive experience not only in career coaching but also in negotiating employment agreements on behalf of executives and corporations and in training executives to be more effective influencers and negotiators. Among the clients he has worked with are the National Football League; National Basketball Association; Avon; Bank of America; Citigroup; Dell; GlaxoSmithKline; Grant Thornton; Grey Advertising; Hitachi;

Howard Hughes Medical Institute; HSBC; IBM; KPMG; L'Oréal; McKinsey & Company; Novartis; Prudential; Reuters; Singapore Tourism Board; Singapore Defense, Science, and Technology Agency; Singapore Ministry of Communication; Standard and Poor's; Sun Microsystems; Toyota Asia; United Media; United States Golf Association; and the chairs, presidents, and senior executives of numerous Fortune 1000 companies.

Miller is frequently a guest speaker at conferences and special events, and he has appeared on CBS's *Early Show*, ABC's *Good Morning America*, *Fox and Friends*, NBC's *Today New York*, CNBC's *Power Lunch*, MSNBC's *Economy Watch*, and NPR's *Morning Edition*. He has taught negotiating tactics to executives receiving outplacement at Right Associates and Lee Hecht Harrison. In addition, he has taught negotiating and influencing strategies at Columbia Business School, Wharton, Princeton, and the Harvard Business School alumni associations; the New Jersey Department of Labor's Professional Services Group; Financial Executives International; the Society for Human Resources; and the American Management Association.

Miller can be contacted by e-mail at Negotiate@earthlink.net.